# Affiliate Selling

# Affiliate Selling
## Building Revenue on the Web

Greg Helmstetter

Pamela Metivier

**Wiley Computer Publishing**

**John Wiley & Sons, Inc.**

NEW YORK · CHICHESTER · WEINHEIM · BRISBANE · SINGAPORE · TORONTO

Publisher: Robert Ipsen
Editor: Cary Sullivan
Managing Editor: Marnie Wielage
Text Design & Composition: Publishers' Design and Production Services

Designations used by companies to distinguish their products are often claimed as trademarks. In all instances where John Wiley & Sons, Inc., is aware of a claim, the product names appear in initial capital or ALL CAPITAL LETTERS. Readers, however, should contact the appropriate companies for more complete information regarding trademarks and registration.

This book is printed on acid-free paper. ∞

Published by John Wiley & Sons, Inc.

Published simultaneously in Canada.

This publication is designed to provide accurate and authoritative information in regard to the subject matter covered. It is sold with the understanding that the publisher is not engaged in professional services. If professional advice or other expert assistance is required, the services of a competent professional person should be sought.

*Library of Congress Cataloging-in-Publication Data:*

Helmstetter, Greg, 1967–
    Affiliate selling : building revenue on the web / Greg Helmstetter, Pamela Metivier.
        p. cm.
    Includes index.
    ISBN 0-471-38186-1 (pbk. : alk. paper)
    1. Selling—Data processing. 2. Internet marketing. 3. Business enterprises—
    Computer networks—Management. 4. Internet advertising. I. Metivier, Pamela. II. Title.
HF5438.35 b.H45 2000
658.8'0025'4678—dc21                                                          99-089704

Printed in the United States of America.

10 9 8 7 6 5 4 3 2 1

*This book is dedicated to my family.*

—Pamela Metivier

*Me too.*

—Greg Helmstetter

# Contents

# Acknowledgments

Perhaps it is the wish of any author to issue one completely original idea after another on every page of manuscript, but we acknowledge that many of the concepts in this book have been adapted or synthesized (or borrowed outright) from sources too numerous to remember, let alone name, including that guy in line to buy a hot dog at a trade show; gossip overheard at—which Christmas party was it?—and more *Industry Standard* articles than its top-notch writers and editors will ever know. These and a host of other sources collectively form the resource base we referenced to write this book. So, just to be safe, we'd like to express deepest heartfelt thanks to everyone we've ever met, the authors of anything we've ever read, and anyone else whose mental vibes twanged the cosmic consciousness that we tap into during really weird dreams.

There are, however, a few individuals who escape the Scylla and Charybdis of forgetfulness and poor recordkeeping, folks we couldn't help but remember to mention. We give extra special thanks (in no special order except for putting our publishers first because they pay us) to: Cary Sullivan, Christina Berry, and Marnie Wielage at John Wiley & Sons, Inc., for making this project a reality; Chia-Lin Simmons (Clip2.com), Jennifer Roy (BeFree), Rebecca Foisy (Tripod), Tricia Travaline (BeFree), Cathie Watson-Short (PeopleScape), Allan Gardyne (AssociatePrograms.com), Scott Horst (Commission Junction), Holly Harper Dodge (The Mother's Heart), and Johnson Ma and Grant Shirk (Cross-Commerce).

Extra extra special thanks to the teams at Clip2.com and CrossCommerce for their infectious vision of worlds to come.

# Introduction

During the latter half of the 1990s, with blinding speed, Web-based businesses began to proliferate in the U.S. market (and to a lesser extent so far, throughout the rest of the world). The low-hanging fruit was picked clean by the first generation of Web entrepreneurs; currently, there are several large, entrenched companies devoted to every major business category you can think of, including travel, finance, parenting, sporting goods, pets, and dating. Then common, it is now a rare and newsworthy event when a college student in his or her dorm room comes up with a simple idea for a Web site that immediately draws staggering Web traffic. It's rarer still to hear of a site that makes any money without first requiring investments in the million-dollar range. Nowadays, lots of money and sophisticated teams of experienced Web veterans are generally necessary to enable entrepreneurs to reach farther and farther up the tree of Web opportunities, to grab the increasingly harder-to-reach fruit. In fact, for a time, it looked as though the top branches were beyond the grasp for most would-be entrepreneurs.

Moreover, many of the entrenched so-called category killers—that is, the best-of-breed sites—had been built on the Field of Dreams premise: If you build it, they will come. And come they did, but the dollars did not always follow. Many of these companies developed their sites by selling banner ad impressions to advertisers for $30 per thousand. Some of them made good money—that is, until consumers learned to tune out banner ads, and advertisers became increasingly less willing to pay money to display banners to people who never clicked through to the advertisers' sites.

But in the wake of these early adopters arose a new field of opportunities—the second-generation sites. These are sites and business models that could only exist in the world today; they have been created as a result of the changes brought about by the first-generation sites.

One such model, *affiliate selling*, is engulfing the Web and changing the rules for everybody. Affiliate selling is pumping new lifeblood into the Web. The premise is simple: *Anybody* with a Web site can earn commissions by directing visitors to other sites that actually sell something. The idea is easy to implement, it doesn't require a degree in computer science, and, best of all, it works because site visitors are often more likely to click on a particular, well-chosen product than they are to click on a random banner ad. Furthermore, commissions ranging from 2 percent to 50 percent of the purchase price can often generate stronger revenues than can be made by the cost-per-thousand (CPM) impressions model that most people use for selling banner ad inventories.

This book is written for three groups of people: First, anybody who is interested in learning about this exciting new method of—to use the jargon du jour—*monetizing traffic*, or converting current visitors into revenue without having to bog oneself down with the difficult business of selling ad space or selling and shipping actual products yourself. Second, this book will be of value to individuals and companies who are thinking about building a new site or expanding a site into new areas. We'll show how affiliate selling opportunities can actually drive decisions regarding what a site should be about and whom its intended audience should be. And third, by pointing out what is important to affiliates, this book will be of great value to merchants interested in developing an affiliate program of their own.

Almost three years ago to the day, I completed the manuscript for *Increasing Hits and Selling More on Your Web Site* (Wiley, 1996). In that book, I made some predictions about the future of the Web that I felt were perhaps a little risky at that time, (for those of you who remember) when some were still decrying the Web as an overhyped toy of the techno-elite or as just a passing fad. As we began researching and writing this book, I went back to *Increasing Hits* to review my predictions with respect to their accuracy. As the folk wisdom goes, yesterday's outlandish predictions that prove true are regarded after-the-fact as things that should have been obvious to all. This has never been more correct than with the rapid and dramatic spread of the Web into every facet of life (at least in the United States, with numerous other nations quickly following suit). A few of the naysayers have changed their flavor of nay from "it will never happen" to "okay, this happened but that's where it ends." But the majority will tell you (and, I believe, truly believe this themselves) that they "knew it all along"—that the Web would be a very big deal indeed. Knew it all along? Really?

Today, it seems that just about anybody who planted a stake into the ground three years ago (or bought stock in somebody else's stake) now owns something at least modestly valuable in terms of either equity or skills. They are the people who did know, and did plant, and they now do own something (perhaps hugely) valuable, as we are reminded daily by the financial news that announces initial public offerings, multimillion-dollar acquisitions, and the newest twenty-something billionaires, who look, for lack of a better description, happy-bewildered.

Here, we reiterate some of the predictions made in *Increasing Hits* (particularly those that came true or that soon will undoubtedly come true), not only because they relate directly to this book's discussion of affiliate selling, but because we want to impress you with demonstrated clairvoyance and, we hope, make you that much more willing to accept any seemingly crazy claims we make regarding the next three to five years of the human experience in this Webified world. Here goes—and remember, these will sound obvious to you now that they've come true:

> **Every company will need to be on the Web.** Obvious? Three years ago, many company owners didn't even know what the Web was. Many who did thought this prediction was an attempt to get their money. "Web site? Why would I need a Web site?" (Hearing this now makes you cringe doesn't it?) Today, of course, anybody who's anybody is on the Web, as are many people who don't qualify as "anybodies" to the likes of *Forbes* and *Business Week*—teenage babysitters, for instance, who enable neighborhood parents to book babysitting nights through a Web-based interface. Oh, sure, there are still a few shoe repair shops and Philadelphia delicatessens without a Web presence, but they're becoming increasingly less representative of the small-biz, owner-operator world. They'll all be online soon enough, even if they offer little more than basic yellow pages-type information such as location and hours of operation.

> **Eventually, Nike will sell direct via the Web.** These words were regarded as heretical three years ago. "Their distribution channel partners will never tolerate selling direct," claimed the experts. Wrong. It turns out that Nike's customers would not tolerate not being able to buy direct. True, Nike was slow and, perhaps, appropriately cautious to move to direct sales via the Web. Similar arguments raged within companies in every industry. Eventually, however, the writing was on the wall in most firms, "One day we will sell direct but we won't do it until our competitors do it." And everyone waited for the other guy to go first, sometimes experimenting gingerly by offering online only hard-to-find items or items at prices higher than could be found in their respective reseller channels. This cautious, slow advancement left doors wide open and territories uncontested, enabling new companies (or those with no traditional physical reseller channels) to get a foothold—witness Compaq, IBM, HP, and others, all of which waited around, looking at one another while mail-order PC-maker Dell Computer swooped in and ate their market shares for lunch by selling a million dollars worth of PCs *per day* through its Web

site. Only when this began to hurt enough did many of the big-name manufacturers start selling direct, despite the bitter cries coming from their distribution channel partners.

**Sites will get more complex and more expensive to build and maintain.** Some folks knew this three years ago because they had already begun creating big sites that had a voracious appetite for new daily content; or worse were the sites run by growing, complex programs that served up dynamic content on-the-fly. Other people, however, were still over-emphasizing the potential of the Web to reduce costs by means of making obsolescent some people's jobs. On the whole, the Web can help cut costs, as in the case of reducing customer support calls and by helping customers help themselves. However, good Web sites generally require a net *increase* of employees; and just about any site that does anything interesting (like generate money) ain't cheap.

To me, three years ago, these three predictions spelled doom for the leveled-playing-field, democratized-utopian-ideal, patchwork Web of small sites. But I also predicted that there would always be an opportunity for small, nimble sites to "out-niche" their huge lumbering competitors. And despite another correct prediction—the importance of forging business alliances between sites—I never imagined the 360-degree about-face that would occur. Yes, all of these predictions came true, but yielded a dramatically different outcome:

*It is now possible for small, nimble sites to "out-niche" big sites—by partnering with hundreds of big companies, which sell direct, utilizing huge expensive sites.*

We are speaking specifically of affiliate selling. If you missed the first wave of the Web, hang on tight. The second wave is about to hit hard, and opportunities abound. Best of all, anybody—big or small, funded or not, technical or not—anybody who wants to can participate. We wrote this book to tell you how to do it.

PART

One

# The Basics

# 1

# Affiliate Selling:
# The Next Big Thing

In July 1996, Web retailing giant Amazon.com introduced the Amazon Associates' Program, making it possible for anyone with a Web site to refer customers to Amazon's site in exchange for a commission on any purchase the customer made once there. Suddenly, site owners from high school students to Fortune 500 companies could start earning revenues—assuming they had a site with traffic—with no more effort than it takes to fill out a form at Amazon and then cut and paste a link into their own site. Site owners can (and do) literally sit back and wait for a check to arrive in the mail, courtesy of Jeff Bezos, CEO of Amazon.com.

We assume that because you've made the decision to pick up this book, you most likely fall into one of three categories:

- You're thinking about adding commissions as a revenue stream to your *existing* site.
- You'd like to create a *new* site that generates affiliate commissions.
- You're a *merchant* who would like to create your own affiliate program.

At the risk of sounding completely cheesy, let us say that you are about to embark on an exciting journey. No joke. This great new Web invention called *affiliate selling* is changing all the rules about who can do what on the Web, who holds the cards, who "owns" the customer, and who makes the money. For those of you who feel as though you've already missed out on the biggest land-grabby, gold-rushish opportunities created by the Web a few years ago, relax; if you missed the first train, the second train is about to leave the station, and it's bigger, faster, sleeker, and sexier than the first.

Sound like hype? That's okay. So did the Web, at first, and we've all seen that the hype was right on the money. If you don't buy into the hype, that's okay, too, but nearly all of the Web entrepreneurs we've met—whether rich or struggling—had a special gleam in their eye that hinted at their personal vision and deep-seated excitement about a yet-unrealized potential world that they, and thousands like them with similar gleams, were working hard to create. The point is, if you possess that gleam, read this book, both to discover wildly new ideas as well as to learn basic points to help support or augment the ideas you're already developing.

## Don't Have the Gleam?

Not everybody reading this book is burning the midnight oil trying to build on his or her own chunk of real estate on the Web, be it big or small, serious grind or hobbyist's flirtation. That's okay, too. Far outnumbering the crazy wildcat Webpreneurs we've met at Silicon Valley happy hours are those who Robert X. Cringley, author of *Accidental Empires: How the Boys of Silicon Valley Make Their Millions, Battle Foreign Competition, and Still Can't Get a Date* (HarperBusiness, October 1996), calls "the Infantry": professional managers brought in to convert skunkworks projects of love into refined, stylish, branded-to-the-teeth sites that bankers can bank on.

---

**INDUSTRY SPEAK: WHO QUALIFIES AS AN AFFILIATE?**

Is Yahoo! an Amazon affiliate? Different companies and contracts define words differently, but any business partner could, technically speaking, qualify as an affiliate. In typical Web industry usage, however, affiliate usually refers to a cookie-cutter agreement written by one company that is used without modification or negotiation by many companies (its affiliates). Special deals are struck constantly between Web companies, but these so-called business development (*bizdev*) deals refer to the other party as *strategic partners, partners*—or, sometimes, *portal tenants* in the case of merchants that occupy space on a long-term basis on portal sites. Given that large affiliates can sometimes negotiate more favorable terms than the cookie-cutter contract would dictate, there is actually some blurring between strategic partners and mass-produced affiliates. While any site that earns commissions for referring customers to merchants is, in essence, an affiliate, egos prevail and some of the largest Web sites would not consider themselves to be anybody's affiliate; and they don't call it "taking a commission." Instead, they call it "revenue sharing."

## WHAT EXACTLY IS E-COMMERCE?

*E-commerce*, short for *electronic commerce* simply means selling things over the Internet, usually via the Web; but the term also refers to sales made via e-mail and other Internet mechanisms. Most people think of e-commerce as the process of entering a credit card number into a form at the site of some Web retailer like CDNOW and receiving a UPS package a few days later containing the compact disc he or she ordered. But e-commerce also includes purchasing nontangible goods and services (such as newsletters, reports, software downloads, insurance, and other professional services). And payment mechanisms are not limited to credit cards; checks, credit, electronic funds transfer (EFT), and digital cash can all be used as exchange media. Moreover, exotic variants like barter and other noncash-equivalent mechanisms could be thought of as e-commerce at one level, but they are not likely to be included in many analysts' estimates and projections.

We've heard the same story many times. The VP of marketing at Web Company X is at a staff meeting when he or she either tells an underling (or, less frequently, is told by an overling) these exact words that deliver a numbing chill into the hearts of even the most seasoned of Web marketing managers: "We need to add e-commerce to our site." Everybody looks around in awkward silence until a consensus of glances eventually is directed at the same person. That person gulps, understanding that he or she is about to become responsible for "adding e-commerce to our site," whatever that means.

Not too long ago, adding e-commerce meant building a complex business and technical partnership with a site that already did e-commerce. Or worse, it meant actually taking peoples' credit card numbers and shipping something to them. Now, thanks to affiliate selling, adding e-commerce to your site can be done in half an hour. But, okay, sure, you want to do a smart, thorough job; well, that might take a few days. Fortunately, it's a few days of relative ease— dare we say fun?—during which you won't have to make a single phone call to a business development manager of another company or—worse—achieve a feat of engineering. Grandmas in rocking chairs knitting afghans can become affiliates. Well, maybe , but suffice to say, it's *very easy*.

But don't let the ease of implementation fool you into thinking affiliated selling is for lightweights. It is extremely flexible and powerful, and becoming more so every day, as we will discuss. Web design hotshots and paradigm-shifting tycoons of tomorrow are already having a field day with this stuff.

The ease and simplicity of implementing affiliated selling is again making the Web accessible to all. You don't even need to know HTML or have your own site to become an affiliate (see Chapter 5, "Don't Have a Web Site?"). Affiliate selling has begun to change everything—again. But before we delve deeply (and we will) into the current and future opportunities generated by affiliate selling, let's step back for a moment and put the new realities into context. Let's take a moment to see how the Web got to where it is today.

## How Quickly Things Have Changed

Just three years ago, I wrote in *Increasing Hits and Selling More on Your Web Site* that, one day, our grandchildren would ask us how we used to check ski conditions before we had the Web. I replied that we would baffle them by saying, "We used to call the radio station." Well we don't even have kids yet, let alone grandkids, and we're already baffled by this. Can you imagine calling the radio station for this kind of information? It boggles the mind to think of how limited our information resources were before the advent of the Web. It is even more mind-boggling to remember that we're talking about a time only three short years ago—just over a thousand days.

Forrester Research has identified the youngest Net users—the "Net-powered generation"—as different from earlier adopters because they are coming of age and solidifying their identities in a Web-enabled world, as opposed to those of us who "added on" the Web to our lives or adapted our preexisting habits to conform to the newly enabled Web world.

Remember, there was a time not so very long ago when merely *having* an e-mail address labeled one as a geek by the average sorority girl/fraternity guy; nowadays, *not having* an e-mail address is tantamount to contracting leprosy in terms of limiting one's social access at a typical U.S. college campus. All of this notwithstanding, we find ourselves questioning Forrester's claims about the new Net youth because, quite frankly—and despite having been among those who "added on" the Web to our already-solidified self-identity—we think we (and many of you out there) wanted something like the Web to happen long before it actually did. Moreover, we can imagine how the Web could be even better, and we are frustrated by the various aspects that haven't been quite worked out yet. One thing's for sure: We now have a hard time even remembering what it was like calling the radio station for ski reports or driving to the grocery store and hunting through the newspaper to find out when a movie starts (for any Net-Powered Gen people reading this, movie listings and all kinds of other neat content used to be prime resources of the semi-dynamic but highly portable legacy format called "the newspaper.")

If you haven't figured it out by now, our first point is that things have changed very dramatically and very quickly. Our next point is that the changes are nowhere near over. And if you take a step back, you can see patterns begin to emerge among all the changes. The future is partly visible, and from where we're sitting, it looks like it's going to get really interesting.

## A Revolution Every Six Months

During its infancy, between 1991 and 1992, there were only about a dozen Web sites in the world, mostly hosted by academic institutions. Then in 1993, Mosaic (the first graphical Web browser, and the precursor to Netscape Navigator) hit the scene and Web traffic grew at a rate of 341,634 percent annually. The number of sites quickly outgrew users' ability to memorize all of the URLs out there, so Jerry Yang and David Filo created a nifty site index called Yahoo! to keep track of them all. Then, amid much controversy and policy debate about how commercializing the Internet would ruin it, a few simple Web sites started selling things online to the small number of users that browsed the Web at that time.

Before long, there were millions of sites of all kinds, including thousands that sold things. The developers of Yahoo! and the then-new competing search engines realized that they could make money, partly by running ads and partly by "recommending" particular sites whose owners paid for the privilege of being endorsed. Naturally, the only sites willing to pay for this service were the very same sites that were trying to make money themselves; these were the early *e-merchants*.

The developers of Yahoo! more or less sat back and started earning revenues, drawing traffic with little effort, thanks to Yahoo!'s position as Netscape's top default Web directory (meaning that Yahoo! was one of the first sites seen and, thus, used when a new user was introduced to a Web browser. That all changed one day when Netscape, with no warning, dropped Yahoo! into the "other search engines" category and replaced it with a different search engine. Yahoo!'s owners learned in a couple of hours one morning that, if it were to survive, it would have to be able to draw and retain traffic on its own, with or without Netscape's help. An aggressive plan was devised to make Yahoo! more than just a search engine, specifically, to make it the one place where a user would always return by default, regardless of his or her browsing habits. This was accomplished by metamorphosing the search engine into the be-all-end-all central location for using the Web. The *portal* was born, and its inventors intended it to become *the* starting point for Web users, by providing an exhaustive array of content and services.

Meanwhile, category-killer e-merchants like Amazon.com demonstrated that the public was willing to buy things online, and in quantities large enough to generate significant revenue streams. Amazon and its imitators also showed that, in order to be really interesting as an e-merchant, they had to invest millions of dollars to be contenders in the race of bigger, better, and faster—in all directions: the servers serving product information, the customizability of the store, the quantity of supporting content, the number of products available, and the systems installed to ensure prompt, reliable service. Though limited space continued to be available for highly targeted, small, niche players that offered hard-to-find items, it became practically impossible for these small sites to compete against the new giants that were backed with IPO funding. According to Charlene Li, senior analyst in New Media Research at Forrester, the "Wal-Marting of America," became evident as public-market-funded e-merchants started building $5 to $20 million online stores, pushing out most would-be small and medium-sized Web retailers.

Next came PointCast, bringing with it the concept of *push*. This was a major milestone on the Web timeline. Are you laughing? Careful—did you laugh at Ross Perot? It was easy to do so, but remember, he changed the political process by using PowerPoint slides to educate anyone who owned a television about a growing and previously ignored crisis called the national debt. Comical or not, he changed American politics. Similarly, PointCast became a laughingstock to some, but nevertheless changed the Web forever.

PointCast offered an alternate, default point-of-entry to the Web, which got Microsoft, Yahoo!, and AOL more than just a little concerned. The idea was to let users customize a browser that would allow content providers to deliver, or "push," content to users each day rather than the user having to actively search for it. PointCast never managed to hit a home run, however, but its basic idea has become the mainstay of every customizable portal—My Yahoo!, My Excite, My MSN.com, and the like. These let you filter content that gets pushed to your site each day. With the failure of PointCast, the term push has fallen out of favor and it's now fashionable to call the idea *smart pull*. (In fairness, smart pull is choosier than push in terms of how much and which content is delivered. Still, the experience is more or less the same for the user.)

And somewhere along the line, banner ad exchanges and syndicators like Link Exchange and Double Click figured out that the many-to-one-to-many model was a great way to solve a lot of problems by aggregating the dual tasks of collecting content on one side of the equation and then distributing it on the other. Rather than having thousands of tiny Web sites each trying to sell their limited inventory of banner space by calling on thousands of advertisers with ads to place, it made sense for an *infomediary* to step in and aggregate all of the advertisers' ads, as well as all of the available ad slots, thereby eliminating much cost and trouble for all involved, as well as achieving network efficiencies in the process.

But one of the biggest innovations was yet to emerge. While technically not the first of its kind, Amazon.com launched its affiliate program in July 1996, allowing anybody with a Web site to sign up, cut-and-paste product links, and start earning commissions if his or her site visitors clicked through to Amazon and made a purchase. The idea for the program stemmed from a conversation between Bezos and a guest at a cocktail party; its success took Amazon management by surprise, with its remarkable growth rates. Within months, Amazon had more than 100,000 affiliates (it's up to 320,000 as of this writing, three years after the program's launch). Suddenly, every hobbyist Web site owner in the world could start converting his or her pastime into a business without even so much as providing a form for filling in credit card information—let alone the more difficult process of convincing a bank to let him or her open a VISA/MC merchant account when working from home or dorm room.

But two other immediate results were even more impressive than seeing hobbyist sites provided with a means of earning income. First, professional sites—even those that already sold their own products or services—began using the Amazon affiliate program to *cross-sell* to their visitors. Rather than adding additional products to their own inventory (which incurs associated costs and risks), these merchants were able to make reasonably good returns taking a commission on sales they passed through to Amazon. Even though some sites risked losing some visitors once they clicked over to Amazon, in many cases, they were the ones who probably were not going to buy anything at the referring merchant's site anyway. On the whole, the trade-off has definitely been worthwhile for many firms. At least one survey reports that sites that sell their own wares make more money from their affiliate revenues than do sites that don't sell anything of their own. (See this book's companion site, www.affiliateselling.com for recent survey statistics.)

The other significant and—I'm willing to bet—*unanticipated* consequence of Amazon's program was that *brand-new* sites started sprouting up like mushrooms to take advantage of the new opportunity: Web-based revenues with almost no barriers to entry. The traditional spiel was (and continues to be) aimed at "anybody with a Web site." But forget about that; suddenly there was a reason for lots of people without sites to actually build them from the ground up just for this new purpose. Sites of all kinds—big, small, pretty, ugly, professional, shoddy, single-product, multiproduct—started to recommend books and point visitors all to the same place: Amazon.com. Some reports estimate that as much as 30 percent of Amazon's total revenues come from its affiliate channel (with 17 percent being the average among e-merchants that have affiliate programs). The business model became very important very fast, and now there are more than a thousand e-merchants with affiliate programs of their own.

We spent a few paragraphs describing the history of Web developments not just for your pure reading enjoyment, but to provide a framework for something quite profound that's going on, which a lot of people don't yet recognize (though it may be well-known by the time you read this); that is, the power is shifting in the makeup of the Web as a whole. Affiliation is beginning to have far-reaching effects, every bit as important as what occurred when Yahoo! went from being merely a directory to a full-fledged portal.

But before we make any outlandish claims, let's get a perspective: the Web economy generates new outlandish claims every few weeks. In fact, the whole Web economy has a tendency to go topsy-turvy every few months, whenever somebody suddenly launches something into the mainstream that captures everybody's attention, as Table 1.1 illustrates.

**Table 1.1**   The Constantly Evolving E-Commerce Landscape

| EVENT | THE INDUSTRY'S REACTION |
|---|---|
| Amazon launches best-of-breed, bookselling site. | "Disintermediation"—Barnes & Noble is dead! |
| Barnes & Noble launches darn good site, too. | Web-based companies that also have "brick-and-mortar operations will dominate due to their lower-cost distribution—Amazon is dead! |
| Yahoo! goes IPO and its stock price skyrockets as the company attains profitability—despite the fact that it became profitable not on its operations, but on the interest earned by its new IPO war chest! | "Portals" control the eyeballs and therefore the money—Amazon is dead! |
| Amazon starts selling music. | Economies of scope—CDNOW is dead! |
| Amazon starts selling videos. | People memorize merchants' URLs. Once they find Amazon through a directory, next time they'll go straight to Amazon—Yahoo! is dead! |
| Amazon acquires a major book distributor. | "Reintermediation"—Barnes & Noble is dead! |
| Major media companies start buying portals. | Economies of scale and scope—Amazon is dead! |
| Amazon offers gifts and starts building regional warehouses. | Economies of scale and scope—Amazon "gets" "brick-and-mortar"—Wal-Mart is dead! |
| eBay goes public. | "C-to-C" (consumer-to-consumer) is the future—Amazon is dead! |
| Amazon adds auctions to its site. | eBay is dead! |
| eToys and Furby do Christmas '98 in a big way. | Traditional companies "don't get it"—Toys 'R' Us is dead! |
| Toys 'R' Us announces major deal with Benchmark Capital to do e-commerce right: toysrus.com. | Big brand meets Silicon Valley know-how—eToys is dead! |
| Toys 'R' Us/Benchmark deal is scrubbed. | Traditional companies "don't get it"—Toys 'R' Us is dead! |
| Wal-Mart signs deal with mail-order giant, Fingerhut. | Big brand meets mail-order know-how—Amazon is dead! |

Do you see a pattern emerging? Every time something happens, the industry interprets the results as though it were the last move in a game of chess, in which the opponent loses because he or she didn't get a chance to respond. In reality, firms not only sometimes respond, they *always* respond—sometimes too little, too late, or too incompetently, but they always respond.

And this game of cat-and-mouse is going to continue for a while. It might take 10 or 15 years, but, eventually, it will probably stabilize, just as the PC market more or less has stabilized, and just as every other industry eventually has. That's not to say that industries become permanently static. In the process of stabilizing, however, they do shake out a lot of players—either through bankruptcy or consolidation (acquisitions and mergers)—and end up with a smaller number of reasonably strong firms remaining to fight over what usually ends up being smaller and smaller margins with less and less differentiated products (in the automotive industry, for example, notice how 80 percent of all cars look alike, every company now offers a sport-utility vehicle, and there hasn't been a DeLorean-like startup since, well, DeLorean).

In a very small way, we have begun to see some of the first, albeit small, inklings of stabilization of the Web—witness the ridiculous number of technology-play acquisitions and ISP and Web service provider acquisitions; even our favorite underdog, Netscape, exited the fray by getting glommed onto AOL. Despite this, the Web promises to change a lot more in the years ahead, if not for all of the great ideas that have yet to be thought up, then for all of the obvious major opportunities that simply haven't happened yet: non-PC-based, wireless Web access and widespread broadband access, to name two. And, of course, let us not forget the opportunities created by the fact that the vast majority of the industrialized world is not even online yet. According to International Data Corp., there were 142 million Web users in 1998 (about half of whom were American), but that the number will grow to half a billion users by 2003. To put it bluntly, we ain't seen nuthin' yet.

# The Current State of Web Commerce

At the risk of stating the obvious—we'll state it anyway with a big, gloating "we told you so!" to the naysayers of three years ago—e-commerce is indisputably big business, and it's here to stay.

Analysts' projections vary dramatically and are updated so frequently that it's difficult to understand why anyone bothers to give credence to the numbers they predict for online sales for next-year's holiday season, let alone the wildly varied guesses as to how much e-commerce will happen ten years from now. But businesspeople like rough estimates better than no estimates at all, so we cite them here*:

**E-commerce is big.** Total global e-commerce in 1999 was estimated to be $95 to $109 billion, with $36 billion coming directly from online consumers (see the sidebar titled B-to-C versus B-to-B).

**E-commerce is growing.** Global totals are expected to hit a whopping $1.3 trillion in 2003 (doubling every 12 to 18 months between now and then). The 1999 Christmas season alone was expected to deliver 1.3 billion visits to Web retail sites, an increase of 71 percent from the previous year's holiday season.

**E-commerce is mainstream.** Over 40 percent of U.S. teenagers and adults use the Internet, and the percentage grows higher each day. Of those, approximately 70 percent shop online and 25 percent have purchased something online in the past three months.

**TIP** To keep up to date on the latest e-commerce jargon, visit this book's companion Web site at www.affiliateselling.com.

Taken together, these statistics and predictions indicate that, not only is the Web a big deal today, but more important, it's going to be the *only* deal tomorrow. Yes, brick-and-mortar retail will still exist, but the volume of commerce that will flow through the Web will become increasingly larger, relative to the volume of brick-and-mortar-only commerce. One study suggests that, of all e-commerce, only 10 percent is incremental (sales that would not have happened otherwise). That means a full 90 percent of e-commerce is coming directly from sales that would have been made through traditional channels—meaning one person's gain is another person's loss. In the future, the scales may tip such that e-commerce is more prevalent than traditional-commerce (t-commerce?), though the distinction will become even more difficult to measure than it is today due to "click-and-mortar" business models. Hybrids between e-commerce and t-commerce will soon combine the best of both worlds; for example, trying on a pair of jeans at the Gap nearest you then using a Web kiosk in the store to order the jeans in a special color or fabric, to be delivered to your house in a few days.

Furthermore, the percentage of e-commerce originating from affiliate sites is growing, and is expected to reach 45 percent by 2003, according to Forrester. Some would call this figure ridiculously optimistic, but we feel it's conservative.

*Sources: Forrester Research (www.forrester.com), U.S. Department of Commerce (www.doc.gov), Intelliquest (www.intelliquest.com), and Net Effect Systems (www.neteffect.com).

## B-TO-C VERSUS B-TO-B

Most of us think of e-commerce as a retail-like shopping experience moved onto the Web. This is called *business-to-consumer* (*B-to-C* or simply *B2C*), and the companies that sell products to end consumers are typically called *Web merchants*, *e-merchants*, or *e-tailers* (short for e-retailers).

Behind the scenes, invisible to the average consumer, sits the huge industrial sector of e-commerce, where companies buy things from one another. In Web parlance, this is called *business-to-business* (*B-to-B* or simply *B2B*). Examples include Kellogg's buying corn to make cornflakes, Ford buying tail-light assemblies, or an insurance company buying a thousand desktop computers or copies of the latest version of Windows for its employees.

It's important to remember that, across the world economy, the total (as opposed to Web-based) B-to-C will *always* be greater than the total B-to-B, simply because all companies' costs end up as part of the price of the products and services that end consumers actually buy online and offline. However, until 100 percent of world commerce happens online (which will not happen until the world becomes completely cashless—possibly never), online B-to-B can be—and is currently—much larger than online B-to-C. This is due in part to the fact that companies have been quicker to move online than consumers and because companies tend to place very large orders.

With respect to affiliate selling, the important consideration is that, as of this writing, most affiliate programs are provided by merchants that provide products and services to end consumers (that is, B-to-C). By the time you read this however, some of the best opportunities may be found serving business-to-business markets, due to the simple fact that these markets are largely invisible or mysterious to—and thus left unaddressed by—many of the small firms creating sites dependent upon affiliate revenues for their sustenance.

Here's why: Almost every one of the significant breakthroughs of the Web involved innovative ways to make more things more accessible to more people for free. Think back to when getting stock quotes and Web page hosting cost money; free Web-based e-mail wasn't even a glimmer in its father's eye yet, let alone something that every portal site had to offer if it didn't want to be out-gunned in the stepped-up tech-arms race—whose only winner, by the way, is the user (along with all the little firms that get acquired for their intellectual property—the guns of this arms race).

Knowing what we know today about the Web, think back to the world of three or four years and consider the following questions:

- Will users' resources become more or less accessible on the Web? (*Answer:* More)

- Will resources become more or less expensive? (*Answer:* Less.)

- Will user functionality become more or less accessible on the Web? (*Answer:* More)

- Will functionality become more expensive or less expensive? (*Answer:* Less.)

- Will it become easier or more difficult to build a basic site? (*Answer:* Easier.)

- Will it become more or less expensive to build a basic site? (*Answer:* Less.)

- Will advanced technology become more or less accessible to Web firms? (*Answer:* More.)

And so on.

You may be thinking that Web sites are more expensive to build than ever. That's true, but the sites are capable of doing much more than sites of their predecessors—the bang for the buck is tenfold. Every feature of yesterday's sites had to be engineered from scratch, whereas today we have at our disposal a rich and diverse arsenal of off-the-shelf solutions, shareware tools and tidbits, countless samples of what works, innumerable been-there-done-that contractors/consultants/employees, and—best of all—freebie Web-based services.

Try this on for size:

The Law of Web Trends: Anything possible, though difficult and expensive, on the Web today will be easy and cheap or free tomorrow.

This gem probably won't be quoted as often as Moore's Law, but the reasoning behind it is sound:

- First, we've already seen it come true over and over.

- Second, concepts that are difficult to implement or problems that are difficult to solve initially on the Web usually are extremely easy and less expensive to copy (despite the recent trend in patenting business methods). In fact, certain Silicon Valley venture capital firms are notorious for doing nothing but knockoff duplicates of any sites out there that seem to be doing well. This "me too" model is making lots of folks rich.

- Finally, we don't just see existing companies knocking off copies of their competitors' ideas, we see *brand new* companies formed just to mass-produce any new interesting idea/technology/feature/model and give it away for free—if only to make money selling value-added services (like consulting or customization) or even less, like merely selling ad space on the page where you access your free service which six months ago would have cost a company millions of dollars to build from scratch (think Web-based calendaring, scheduling, and a whole host of free, out-sourced services).

Some more laws to keep in mind:

The interconnectedness of everything will increase, not decrease.

Technology and media assets that were expensive for the giants to build the first time will be mass-produced for all.

# The Punch Line

We could have written this book because affiliation is a neat little "toy" that allows little Johnny's game site to earn him enough money for his trip to Washington, DC this summer. But we didn't. We don't think affiliated selling is merely the next gem on a string of pearls. It is not just the next neat thing affecting e-commerce. We believe that affiliated selling will become the string that holds all the e-commerce pearls together. We wrote this book because we also believe this is the dawn of something monumental, second, perhaps, only to the creation of the Web itself. Affiliation is going to change everything, for everybody, both meek and strong in the current online environment. Bold claims? You bet.

## The Future: A Hyper-Enabled World

We'll say it again: The interconnectedness of everything will increase, not decrease. Technology and media assets that were expensive for giants to build the first time will be mass-produced for all. What if we were to tell you that every Jimmy and Jane out there in the world (and every classroom, school, club, company, and nonprofit organization) could have their own private-label version of Amazon.com, selling not just books, videos, and whatever new "tabs" (the navigational things along the top of Amazon's page) Amazon has in store (so to speak), but literally *every* product imaginable? And let's add to that the capability for all these Jimmys and Janes to include on their sites— often at no cost to them but for a small revenue share—any piece of content related to each product: photography, video, technical specs, professional third-party reviews, and so on? How will this ever be possible?

But wait, it gets better. Imagine that a visitor to, for example, Jimmyzon.com buys some things using a credit card form page that looks like every other page of Jimmyzon. When the box arrives via courier a few days later, it's got a packing slip with the Jimmyzon logo. And let's say the order is incorrect in some way; all the end user has to do is call an 800-number where a pleasant-sounding, well-trained customer service rep—who just happens to be sitting at a phone center in Blaire, Nebraska—says, "Jimmyzon customer service; how may I help you?" The name Jimmyzon even shows up on the credit card statement.

Now keep in mind that Jimmy is still just Jimmy; he's not doing any of this himself. He's plugged into the mother of all affiliate programs, some beast that doesn't exist yet that has been assembled by thousands of companies working together, enabling each part of the value chain to be redirected or outsourced, using accepted protocols and standards. These conventions and relationships will enable the passing, in one direction, of merchandising content (prices, photos, descriptions, specs) from thousands of merchants, while customer information (credit card numbers, street address, preferences) passes in the other direction.

And somehow, magically, it all just works. Sound like fiction? Pure fantasy? Consider this: As you read these pages, elements of the "hyper-enabled" world we've just described have already been assembled. Companies like CrossCommerce (www.crosscommerce.com), Affinia (www.affinia.com), and Vstore (www.vstore.com) are enabling Web site owners to pull merchandising content from thousands of e-merchants. Many technology companies are attempting to build merchant-independent shopping "carts" that reside on the client's browser and allow him or her to select multiple products from multiple merchants but with only one credit card transaction. And where the tire literally hits the road—physical distribution—companies like Ingram Micro are retooling their longstanding bulk distribution systems to drop-ship "unit of one" packages to individuals.

And though many of the enablers described here are currently directing their efforts at large companies or well-known sites with lots of traffic, as stated previously, once the difficult initial implementation work is, these sorts of technologies will be cheap to emulate and duplicate, and thus will become widely available, first to other substantial business sites, then to greater numbers of GeoCities and Homestead sites of the world, for better or worse.

### For Better or Worse

Why "for better or worse?" When imagining the impact of these developments, it's helpful to take a step back and think about the value chain from manufacturers to end consumers. Who provides value along the path, and how easy would it be for somebody to attempt to steal another's share? Currently, e-merchants such as Amazon.com do a handful of important things: They aggregate existing products from multiple manufacturers (publishers, in the case of books), they aggregate product information (photos, descriptions, etc.), and they create some of their own product information (reviews, etc.). They also attract the consumer (through advertising and promotions), take a credit card number, fulfill the order, and offer customer service to back up the sale.

This book is written based on the fact that affiliates are drawing a lot of these merchants' traffic (and the percentage may grow to about half of all e-commerce traffic by 2003). That means affiliates have usurped part of the value chain from Amazon; and affiliates get paid commissions for being good at this. Similarly, other third parties are grabbing segments of the value chain: Merchandising content aggregators are collecting product data (and soon will also be getting it directly from manufacturers, not just e-merchants); shipping specialists will make it cost-effective for manufacturers to drop-ship onesies-twosies; and customer service specialists will handle the returns, complaints, and possibly even the upselling opportunities. Where then, does that leave the Amazon.coms of the Web world? As J. Gurley of Benchmark Capital has stated, "Taking an order and putting it in a shopping cart is already a commodity." Will anybody still need the e-merchants?

The answer is yes. Amazon and the other e-merchants will have a place, albeit a diminished place in the e-commerce landscape of the future. At a basic level, there are two types of shopping behavior: *directed* and *serendipitous.* Directed shopping is when consumers know what they want to buy and they go somewhere to buy it. E-merchants efficiently address this type of behavior, as do affiliates that cater to niche categories of directed shoppers. The other category, serendipitous shoppers, is composed of those who don't necessarily intend to buy. They browse, and perhaps end up finding something they want to buy. (Impulse shopping is an extreme form of serendipitous shopping. There are other kinds of shopping behaviors as well, such as when a user is looking for product reviews. He or she may not have been intending to buy that moment, but if he or she ends up finding exactly what he or she wants, he or she may go ahead and buy it. This is partly directed and partly serendipitous, but not impulsive.)

There you have it. Web users will buy both from stores as well as from content-oriented affinity sites (in other words, sites that address a particular topic or targeted toward a particular group of people). E-merchants that resist affiliate empowerment may lose some market share to those merchants (and original manufacturers who sell direct) that embrace affiliate empowerment. There will be a dramatic shift in Web distribution power, though no category will completely cease to exist as a result. Affiliates will comprise one winner group—at least, those affiliates that do a good job of attracting users and offering value, be it in the form of editorial content, site functionality, or product selection. Consumers will be the other big winner group; they will have greater access to more intelligently placed opportunities to buy products and services they actually might be interested in buying.

We don't pretend for a minute that the Web marketplace would be very interesting if it were nothing but a bunch of private-labeled Amazon.com duplicates. That said, we have to face the fact that the emergence of infomediaries in every space (banner ads, merchandising information, contextual content, functionality, private-labeled cross-merchant shopping carts, and so on) will begin to homogenize much of what we see from one Web site to the next; this is apparent already. Every day, for example, there are fewer finance-oriented sites that don't offer stock quotes. At the same time, fortunately, there will be so many ways to combine the vast syndicated resources out there that, in addition to lots of exact copies (which draw few visitors), there will be lots of highly unique sites despite their comprising components of broadly available media resources. Moreover, there will always be—as there is today—a premium placed on good, original content that can't be found elsewhere. The question is, if you were creating great original content, wouldn't you want to distribute it on as many sites as possible, if not for more revenue, then at least for broader exposure? Yeah, a lot of people think that the cult of rampant commercialism has been a bad thing for the Web, but even they don't want to create something that nobody else will ever see. Think memetics: information wants to spread. And information that is worth spreading will outspread that which isn't good in this dog-eat-dog, Darwinian battle between bits and bytes.

The interesting sites, ideas, and services will pull ahead for a while until copycats reproduce what worked until it's no longer interesting. And then something else will become interesting—a cycle that happens across all realms of creativity and behavior: film, literature, fashion, automotive, and public issues. This is the essence of democracy—the mechanism of which is designed to allow all ideas to be heard and voted either into prominence or oblivion. And commercial markets enable a much purer form of democracy than our government could ever hope to achieve. The consumers vote every time they choose one brand of bottled water over another, whether because its label is prettier, or because it's ten cents less, or because it's situated in a mini-mart 100 feet closer to your house. This new dawn of affiliation is, in our opinion, breathing back into the Web the initial hopes for a democratized, level playing field that many of us perhaps naively hoped for, only to see Wall Street swoop in and say, "Nope, business as usual." (Though we must point out that we vote in true democratic fashion every time we place a put option on fifty shares of eBay stock.)

The new commercial democracy will be enabled by the new wave of infomediaries we described. Through complex technologies, the best of them will manage to make it simple for companies and organizations of all sizes (from the one-person show to large companies) to erect e-commerce storefronts that are customizable right down to individual user habits (driven by *personalization engines*, another technology currently available only to the big players but that will soon be available to all—for a small revenue share, of course). To the typical consumer, the megasites will look as though they were built from scratch by an individual or by a company's in-house Web development team.

In Table 1.1, we poked a bit of fun at the industry experts who make definitive statements, seemingly based on every new headline they read regarding the Web economy ("Amazon adds auctions to its site—eBay is dead!"). Are we guilty of the same? Are we predicting that affiliation is going to fundamentally hurt party A and help party B? No. In fact, we're saying that affiliation per se is just as likely to help any company (e-merchant, content producer, or eyeball capturer) whether it chooses to play on the left side (syndicating content or product data), the right side (using syndicated content or data), or on both sides of the new infomediary-enabled distribution model. We believe that the only losers will be the companies that fail to participate at all or that get onboard too late to make a difference. Certainly, there will be some winners among the infomediaries (those in the middle of the equation), though the race promises to be more competitive than any we've seen so far.

## Summary

The short take is that affiliation is going to be important beyond words, driving a true—dare we use the tired phrase—paradigm shift, one that could give the strongest legs to all global e-commerce and carry it forward into the next century. This continues to be an exciting time, during which countless heretofore unknown big winners will emerge; conversely, there will probably be some loud crashing sounds coming from this or that publicly held company that has failed to maneuver through the next stretch of bumpy road. If you work at a medium- or large-sized Web company, pay attention; things are going to change—again. If you are just an eager do-it-yourselfer, pay attention as well, because things are about to get really, really fun.

# 2

# Types of Programs

Affiliate programs are rapidly becoming a very popular way for online merchants to target their customer base, by rewarding those who generate traffic to their Web site. There are many different types of affiliate programs available on the Web. Some pay a percentage commission or a flat amount for every successful sale made to a visitor you send to their site; others pay you to simply encourage your visitors to click-through to their site, thus earning money for you whether a sale is made or not; still others pay you a couple of cents every time one of your visitors follows a link to their site; finally, there are those that pay upward of 50 percent of commissions for every sale made to a person you referred to their site.

If you already have a Web site or are looking to start a business, affiliate programs are a great way to generate and build revenue, add content and value to your Web site, and increase traffic by offering products and services relevant to those offered on your site. To succeed with affiliate selling, however, it's important that you choose the right type of program for your business.

There are four basic types of affiliate programs:

- Commission-based programs (also known as pay-per-sale programs)
- Bounty/flat-fee referral programs (sometimes called pay-per-lead/new customer)
- Click-through programs (also known as pay-per-click programs)
- CPM (cost-per-thousand impressions) programs

And for each of these types of programs, there are two types of reward calculation methods: money and incentives.

The type of affiliate program a merchant sponsors depends on the type of products or services they offer on their Web site. For example, if a merchant runs an online sporting goods store that sells work-out apparel, exercise equipment, and nutritional supplements, it might have an affiliate program under which its affiliates earn 10 percent commission on every purchase made by a visitor that was sent by an affiliate site. This is an example of a commission-based program. On the other hand, if the merchant's site doesn't sell a product but, rather, provides content such as sporting news, it might pay its affiliates $5 for every visitor they send to its site who signs up to receive the sporting goods site's newsletter. This is a flat-rate program. And in the case of affiliate program providers that don't sell products directly but that offer news, real-time scores, or statistical data, for example, affiliates might be paid a small amount of money for each unique visitor they send to the program provider's site. This is done for the sole purpose of increasing traffic to the provider site. This is a click-through program, sometimes referred to as *pay-per-click* (PPC). Examples of click-through programs include those offered by Lycos and the comparison-shopping service mySimon (www.mysimon.com). Finally, an affiliate program provider might offer a percentage of the revenue earned from banner advertisements viewed by visitors on affiliate sites. This is a CPM program. Bottom-dollar.com, for example, offers an affiliate program that pays from $.02 to $.12 per click-through to its shopping search engine, and $5.00 per 1,000 pageviews seen after the referred visitor performs a search.

The type of reward calculation method used by merchants is less dependent upon the types of products and services offered than the goal they are trying to achieve. For instance, CDNOW's Cosmic Credit affiliate program enables you to earn CDNOW store credit when a visitor to your site uses the link there to CDNOW and makes a purchase. You can use this so-called Cosmic Credit to buy anything at CDNOW. In this way, not only does CDNOW gain a visitor, it also can be certain that you'll return to its site occasionally to redeem your credit. Thus, CDNOW offers incentives as a reward for its commission-based program to guarantee repeat visitors.

## Commission-Based Programs

Commission-based is the most commonly used type of affiliate program. These programs pay you a percentage of the revenue generated by the sale of a product or service made to a visitor who was referred by your site. Typically, the commission percentage rate is fixed (15 percent, for example). However, some programs offer higher commissions (or *bonus commissions*) to affiliates with high-volume traffic and/or with proven track records.

## Advantages

A well-selected commission-based affiliate program can greatly enhance the value of your site because it enables you to add relevant content that would otherwise have to be provided by content providers. For example, let's say you have a Web site that reviews skiing equipment for the sport's numerous enthusiasts; clearly, it would be very convenient for your visitors if you also provided an easy way for them to purchase the equipment you just recommended to them. If you also make an effort to annotate your recommendations, you can earn a significant amount of money. To take another example, let's assume we're major fans of German board games and that we visit a board game review site to read a review about a brand-new, supposedly great, German game. Chances are, we'd be open to a simple, convenient way to buy the game or other games like it if the reviews confirm that the game is indeed worth buying. (Naturally, reviewing products that you also promote for sale raises strategic and ethical issues, not the least of which are how to maintain objectivity and integrity, both of which you'll need to address. See Chapter 8, "Planning Your Implementation," for more information.)

If the affiliate program you've joined enhances the content of your site, you are likely to get good results from a commission-based system. But it's important to point out that in conjunction with the affiliate program, it's imperative that you establish, then maintain an interesting site, so that you develop a credible reputation with your visitors. Once you do, your visitors will come to value your opinion and will be more likely to take your advice regarding products and services that you recommend to them.

## Disadvantages

With the commission-based program model, the primary disadvantage is that the conversion rate—the number of people who click on a link and subsequently make a purchase—tends to be quite low, even if you have a high-volume site. Only a small percentage of your visitors ( the average is 2 percent) will click on a banner ad or link; of that percentage, only a fraction will actually make a purchase. So even if you measure 10,000 pageviews of your site in one day, typically, only 200 (2 percent) of those visitors will click on a banner ad or product link. Of those 200, chances are only one (0.5 percent) will buy something, and thus earn some money for you. Recognize that these are only averages. Highly targeted sites, such as those

---

**PAGEVIEWS AND NONPERFORMERS**

Despite the pageview requirements set forth by some affiliate programs, we managed to join a few of them using a test home page that generates a whopping 10 pageviews a month. But these programs did specify in their Terms of Agreement documents that if we didn't generate the required pageviews in the first month, we'd be removed from the program. That said, we also learned from one program provider that it's really difficult to keep track of those numbers, a serious concern of providers. Why? Because having unqualified affiliates in these programs costs the merchants money. They spend more money providing unqualified affiliates with reporting tools, an affiliate newsletter, phone support, and year-end reconciliation payments than such participants can possibly make back for them by posting the affiliate provider's link in obscure, random spots on unrelated or poorly related sites. The bottom line: It's a waste of money and potential revenue for all involved to place irrelevant affiliate links on low-traffic sites.

---

devoted to one specific product (your favorite book or movie, for example) generate lower traffic volumes, but higher conversion rates, because the small number of visitors are finely filtered by virtue of the fact that they have found their way to your narrowly focused site and thus are more likely to buy the product or service.

## Recommendations

Carefully select the affiliate program or programs that you integrate into your site. The more closely the product or service offered by the affiliate program provider matches your content and audience preferences, the more likely your affiliate site will be recognized as a valuable resource by your visitors and the more likely they will be to make a purchase at the merchant's site.

Be aware that many affiliate providers carefully screen their program participants to ensure that the affiliate's site generates enough traffic (read: interest) to generate an adequate volume of sales. This screening process will also help you decide whether the program is right for your business. If, say, a merchant requires its affiliates to generate 10,000 pageviews per month before being eligible to join its program and you generate only 900 pageviews, clearly you need to keep shopping for a more suitable program.

## Example: Amazon.com

You can't discuss a commission-based affiliate without mentioning Amazon .com, the mother of all affiliate programs (well, not really, but definitely one of the founders in this new frontier). As we mentioned in Chapter 1, Amazon's Associates Program was launched in July 1996, and it has been growing like the proverbial weed ever since. Everywhere you click on the Web, there's a link to Amazon. Its phenomenal growth can be attributed primarily to the relevance versatility of the premiere Amazon product line: books. No matter what you offer at your site, there's a darn good chance there's at least one book, if not a dozen or more, that relates specifically to your content. Books also happen to be a popular purchase for the Web's current (though ever-changing) "typical Web user." For these reasons (and many more), books sell well online and make a natural affiliate product link.

Amazon has expanded its reach by affiliating with other products, such as CDs, DVDs, videos, toys, consumer electronics, and computer games. The list goes on and will continue to grow. Founder Jeff Bezos named his company Amazon.com—as opposed to Books.com—for a very good reason: His vision was to create the world's largest channel for moving products, not just books (the Amazon River passes more water through it than any other river). In short, it would be difficult to find a product available via Amazon that doesn't add value and drive traffic back to your Web site.

As a participant in the Amazon.com affiliate program, you can recommend specific products, or simply link to the main Amazon home page. You get paid on all products bought by visitors that you refer, regardless whether your site specifically relates to the product they end up buying. Customers using your product link may click over to Amazon, then browse around at Amazon's site and end up buying something totally unrelated to your product or service; nevertheless, you get the commission if the purchase occurs during the same visit, or "session." You can even add an Amazon.com Associates Search Box to your site and get paid on all resulting sales.

As of this writing, Amazon.com pays its affiliates 15 percent on more than 400,000 titles, and 5 percent on more than 1.5 million additional in-print titles, CDs, videos, toys, and consumer electronics. And, unlike some other commission-based programs, Amazon does not require its associates to meet sales quotas to receive referral fees.

Figure 2.1 provides an example of an Amazon associate site that promotes itself as *the* place to browse for information about martinis. Here, you can find recipes, share your stories on a discussion group, and—our personal favorite—e-mail a friend a virtual martini. If you search for "martini" using any major search engine, this site will probably show up. As you can see in the figure, the site's designers have taken special care to keep their affiliate links directly relevant to the content on their site. If they have a steady stream of serious martini drinkers browsing their site, chances are good the books they're promoting at Amazon will realize good affiliate earnings.

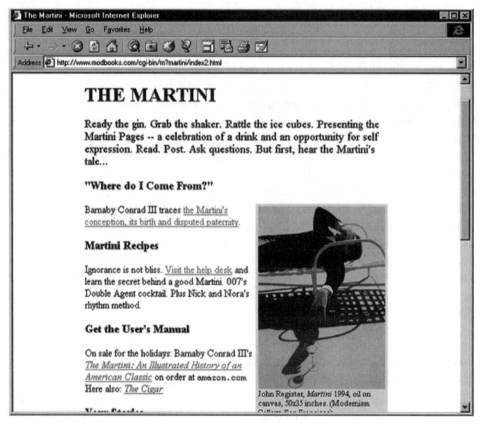

**Figure 2.1** The Martini Expert, an Amazon associate.

## Bounty/Flat-Fee Referral Programs

Bounty, or flat-fee referral, programs are less commonly used than click-through and commission-based programs. Bounty programs pay affiliates a predetermined, flat (fixed) fee for every new visitor (bounty) they send to a merchant's site.

Sometimes flat fees are paid to affiliates for visitor actions other than purchases. These may include the visitor completing a registration form, requesting product information, downloading software, answering survey questions, or joining a mailing list. In these cases, bounty rewards are usually in the form of money, as opposed to store credit or other noncash incentives.

### Advantages

If you succeed in encouraging a visitor to your site to make a purchase, register, or take some other action at the affiliate provider's site, you will probably earn more than you would by participating in a click-through or commission-based program. Why? Because each qualified action is guaranteed to earn some amount of money for you. Moreover, you only need a few successful signups, downloads, or whatever, before you can start to turn a profit. For example, let's say you earn $1 for every one of your site's visitors who signs up on Clip2.com; if 100 of your site's visitors sign up with Clip2.com to share your links every week, you could earn up to $400 in a month. Not too shabby.

## Disadvantages

The key to succeeding with this type of program is to increase traffic to your site (read: get new users). Some merchant affiliate programs state that once a user visits the merchant's site, he or she "belongs" to that merchant. That means that even if a user made a purchase at the affiliate provider's site by clicking on a link on *your* site, if he or she was a customer of that merchant any time in the past (no matter what route he or she took to arrive at the site), you will not get paid. This clause has been added to many affiliate agreements because some merchants can justify offering affiliate programs only as a means of acquiring *new* customers, meaning they cannot afford to pay to have their existing customers return to their site. This is especially the case with merchants that already offer discounted prices for their products or service; in fact, some merchants even lose money on affiliate transactions, expecting to break even only when that visitor returns to buy something later. The bottom line: Read the small print on affiliate agreements. For some affiliate programs, you need new blood to keep the checks coming in.

## Recommendations

Determine how much you will be paid for each *new referral* versus how much money you could make if you were making a commission *from every sale*, then estimate or test to see how many of your visitors you can convince to buy a product or service that you're recommending/linking to on your Web site.

For example, let's say you're reviewing two affiliate programs from two similar merchants. The first is offering a flat-fee affiliate program that pays $5 for each new customer you refer to him or her. The second merchant is offering a commission-based affiliate program that pays 15 percent of sales. Now let's assume that the visitor you refer purchases $150 worth of products or services. Under the commission-based program, you'd make twice as much money as under the flat-fee program. If, however, the flat-fee program offers $15 per new customer, your referral would have to spend $250 in order for you to receive the same amount of money under the commission-based program. Obviously, if the products being sold have a low per-unit cost (such as CDs or vitamins) there's little chance you're going to make more than $15 in commissions, so a flat-fee program would work better for you. Keep in mind, however, that most merchants won't offer flat-fee compensation to promote low per-unit-cost products and service—at least not until micropayments become the norm.

## Example: Priceline.com

Priceline.com has pioneered a unique e-commerce business model known as a *demand collection system* that enables Web users to save money on a wide range of products and services, including airline tickets, hotel accommodations, cars, groceries, and home equity loans, while enabling merchants to generate additional revenue. Priceline.com offers online shoppers a "name your price" model that works like this: The shopper specifies what he or she wants and how much he or she is willing to pay for it; then the customer provides credit card information. Priceline.com searches for a suitable match in the inventories provided by participating merchants. If there is a match, Priceline.com fills the shopper's request.

As one of its affiliates, Priceline.com's affiliate program will pay you $1 for every "reasonable offer" posted to its service. If you refer more than 50 reasonable offers in a month, you earn $2 for the fifty-first offer and all subsequent offers during that month. For services like Priceline.com that offer big-ticket items, a flat-fee affiliate program is an obvious solution for attracting qualified buyers. And because most of its offerings are frequently used services such as hotel and airline tickets, you stand a good chance of realizing a substantial revenue stream for your related site. Figure 2.2 is an example of a Priceline.com affiliate, Travelsites.com.

# Click-Through Programs

Click-through programs pay affiliates a small amount of money for each unique visitor they deliver to the program-provider merchant's site. Affiliates generally earn between $.01 and $.05 per unique visitor.

## Advantages

The primary advantage associated with click-through programs is that you get paid for every unique visitor you send to the merchant's Web site, whether he or she makes a purchase or not. Another advantage is that most click-through programs are well established and, therefore, provide advanced reporting tools that make tracking your earnings quite easy. Likewise, little effort is required to set up and maintain your affiliate links; you merely add a text-based hyperlink or banner advertisement to your site, and it practically runs itself. Your only responsibility is to encourage a healthy stream of traffic to your site to ensure that enough of your visitors click through so that you can make some real money.

**Figure 2.2** Travelsites.com tells you how to get there cheap.

## Disadvantages

One of the disadvantages of click-through programs, as compared to commission-based or flat-fee referral programs, is that you receive a few cents only for driving a customer to the affiliate provider's destination; you don't earn money for anything he or she buys as a result. Obviously, if the destination site sells high-cost-per-item goods, you could be losing out on substantial commissions.

Additionally, to protect themselves from dishonest affiliates who fake clicks, some banner ad click-through programs limit the maximum payout affiliates can receive, based on the click-through ratio (the number of banner impressions you display that actually lead to a click-through). For example, a program with a click-through ratio limit of 5 percent and a payment $.03 per click-through would limit your earnings to a maximum of $1.50 per 1,000 banners that you display, no matter how many visitors actually click on those banners to access the merchant's site.

Although a 5 percent click-through ratio is considered very successful for most sites (the typical being around 2 percent), if your site contains highly relevant, targeted content in a popular niche, your visitors are more likely to click on a relevant banner advertisement. Therefore, this type of program could limit your upside and hurt your bottom line. In other words, in this case, you're damned if you do.

And if you don't have a high traffic site, then you're damned if you don't, because unless you have hundreds of thousands of pageviews per month, your earnings will likely fall short of paying for that trip to Paris this year. Here's the deal: Let's say that your site gets 10,000 pageviews a month and that you are displaying links for a click-through program that pays you $.03 per click-through. If you get a 2 percent click-through ratio, you will earn $6 for the month. Basically, you'd have to boost your click-through ratio to 5 percent before you could afford even to buy a new CD.

Because it's very costly to mail checks for $6 (or less), many click-through affiliate programs require you to earn a minimum payout amount—usually between $15 and $50—before they'll send a check to you. The good news is that most affiliate programs will send checks either every month or every quarter, and carry over subthreshold balances to the next earning period. So, for example, if you earn $12 dollars through an affiliate program with a minimum payout amount of $15 in May, that $12 balance will be carried over to your June earnings. Consequently, you'll only have to earn $3 in June to receive a check from the program. On the other hand, if you don't have a high-traffic site and you're earning $6 a month from your affiliate program, it will take you three months to receive a that $18 check.

## Recommendations

Always read the affiliate agreement/terms *thoroughly* before joining a click-through program. If your site's traffic measures fewer than 10,000 pageviews a month, you should consider finding a suitable commission-based program. That way, you'll only have to make a couple of sales before you receive a check. However, if you're not really interested in pushing products and/or if you have a high-volume Web site that contains a broad spectrum of content, check out some of the great click-through programs, one of which is described next.

## Example: Quicken.com's Affiliate Network

Quicken built its own Quicken.com Affiliate Network, which enables any individual or company with a Web site to add investment, debt planning, and insurance tools to their Web site. You can place one or many of these tools on your site to enable your visitors to search for quotes, design retirement plans, and even plan for their kids' college education. The Quicken Affiliate Network pays you $.01 every time your visitors use a Quicken.com tool, up to a maximum amount of $3,000 per affiliate, per calendar quarter.

Joining Quicken's Affiliate Network is a no-brainer if your site has anything to do with personal finance (investing, credit, or online banking), retirement, travel, automobile sales, education, or even pregnancy (the "paying for college" factor). Unlike books and music, which consumers buy only occasionally, investment news and personal finance are something many Web users check on and think about on a daily basis. A key benefit to using Quicken is that its tools provide useful information to your users that can help you bring them back to your site. Content is king, and they're paying you to wear their crown. You can't beat that.

Figure 2.3 shows an example of a news site, news-4-u.com, that offers their financial newsreaders access to Quicken's powerful financial tools.

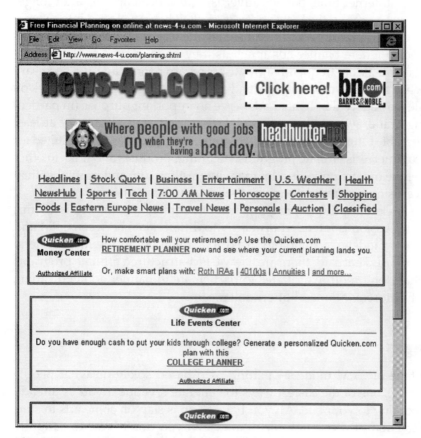

**Figure 2.3**  news-4-u's Finance Planning Tools page.

# CPM (Cost-per-Thousand) Impressions

The fourth and final method frequently used for measuring affiliate activity levels is based on *impressions;* that is, how many times the affiliate program provider's link is *seen* by your visitors, as opposed to how many times your visitor clicks on the link or actually purchases something once he or she clicks through. By generally accepted convention, impressions are "sold" by affiliate sites at some price per thousand, or "cost per thousand" (the M in CPM stands for the Latin for thousand).

CPM-based affiliation models are most often used with advertising banner syndicators such as DoubleClick, AdKnowledge, and LinkExchange. These services work by aggregating the available banner space on their thousands of affiliate sites and then turning around and selling these slots to advertisers that want to display their banners. In this way, small Web sites can sell ad space without having to hire a direct sales force or deal with the advertiser (though some syndicators require that their affiliates meet certain traffic volumes).

Speaking in Internet time, banner advertising has been around a lot longer than affiliate programs on the Web, and as a result, it has developed into a somewhat mature industry, but according to some, one that is in decline since users have learned to ignore banner ads much as they have learned to ignore television advertising. More frequently now, users regard banner ads as a necessary nuisance when they download a page, and are increasingly less likely to click on them. While we believe that banner ads serve an important purpose (in particular, building brand awareness for the advertiser) and are here to stay at least for the foreseeable future, we don't think they are anywhere near as well suited for driving e-commerce as affiliate programs. Including products and links to other affiliate revenue opportunities is a lot more interesting, fun, and profitable than banner advertising programs for you as well as your site's visitors.

Banner ad-related affiliate programs are, therefore, not the focus of this book. This discussion is intended primarily to differentiate between CPM and other payment models/terminology used for affiliation, in the most general sense of the word. That said, there are a few CPM-structured affiliate programs available that don't require affiliates to participate in banner ad syndication, including the aforementioned Bottomdollar.com.

## Advantages

The advantage of CPM models—getting paid based solely on what people see—is that it is one of the easiest ways to generate revenue if you've already got traffic coming to your site. All you have to do is slap on some ads to start earning a fraction of a cent for each pageview; you don't have to carefully select what is displayed on your site nor try to align the ad spots with the interests of your visitors (though ad syndicators can help you do this).

## Disadvantages

Unfortunately, as a thoughtful site developer who spends a lot of time experimenting with the precise look and placement of elements on your site, the last thing you may want is something whose design and content you have no control over. You could, for example, have to display an obnoxious-looking slow-downloading, animated banner ad that has nothing to do with the content of your site. Obviously, not all banners are in poor taste; the point is that you, the site developer, have little or no control over what appears. You also are limited as to the format of banner ads. The vast majority are a standard size of 468 pixels wide by 60 pixels high, which Web designers are forced to design around.

Perhaps the most unfortunate aspect of CPM-based compensation is that it generates an incentive for site developers to entice visitors (sometimes through clumsy or tricky means) to see *more* pages rather than *better* pages. For instance, a less-scrupulous designer might be tempted to break up an article to appear on many small pages in order to be able to include more banner ads, when one longer page would have made for a more convenient and more logical user experience. Well-targeted e-commerce opportunities, on the other hand, are actually regarded by many users as a site enhancement! (Has anybody ever considered banners to be an enhancement to a site?) From our point of view, appropriate product (or service) information can be considered content only if it is relevant and useful within the context of the hosting page.

Not surprisingly, then, some studies have shown that visitors are more than twice as likely to click on a product's name or "buy now" link as they are to click on a banner, because users already know what to expect (more information and a chance to buy the product), whereas banner ads usually do not make clear what the result will be if you "click here." As stated earlier, users are clicking through banner ads less and less frequently across the board (down 95 percent by some estimates), forcing some who sell banner space to lower their rates from a $30 CPM down to a mere $2 CPM. Web companies that promised (their investors) to become profitable are finding that the advertising CPM model doesn't work very well; hence, they are unable to sell their available ad space inventory, despite lowering their CPM. To supplement or replace these programs, former banner-sustained Web sites are turning to the commission-, bounty-, and click-through-based revenue programs that comprise the focus of this book.

## Recommendations

There is no rule that says you can't have multiple revenue models coexisting on your site. In fact, you should experiment with any and all that make sense, given your business, design, and editorial requirements. If you have a good space for banner ads, which doesn't seem well suited to links that use other types of compensation methods, and if the ads won't detract significantly from your users' experience at your site, then by all means, give CPM a try.

# The Exotic Others

Though commission-based and bounty programs continue to be the most popular affiliate programs in use today, some merchants are creating more exotic approaches to acquiring affiliates and their referrals. For affiliates less interested in building revenue streams for their sites and more interested in, for example, getting free stuff, being eligible for special deals and discounts, and even acquiring frequent flyer miles, the rules of the affiliate game change a bit. No longer a matter of earning $.05 here and $5 there, the issue is "What do I get?" A variety of affiliate programs are answering that question in fun and unique ways.

## Incentive Programs

As the adage says, money doesn't always equate to happiness. The developers of CDNOW would probably agree. CDNOW, a top online music store, has instituted a unique payout approach for their affiliate offering. Rather than pay a commission for referrals, it offers store credit known as Cosmic Credit. As of this writing, affiliates with personal Web sites (that is, noncommercial sites) receive 7 percent of all purchases made through their affiliate link. That 7 percent is calculated and paid out immediately as Cosmic Credit, which affiliates can use to buy anything sold at CDNOW's site after the first sale is made. (Affiliate credit account IDs are updated weekly.)

CDNOW's Cosmic Credit affiliate program is a great tool for adding value to your Web site—not to mention for bankrolling your music collection. Just remember: Promote music at your site only if it's relevant to your site's existing content, and focus relevant sections on a specific music genre or an artist or artists. For example, the Angela's World Travels home page features a small section called Favorite Music that contains links to all types of music from Hip Hop to Country & Western. Angela's site is probably less enticing to Hip Hop fans, who would likely opt for Crazy About Hip Hop, a site dedicated to Hip Hop artists that features links to biographical information, albums, downloadable samples, and the latest news about the hottest Hip Hop artists. Angela's site would fare better by featuring Los Mocosos in the Latin American Travels section of her site, Ostad Elahi in the Persian Paradise section, and so on. Put another way, niche + relevance + traffic = repeat customers = $$$.

Figure 2.4 illustrates an example of a well-placed CDNOW affiliate link. Here, the Miss Janet Fanclub site (dedicated to recording artist Janet Jackson)

**Figure 2.4**   Miss Janet Fanclub, a CDNOW affiliate.

provides its visitors with tour dates and locations, news, games, chat, and more. Not only is the link to her current album relevant, it's expected—even if the album was released in 1998.

> **NOTE**   Got lots of traffic coming to your site? CDNOW also offers a commission-based (as in real cash) affiliate program for business and high-volume e-commerce sites. See the Appendix for details.

## Multi-Tiered Programs

Most of the sites we've mentioned so far in the chapter are single-level programs that enable you to earn money (or incentives) for every unique visitor you send to a program-provider merchant's site. But as we mentioned, some

## VIRAL MARKETING

Viral marketing is one of the more important buzz phrases of the many that have been spawned by the Web economy. The term refers to any marketing mechanism that tends to spread exponentially by making copies of itself, such as a chain-letter e-mail that contains, among other things, a commercial URL. There are a lot of superstitious people out there who will always forward any chain letters they receive; in this way, this marketing mechanism succeeds in reproducing, just as viruses trick host cells into making copies of them.

Sending chain e-mails and spam are almost universally regarded as unacceptable (and sometimes even illegal) behavior on the Net, but there are numerous examples of ethical viral marketing. One famous case is that of Hotmail—the first provider of free, Web-based e-mail—which included in the footer of each of its users' e-mail a small commercial for its service. This equated to millions of e-mails per day percolating through the Web with the message, "Get your free Web-based e-mail at www.hotmail.com" and contributed to Hotmail's wildfire rate of adoption among Web users.

Multi-tier affiliate programs are 100 percent viral in nature because their raison d'etre is to self-replicate via thousands of autonomous Web site owners who do the work of attracting new customers to the merchant, while the merchant keeps busy marketing itself in other ways.

Unfortunately, the term viral marketing has begun to carry a negative connotation, as its use has become more frequently associated with spam and other unethical Web marketing practices.

programs don't allow you to earn money from repeat visitors or from referrals from your visitors. For example: We really like the book *Increasing Hits and Selling More on Your Web Site*, so on our Web site we added a review of the book along with a link to it at Borders.com so our visitors can easily buy it. And being good Webmasters, and because we don't want to present only our own opinion, we also added links to reviews and analyses on other sites as well. If you (our visitor) click through to one of these other sites and click on its Buy This Book affiliate link, we won't earn a cent. Though, some visitors undoubtedly will go back to our site to buy the book, the majority will opt for the most convenient method, which means they're going to buy it from the current page they're viewing.

Multi-tiered programs change all that. By signing on with a multi-tier program, you can earn a commission for sales made not only by visitors who follow a link on your site but also those who follow a link on one of your *subaffiliate*'s sites (see Figure 2.5). A subaffiliate is a Web site (or Web site owner) that joins an affiliate program via your Web site, as opposed to signing up

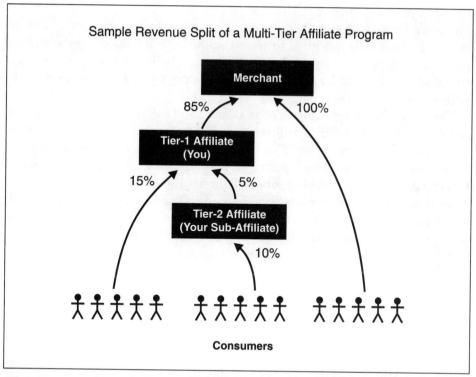

**Figure 2.5** The two-tier affiliate model.

directly at the program-provider merchant's site. Generally, subaffiliates join a program by clicking a Join This Affiliate Program link on your site that takes them to a Sign Up page on the affiliate program-provider's site. By encouraging those of your visitors who have their own Web sites to become your subaffiliates, you not only earn commissions on the purchases made by *your* visitors, but you can earn commissions on purchases generated by your subaffiliates' visitors as well.

The good news for merchants is that multi-tier programs enable them to acquire more affiliates, to help promote their product or service at a grassroots level. The good news for affiliates is multi-tier programs mean that they can get paid for both direct sales to their site visitors as well as for ongoing sales made by visitors who become their subaffiliates. If you choose the right multi-tiered affiliate program, your earnings could start to pile up.

## How Multi-Tiered Programs Work

When you join an affiliate program, you are assigned a unique affiliate ID so that program-provider merchants can identify and reward you for driving traffic to their site. This ID is included in the HTML for a banner or product link that points to a provider merchant's site, product page, and so on. For multi-tier affiliate programs, you can place an additional banner or link on your site specifically designed to advertise the benefits of joining the affiliate program in order to acquire subaffiliates. This subaffiliate banner or link also contains your affiliate ID and points your visitors to the provider merchant's affiliate program sign-up page.

The following sample HTML code is that used by netgenie.com, which (as of this writing) offers $25 to affiliates for each referral that signs up for netgenie's One Fee ISP service, and $5 for each customer generated by an affiliate's subaffiliates. Netgenie.com supports a *two-tiered* program, which means that you can only have one level of sub-affiliation. (The most popular multi-tiered programs are only two levels deep.) This code is used to create a link that reads "Earn money the easy way! Be a netgenie affiliate!" When visitors click that link on your Web site and join the program, they become your subaffiliates, and whenever they generate revenue, you generate revenue.

```
<A
HREF="http://www.netgenie.com/affiliate/signup/index.cfm?id=affiliateID#
here"><IMG SRC="http://www.net-genie.net/banners/subaffiliate.gif"
WIDTH=88 HEIGHT=31 ALT="Earn money the easy way! Be a netgenie
affiliate!" BORDER="0"></A>
```

Figure 2.5 illustrates the two-tier affiliate model.

### Sound Like Multi-Level Marketing?

Whether you're a fan of multi-level marketing (MLM) or you hate it, it has similarities to, as well as distinctions from, multi-tier affiliation, and both are worth mentioning at this point in the discussion.

For those of you unfamiliar with the term, MLM is a business structure that has been around for a long time, predating the Web by decades, and popular in companies such as Amway, Tupperware, and Mary Kay Cosmetics. In MLM, individuals—typically called *distributors*—earn money by selling a company's products directly and by signing up other distributors. For the latter, they keep a percentage of what the distributors they sign up sell, and so on down the line. MLM's reputation has more recently fallen on hard times, partly due to its similarities with illegal (but different) "pyramid schemes"; partly due to results of many who've tried and failed with MLM; and partly due to the misleading get-rich-quick, in-your-face sales tactics used by some of its more energetic practitioners.

Like most things in life, there are good and bad MLM programs and good and bad MLM distributors as well. Generally speaking, we believe that those programs that emphasize actual sales of actual products are far more substantive and viable than those that promote signing up your own distributors without regard to what products or services are actually being provided by those distributors.

As you can see, there are definite similarities between multi-tier affiliate programs and MLM—the most obvious being that they share the same basic financial model. A less obvious similarity is that a lot of the same people are drawn to both, for these reasons: be one's own boss, work from home, earn money in spare time, and so on. Strictly speaking, if you earn a percentage of a sale originated by a distributor (subaffiliate) that you've signed up, it's multi-level marketing. But unlike MLM, most affiliate programs permit only one or two tiers of subaffiliation. For example, if your subaffiliate A signs up affiliate B, who then signs up affiliate C, you don't get a percentage of C's commissions. In this way, most multi-tier affiliate programs pass our sniff test.

Multi-tier affiliate programs are more concerned with generating sales of products than they are with signing up distributors, who spend more time signing up distributors than merchandising the products sold to end users. As a further control, some multi-tier affiliate programs only allow those affiliates who exceed certain sales volumes to sign up subaffiliates. For many mainstream e-merchants, subaffiliation is a land-grab attempt to sign up as many sites as quickly as possible (before they sign up with a competitor's affiliate program); it's not designed to sign up sites that will never deliver significant traffic through to the merchant. This is quite different than many MLM programs that place first priority on signing up your own distributors, especially when people have to pay money in order to join.

This brings up the next important point: Be wary about joining *any* multi-tier affiliate program that requires you to "make an investment" (read: purchase inventory or otherwise give money). By and large (exceptions may exist), these organizations regard the practice of signing up distributors as a revenue model in and of itself—not a means to an end—of capturing the attention of as many end-users (colloquially referred to as *eyeballs*) in order to sell products and services. Though it is tempting to issue the sweeping statement, "*Never* join an affiliate program that asks for money," we can't, for two reasons. First, greater numbers of traditional distribution channels are migrating to the Web and minimum orders have existed almost since the dinosaurs as a means of screening out less than committed resellers. As business-to-business e-commerce becomes more Web-enabled, we may see hurdles erected to qualify those who apply as Web distribution partners; or we may see competition between applicants in exchange for exclusivity or custom services. Clearly, merchants that spend time and devote resources to working with a small number of premium channel partners need to be careful about picking those partners. For now, however, the power seems to be firmly in the hands of those that capture eyeballs, as opposed to those that actually sell something. Amazon.com pays to have its logo on Yahoo!; Yahoo! doesn't pay Amazon for the right to show the logo.

The second reason stems from the launch by Amway of Quixtar.com, its all-encompassing, mother of all MLM/affiliate-programs Web company, where end consumers can buy just about anything, and distributors can sign up, order inventory, and go for financial independence via the online world (using affiliate product links), the offline world (talking to strangers in line at the grocery store), or both. Quixtar is a potential exception to the "never pay to join" rule simply due to Amway's sheer number of distributors, and, perhaps more importantly, it's amazing breadth and depth of product selection.

If it were possible to do away with the unattractive, spammy, in-your-face sales tactics that have made MLM famous (or infamous), clearly there would be something attractive about a flat, purely peer-to-peer distribution model, one that seemingly chaotically—almost anarchistically—shatters the dominant multinational corporate oligopoly-driven economy, which so many of us believe rules our lives. (Microsoft notwithstanding, we're not totally convinced it does.) A more user-friendly version of the basic Amway idea might be considered a potentially democratic and egalitarian new approach to the age-old problem of distributing products with maximal market efficiency. If Amway doesn't quite achieve it, then perhaps all of the other affiliate programs, in aggregate, may come close to the mark. If, however, Amway can pull it off, then look out Amazon.com. Who knows, maybe one day we'll read of the largest merger in history, called Amwayzon.com.

## Buying from Yourself

While many merchants discourage you from making purchases by following your own links, some Web services have built a business model based on buying from yourself. The following are two interesting, though extremely different, approaches to making money without having a single visitor come to your Web site.

### Cheaters Sometimes Prosper

Although many affiliate programs specifically state in their agreements that you can't earn a commission by clicking on an affiliate link on your own site, there are affiliates who have successfully built Web pages from which they alone purchase products and services. And they get paid. How do they get away with it? Well, some merchants either can't or don't bother to police themselves. In the latter case, for example, if an individual builds a page and uses it to establish an ongoing purchasing relationship with the merchant, most merchants chalk it up to "building customer loyalty" because, by doing so, they gain a devoted, repeat visitor. And the cost of acquiring and maintaining a repeat customer is much more expensive than shelling out $1.50 for an occasional book.

You can make (well, actually save) a lot of money buying from yourself if you shop online frequently and/or if you're buying high-ticket items; but if you get caught and the merchant decides not to look the other way, you could be dropped from the program and lose all of your nonpaid earnings.

### Using Affiliation to Buy Stuff for Yourself: ebates.com

There are legitimate ways to get paid for buying for yourself—without adding a single affiliate link to your Web site. One such solution is ebates.com. This site sponsors a free program that pays you in the form of rebates for purchases you make from the ebates.com store. Here's how it works: ebates.com gives you a special e-mail address (victoria@ebates.com, for example) that you use when you make a purchase from its online store. (Note: You can use this e-mail address only to receive messages from merchants!) You shop around the online store, buy stuff, then, when prompted, enter your special ebates.com e-mail address to earn your rebate. In effect, ebates.com acts as the affiliate, passing the commission it makes from your purchases along to you as a rebate. The rebate percentage is usually a flat commission set by the online store. Each merchant's rebate commission is clearly listed on the main shopping page; this makes comparison-shopping a lot easier. Figure 2.6 shows an example of ebates.com's online shopping marketplace.

**NOTE** Certain products are not eligible for rebates, including auction items and prescriptions from an online drugstore, among others. Make sure to read the fine print!

To ensure flexibility, ebates does not depend on only one affiliate model; it also provides a multi-tiered affiliate program. If you choose, you can earn rebates using the "traditional" affiliate model; in this case, by placing a link to ebates in an e-mail or on your Web site where your visitors can click to join ebates. At the time of this writing, when any of your site visitors join, you get 10 percent back on all of the rebates they earn. And if your visitors' visitors join, you get 5 percent back; finally, if those third-level visitors refer new visitors, you get 2.5 percent. The ebates program offers both e-mail referral kits and banner referral kits, so you can choose whether to send your invitation via e-mail or post it on your site.

### Recommendations

If you're intending to use ebates.com's multi-tier affiliate program to make money from visitors who join, be sure to first review the affiliate programs

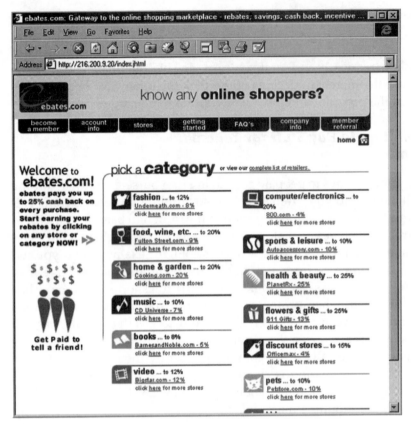

**Figure 2.6**    Earn rebates by shopping online at ebates.com.

offered directly by the ebates merchants. Currently, ebates offers an 8 percent rebate on products at Cooking.com (which means you would make 0.8 percent for items your referrals buy). However, if your site visitor clicked on your Cooking.com affiliate link and went straight to Cooking.com to make his or her purchase, you'd make a whopping 10 percent (as of this writing). Clearly, if all or most of your links are for products sold by a single e-merchant, it makes sense to affiliate directly with that merchant.

On the other hand, if you're not interested in maintaining a Web page for affiliate links, ebates.com offers a nice way to save money while shopping on the Web.

## Content Instead of Cash: iSyndicate

Looking for something different to enhance the value of your site? Consider a program such as iSyndicate Express (www.isyndicate.com). For no charge, iSyndicate will automatically upload updated headline links from resources like Reuters, CNET, Wired, and TheStreet.com to your own customizable news site. With iSyndicate, you can carry links to Web news that you've determined to be relevant to your audience. You simply select the type of headline news you want, and iSyndicate Express will generate a headline news page for you. iSyndicate Express doesn't pay commissions, but it does offer a service that can save you hundreds or even thousands of dollars. From iSyndicate's point of view, the content providers are, in effect, paying for the placement of its news links on your site to drive traffic back to its sites (where the full articles are read by your visitors).

Figure 2.7 is an example of an iSyndicate affiliate site, ForumCenter.com, which provides Internet-related tips, FAQs and general resources.

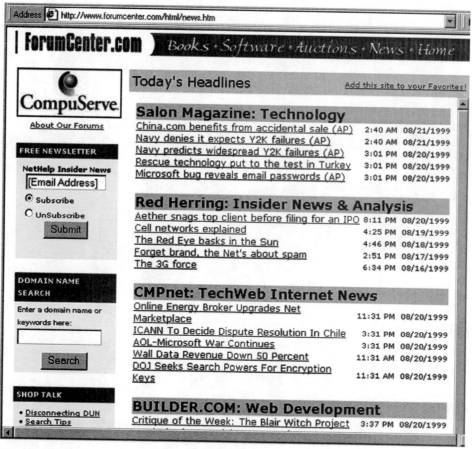

**Figure 2.7** ForumCenter.com, an iSyndicate affiliate.

## Summary

Your first step as an affiliate is to decide which type of program will work best for your Web site. The purpose of this chapter was to give you the background information you need on the various types of affiliate programs available. Chapter 3, "A Strategy for Your Site," provides some guidelines to help you make the choice as to which one is right for you.

# 3

# A Strategy for Your Site

What is the purpose of your site? Is it simply a personal home page? A haven for Java developers? Or the best online resource for antenna tops? Your site's function will be the primary factor when you are determining the most appropriate method or methods for adding affiliate links. To guide this process, this chapter provides examples of various types of sites and the affiliate methods we recommend for each.

## What Does Your Site Do Now?

Before you can choose a suitable affiliate program, you need to consider the nature of your Web site. What function does it perform now and how might that function need to change after you join an affiliate program? Are you seeking a gold mine, a great and long-lasting partnership, or just trying to earn pizza money?

## Vanity/Personal Page

Is yours a *vanity site*, where you, for example, provide links to your favorite places online, discuss the travel books you're reading, post your resume, and show off pictures from your last trip to Venice? If so, you might consider a program that will help to cover the cost of your Internet service provider or that new scanner you bought so you could share your vacation slides online with your grandmother who lives in Detroit.

For a vanity site or personal page, it's probably safe to say that most, if not all, of your visitors consist of friends, family members, and colleagues with similar interests. If this accurately defines your site, you can earn a little cash by joining a well-established affiliate program such as Amazon. Then you could promote the travel books you used to plan your trip to Venice, for example. You'll probably also want to add a few general-topic links to other merchants' programs, such as featured Italian wines at Virtual Vineyard (now Wine.com), as well to cover all of your bases.

Figure 3.1 is an example of a personal page that offers links to commercial real estate, HTML, Web page promotions, along with personal content. It's an interesting mix isn't it? Hey, that's what personal Web pages are for. Notice that this Webmaster has carefully selected products and services he or she

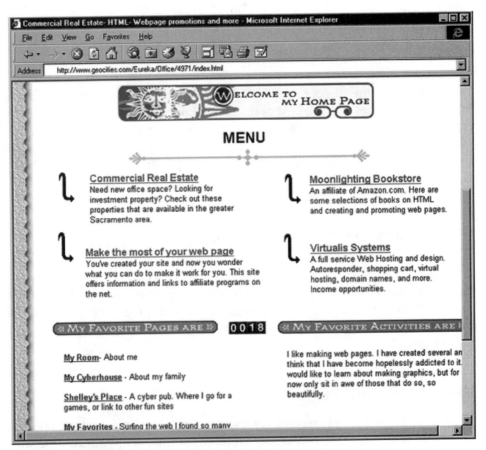

**Figure 3.1**   A personal, or vanity, Web site with affiliate links.

knows will be of interest to the site's target audience—which at the time of this writing consisted of only 18 people, but its future looks bright.

## Topic Expert/Hobbyist

Let's say you are a member of a popular online gaming Web ring where you offer reviews of the latest games, hints, strategies, and add-ons, and you have 10,000 visitors a month who depend on you to be their topic expert. Why not provide affiliate links to the games you're reviewing? Not only will it pay for your online gaming habit, but it will also add value to your content-rich site by providing your visitors with an easy way to get a copy of the hot new game you just reviewed. Ever been to a seminar where the speaker didn't offer supplemental books, tapes, or study aids?

> **NOTE** If you are a topic expert, it is especially important that you take care to join the right affiliate program(s). Shop around for the best prices, best quality, and best customer support for the products or services you're promoting on your site. As an online guru, your visitors will be depending on you to guide them through their purchase decisions, so you'd better take the role seriously. You should update your affiliate links as frequently as needed to ensure you're offering the best solutions. Consider using a service like CrossCommerce to automate your product selection based on your audience criteria, and let it do the work for you. (Read more about CrossCommerce in Chapter 7, "Adding Links to Your Site.")

Another way topic experts can make their sites really interesting is by joining an affiliate program for an online auctioneer. Internet auctions can be a highly successful and financially rewarding business model. In the past, the problem with the auction model for most would-be e-commerce entrepreneurs has been the technical difficulties and financial investment needed to build and promote such sites. Now, however, one program, utrade.com, lets you to create your own customized auction house. You can select specific categories of items—say Beanie Babies, antiques, and sports memorabilia—that you want to sell. Think about it: Your site is already tailored to the needs of your fellow enthusiasts, so why not provide them with a way to buy and trade the things they're interested in? Figure 3.2 shows an example of an auction site customized using the utrade.com program.

If you don't want to spend time customizing an auction site, an option is to join a program like the Sporting Auction and earn $1 or so for every lead to someone who registers a bid on the site. This takes about 10 minutes and provides incredibly valuable, dynamic content to your site. And, as a Webmaster, you know that dynamic content means repeat visitors.

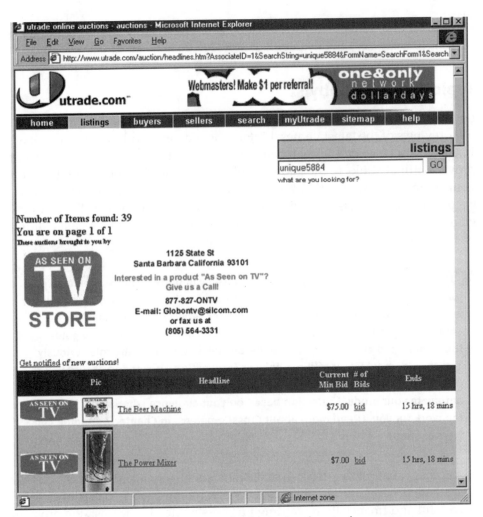

**Figure 3.2** The As Seen on TV Store established using the utrade.com program.

Figure 3.3 illustrates one of the many examples of an Amazon.com affiliate, in this case, as implemented by the Ayn Rand Institute. Dedicated to one of the more influential (if controversial) authors and philosophers of this century, the Ayn Rand Bookstore site provides visitors with convenient access to all of her books, as well as more than 150 Objectivist audio and video lectures and courses. This is a real service, because these items are typically very difficult to find and thus are clearly of value to this site's target audience. Notice in the figure the effort taken by the site's owners to annotate the books they recommend. This will certainly increase their click-through rate and probably the conversion rate as well. In this case, the chances are good that visitors will buy the book here, rather than go directly to Amazon.com, because they've

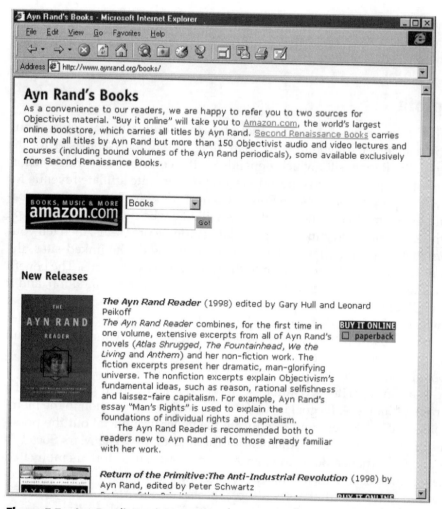

**Figure 3.3** Ayn Rand's Books, an affiliate of Amazon.com.

been given in-depth information from a site that caters to their specific interest. If you were an Ayn Rand fan, who would you be more likely to trust: Amazon .com's editorial staff or the editor of the Ayn Rand Institute's Web site?

Notice, too, in this figure that an important piece of merchandising information is missing: the price of each book. Pricing data is essential in terms of increasing click-through rates, so why isn't it shown here? Believe us, it's not a major oversight. It's because program-provider merchants change their prices frequently, so most discourage, or prohibit, their affiliates from displaying prices, for fear they'll show the wrong price. (From a merchandising perspective, the only thing worse than showing no price is showing an incorrect price.) But if you generate your links through a real-time merchandising content provider like CrossCommerce.com, not only can you can display prices, but you can also rest assured that the price will be automatically updated with no additional effort on your part.

## Nonprofit

But what if you're not out to earn enough cash to quit your day job and buy your own small jet. Maybe in your spare time, you're the Webmaster for the Border Collie Rescue site, which depends on the contributions and sponsorships of others to make ends meet. How do you generate affiliate revenue for a site whose purpose is to rescue Border Collies? It's easy. To begin, it's probably safe to assume that visitors to the site will likely be dog owners. The next step, then, is to find and join a few pet-related affiliate programs; then tell your visitors that each time they make a purchase at one of the linked sites, the revenue earned by your site will go to the foundation as proceeds. The benefit of this is twofold: It enables you to generate money for the foundation, and it offers an interesting way for your avid dog-loving visitors to contribute to a worthy cause. In fact, it's far more likely that they'll make a purchase under these conditions than they would otherwise. Again, give your visitors a fun way to contribute to your cause and they will! After all, how many times have you bought a $3 candy bar from a knee-high Cub Scout?

The Mars Society site (www.marssociety.org) is an interesting example of a nonprofit affiliate site. Its goal is twofold: to provide information to the members of The Mars Society and to educate the general public about the possibilities of exploration and settlement of the Red Planet. The Mars Society's Laws and Governance Bookstore, an Amazon Associates store, is motivated by these same goals, which it meets by offering a comprehensive list of recommended titles about the scientific aspects of exploring and colonizing Mars. The bookstore also includes titles relating to political, ethical, and economical perspectives. Figure 3.4 shows the bookstore's Science and Terraforming page. The Mars Society receives a 15 percent contribution (read: nontaxable commission) from Amazon.com for every book sold through a link on this page.

**NOTE** Many online merchants offer special affiliate programs for nonprofit Web sites. See this book's companion site at www.affiliateselling.com for a list of nonprofit-related affiliate programs.

## Corporate (Web Presence)

Do you work for a corporation that finally bit the bullet last year and built that Web presence your customers were hounding you for? Congratulations! But if

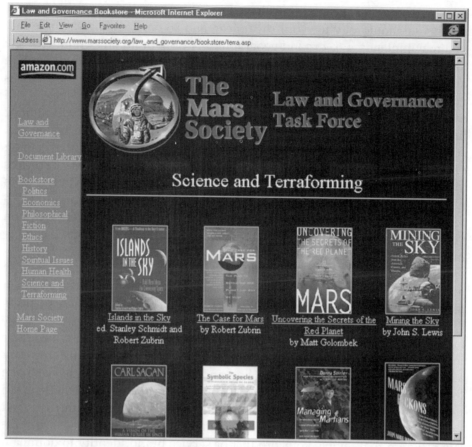

**Figure 3.4**   The Mars Society Bookstore.

your site is already a year or two old, no doubt your customers are beginning to expect more from it. To keep them coming back, you have to give them a reason to do so, whether it's for updated company information, contact information, service descriptions, whatever.

To keep your site fresh and interesting, perhaps you decide to hire a Web team to deliver the goods. The question is: How will you pay for it? First, you need some interesting ways to drive new visitors to your site. (See Chapter 10, "Increasing Hits and Selling More on Your Web Site," for some ideas.) Second, you need to find a way to make the site pay for itself without detracting from its primary purpose—to promote your company. The good news is, it's even possible to use affiliate links to enhance your corporate image. Read on.

Let's say you're the VP of marketing for Angela's Classic Cars, a company that buys and sells vintage automobiles. Your site provides information about classic car maintenance, what to look for when shopping for a classic, how much you should pay for your dream car, and so on. Let's also assume that you're not intending to expand geographically or to build an e-commerce site to sell car parts online (you've done your research and you know there are already many big companies doing that, and, besides, selling car parts online is not your thing). Even in light of all these criteria, your Classic Cars site can still make money through affiliate selling: First, you might want to add affiliate links to books about classic cars that are available from Barnesandnoble.com. And you can turn your repeat visitors into a steady revenue stream by joining programs such as: 411autos.com, which specializes in classic car parts; CarPrices .com, where you can make $3 from every *new* car price quote your visitors request (no purchase necessary); and TheCarLine.com, where you can link to recommended classics you don't have available in your own inventory. Soon your site will be a full-featured place where car buffs will go to get the information they need and the products they want.

If you succeed in making the flow from your site to the program-provider merchants' sites appear seamless, your visitors will continue to use your site as the front door through which they'll go to make linked purchases. This is where affiliate programs that offer co-branded point-of-sale sites are important. Co-branded point-of-sale sites are storefronts, eShelves (described later in the chapter), or other types of virtual stores that you can customize by adding your logo, color scheme, tag line, and other stylistic elements that make them appear at best, *part* of your site, and at least *associated* with your site. We recommend co-branded programs when the merchant running them is well known and has a good online reputation. Ideally, you want to choose an affiliate program that allows your product or service brand identity to dominate the pages that lead up to the sale, as well as the page where your visitor completes the transaction.

By co-branding the site where your visitors will make their purchases, you are essentially giving your stamp of approval on the entire sales process. And, note, if your brand is better known than the program-provider merchant, your visitors will assume *you* are endorsing the merchant. Usually, however, the program-provider merchant's brand will be better known than yours. That's okay, too, as many small sites or brick-and-mortar companies with a great reputation can bolster their brand images by partnering (affiliating) with highly respected online companies. In any case, you can see how important it is to take special care when choosing an affiliate program to join. Just one disgruntled customer can cost you not only his or her repeat visits to your own site, but also any and all commission revenues he or she might have made for you on subsequent visits to your affiliate sites.

See Chapter 7, "Adding Links to Your Site," and the appendix of this book for details on selecting affiliate solutions providers and merchants that facilitate co-branded merchandising and point-of-sale environments.

**NOTE** Keep in mind that some affiliate programs have a clause in their agreement that states that you will only make a commission on the *first sale* made by your visitor. In other words, when a visitor goes to the merchant's page (co-branded or not) from your site, the merchant "owns" that visitor for all future purchases after the current shopping session. You will not make a dime for repeat traffic to that merchant's site. But no two programs are alike, so be sure to thoroughly read the affiliate agreement for each program you're considering. (See the Affiliate Agreement section in Chapter 4, "Joining the Right Program(s).")

CBS SportsLine is a great example of a co-branded affiliate site. CBS SportsLine is an Amazon.com associate (as you've probably figured out by now, Amazon calls its affiliates "associates") that has integrated Amazon's links and banner ads into its online store. The developers of CBS SportsLine know that Amazon has an excellent reputation as an online merchant that consistently provides excellent customer service; an easy, secure ordering process; a reasonable return policy; and custom delivery service.

The developers of CBS SportsLine also no doubt are aware that some of its visitors have probably already made purchases at Amazon in the past. Therefore, CBS SportsLine might not necessarily be able to earn a commission for anything those visitors buy. But here the Amazon affiliate links can serve a different purpose: to provide a convenient shopping area for the site's regular visitors. Perhaps CBS SportsLine is more interested in driving repeat traffic to the site than in earning affiliate revenue. With this model, however, it can do both. And in all likelihood, the developers of CBS SportsLine negotiated Amazon's affiliate agreement. (See the upcoming sidebar titled *Are Affiliate Agreements Negotiable?*)

Figure 3.5 illustrates CBS SportsLine's confidence in driving its users to its store without the assistance of a well-known partner. Notice that the section heading is simply Shopping. Not until the main shopping page (see Figure 3.6) do visitors realize that the CBS SportsLine store is actually an Amazon associate store.

## Publishing/Content

Is your site so rich with dynamic content (news and reviews, for example) that you have no idea how to begin to choose the right program to join? No problem. You can either use a third-party service like CrossCommerce.com to manage and update your affiliate links or you can join many different affiliate programs to supplement your ever-changing content. For example, you could join eToys.com's affiliate program so that the next time you publish an article about Christmas shopping for children, you've got links to the latest must-have toys. Running a story about the MP3 craze? Add some links to the hottest tunes at MP3.com. Are your readers looking for help to recover from a crazy

**Figure 3.5** CBS SportsLine's gateway.

**Figure 3.6** The CBS SportLine store integrated with Amazon.

## ARE AFFILIATE AGREEMENTS NEGOTIABLE?

If your online business is big enough or important enough to matter to an affiliate program-provider merchant, then the adage "everything is negotiable" is true. We know of one company that has several large sites and that belongs to more than 70 different affiliate programs. As a standard practice, this company always asks for a better deal from program merchants. Some merchants are quick to make concessions, others will do so only after much wrangling, and a few refuse to budge unless the site under negotiation boasts truly gargantuan traffic volume.

And even if you're not considered big or important by program-provider merchants, another adage holds true: It never hurts to ask. If you're under a million pageviews per month, don't be put off if Amazon is slow to return your calls. So what if you don't have a nationally recognized brand. You can still take advantage of the opportunity afforded by affiliate programs to partner with a merchant with a killer online identity. Use a third-party affiliate solutions provider like CrossCommerce (see Chapter 7) to get your company's name and logo on the same page as one of the big players—and, of course, get paid a commission for participating in that affiliate partnership. The Mother's Heart (our next example in this chapter), which syndicates maternity-related content to hospitals, has signed up with CrossCommerce to seamlessly integrate eShelves to its site. An *eShelf* is a space allocated on an affiliate site that pulls real-time content from CrossCommerce.com (for example, current product prices) and displays products to the end user. eShelves can contain either fixed products (hand-picked by the affiliate) or a dynamically updated (rules-based) selection of products that are placed alongside an affiliate's content on a Web page. As Figure 3.7 shows, when visitors to The Mother's Heart click through to buy a product from the site's co-branded BabyCenter.com eShelf, they'll likely notice that The Mother's Heart is partnering with BabyCenter, whose site, as of this writing, is ranked as the number-one online baby store. This co-branding gives the impression that The Mother's Heart is important enough to an e-tailing giant like BabyCenter to give up some real estate on its point-of-sale page.

*Continues*

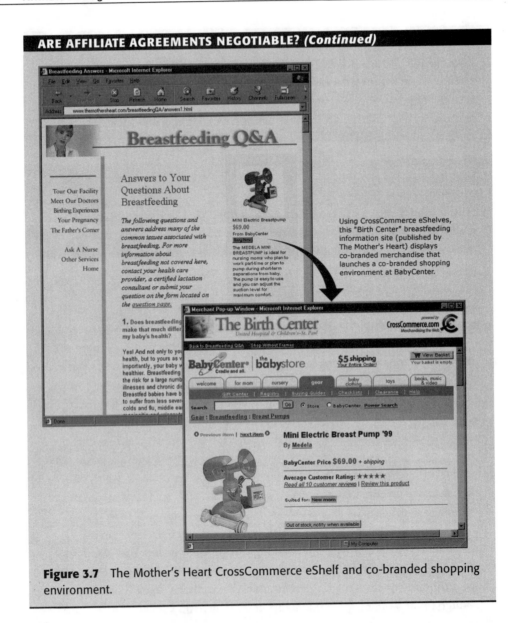

**Figure 3.7**  The Mother's Heart CrossCommerce eShelf and co-branded shopping environment.

holiday season? Sounds like a prime spot for an affiliate link to Body Matrix! You get the picture.

In Figure 3.8, you can see that AOL.com acts as an affiliate for Cooking.com (and many others) on its Food & Cooking page. AOL.com provides the content and navigation, and sprinkles just enough affiliate links on special-interest content pages to make it fun for its readers, who get the feeling that if they return tomorrow, there will be another interesting article to read and another opportunity to buy some cool kitchen gadgets.

**Figure 3.8**  AOL.com, a Cooking.com affiliate.

**NOTE**  Notice in the previous paragraph that we used the phrase "acts as an affiliate." It's usually safe to assume in such a case that Cooking.com and AOL.com have a special, negotiated partnership agreement, one not available to everybody (refer again to the sidebar titled *Are Affiliate Agreements Negotiable?*). However, Cooking.com does have an affiliate program that is available to everyone.

Now what if your site's main focus is the national news, but you want to keep local readers from tuning out after they get their fill of the bigger picture. In this case, you could use a Lycos Content Box to get paid every time one of your site's visitors uses Lycos' search box to get customized local news (www.lycos.com/affiliateprogram/). Lycos provides this pay-per-click solution that not only guarantees earnings for owners of great content sites, but also provides the sort of value that will encourage visitors to return for more.

> **NOW THEY'RE PAYING US**
>
> Almost five years ago, we added the Webcrawler search tool to use on our site. At the time, it was a big deal to be able to use this tool for free, as it cost money to use similar tools. Now, Webcrawler is paying *us* to use it. Isn't the Web great?

## Communities

If you're an owner of a site featuring message boards, chat rooms, forums, and other community-related offerings, you might wonder how you can effectively target different segments with the same affiliate programs, products, and other links. It's really quite simple. The easy way is to use a generalized description of your typical chat users (which, for this discussion, we'll say has been defined as Caucasian males, 25 to 34 years old, college-educated, employed at the manager level or above, with no kids) and determine what some of their interests are before you start inundating them with banner ads. Heck, just look at the development of the Web to figure out what they're into (online gaming, streaming video, MP3s, online trading). After you've determined their interests (computer games, music, auctions, and so forth), join the appropriate affiliate program(s) offered by BRE Software, MP3.com, and/or EBid and add relevant affiliate links to your community.

You can take the more difficult, but definitive, road to target your programs even more effectively. For instance, you could add the Ancestry.com Global Search Template to the top level of your Genealogy message board to enable your users to search for family history records for more than 274 million surnames. Not only would you be providing your users a tool that is pretty much free of charge (although some of the more juicy features require them to register), you're likely to make a few bucks ($3 to $20) for each visitor who thinks it's cool enough to sign up and start using it. If you have 5,000 unique visitors posting to your Genealogy message board a week, and 5 percent of them click on the link (that's 250), even if only 5 percent of those 250 individuals become annual subscribers, you can make about $187.50 per message board per week. Five percent might sound high for a click-through rate, but someone who is using a message board as a tool for researching his or her family history will likely fork over a small amount of money ($20/year) for access to birth records, marriage records, pedigree charts, and other difficult-to-find information.

To continue with the Ancestry.com search tool example, you could also link to Cemetery Records on the Internet (www.interment.net), which offers The Cemetery Column, described as "An electronic journal of everything six feet under." It also contains great tips for using your Palm V to record tombstone inscriptions, a cemetery bookstore (operated in association with Amazon, of course), tours of cemeteries, a mailing list, research tips for finding cemetery records, and more. And, of course, it has the Ancestry.com Global Search Template (see Figure 3.9).

## Already an E-Merchant?

Does your site contain some content, but its main purpose is to sell products or services? You might be thinking that none of this affiliate stuff really applies to you—unless, of course, you're considering starting an affiliate program yourself. That's not a bad idea, but consider this, too: A single Web site can act as both an affiliate and a merchant. We recently read about a company that sells its *competitor's* products through its own site as an affiliate; in this way, the company is guaranteed to make money, even if the customer chooses to buy its competitor's widget.

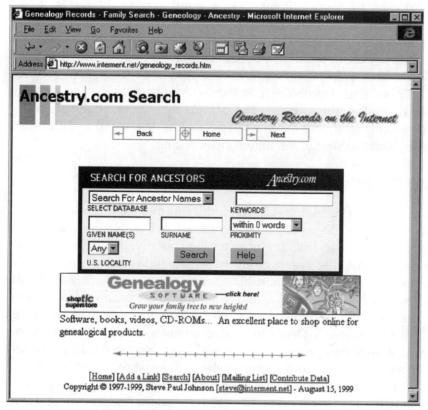

**Figure 3.9**  Cemetery Records' ancestry search.

We're not recommending that you follow this strategy, but it does raise an interesting question: If your company sells a product or group of products, should you use affiliate programs to promote other related products or services? The answer? Of course! Let's say that you're selling transistor radios—all types, all sizes, all prices. You could make a nice commission by enabling your visitors to link to sites that sell AA batteries in bulk at a great price. The idea here is to find a program or programs that provide products or services that mesh well with those you're selling, but that don't necessarily compete directly with your product line. Look for a natural partnership, and leverage someone else's successful business idea to generate more revenue and to create a broader reach for your existing e-commerce site. This concept, called *cross-selling*, is not new. But there are always new and interesting combinations, such as being able to buy microwave popcorn at Blockbuster Video stores. Makes perfect sense, doesn't it?

Think of it this way: You've done a lot of work to get a particular customer to your site for a specific reason. But what if he or she wants more than you're willing to offer at your own site? Obviously, you don't want to lose this customer, but on the other hand, you probably can't (and wouldn't want to if you could) start stocking obscure items in an attempt to meet the needs of each customer, thereby weakening the focus of your core objectives or requiring expertise or capital that you don't possess. Affiliate programs provide the perfect solution. Case in point: One of BabyCenter.com's most successful affiliates is a site that sells porcelain figurines. Why? Maybe people give collectible keepsakes to parents of new babies. Maybe babies keep breaking collectible keepsakes. Who knows. The point is that the porcelain site's visitors also buy baby stuff, and this clever affiliate has developed a strong ancillary revenue stream through intelligent cross-selling.

## Born on the Internet

Are you running a site that was born *on* the Internet *for* the Internet? Like Deja.com for example? Deja.com, formerly known as Deja News, was founded in 1995 to provide a user-friendly interface to an archived version of Usenet, the original Internet discussion group network. Today, Deja.com provides Web users with access to more than 40,000 online discussion forums. The site makes its money from advertising and from links to e-commerce merchants. It turns out that many shoppers looking for product recommendations seek this information through Deja's extensive archive—if you want to know what kind of surfboard a beginner should buy, somebody has certainly asked the question before and someone else has answered. Deja.com recognizes that once a customer makes a decision about purchasing a product, he or she is usually eager to act on that decision. To capitalize on that tendency,

## AFFILIATE SALES AS A REVENUE MODEL

Spend some time browsing the Web and you'll quickly see that many new venture capital-backed Web startup sites contain no advertising whatsoever on their sites. Of course, they're Web startups and no one is concerned about revenue yet, right? Not long ago, the statistic that mattered was number of users. Later, monthly pageviews was the number to count. And as of this writing, the more traditional revenue factor is resurfacing. (The even more traditional profit factor has yet to make its comeback.) Investors want to know how startup entrepreneurs plan to earn a living when their venture capital runs out.

The point: If you're a startup, be prepared. If your revenue models aren't clear yet, find a way to include affiliate sales to generate revenue for your fledgling Web company. Haven't hatched your million-dollar idea yet? Build a model around affiliate revenue opportunities from the ground up (as did Epinions.com, which in record time raised $8MM in its first round of venture capital). For new Web-based companies, there has never been a quicker, more viable, easy, turnkey solution for generating real revenues immediately. (For links to startup consultants, visit www.affiliateselling.com.)

Deja.com places contextual links to e-commerce retailers throughout its Web service.

Here's how the Deja.com setup works: We searched for a Usenet discussion about avocados to try to find out why a bowl of guacamole won't turn brown for days if you leave the avocado pit in. Though we never found the answer to that question, we were offered links to books about avocados available at Amazon.com. We were also given the chance to participate in an auction for some gorgeous "avocado-green clip-on earrings." Okay, okay, Deja can't make a perfect match every time, but you get the idea; and more often than not, you will find exactly what you're looking for. The method is this: Grab the users while they're interested and give them the ability to act on their interests immediately—impulse shopping at its best!

Figures 3.10 and 3.11 illustrate Deja.com's impulse shopping feature. Figure 3.10 shows Deja's results for a search on avocado, and Figure 3.11 shows the Amazon.com page that is the result of clicking on the avocado link on Deja.com's page. What makes this so interesting is that Deja.com shows everything available that might be of interest to someone looking for information about avocados, then goes one step further, guiding the user to a new source for information. Not only is it convenient, but Deja also earns a commission on any book, video, music item, or auction item purchased.

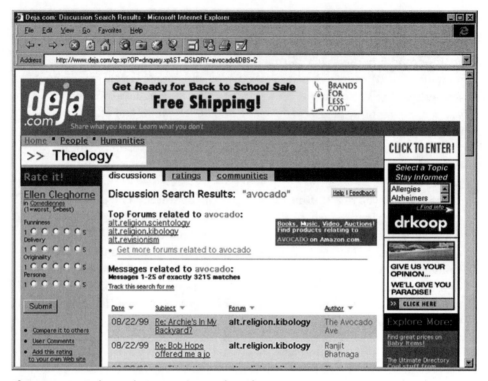

**Figure 3.10**   Deja.com's Amazon's search tool.

## Self-Service Sites

Many Web sites have self-service functionality, enabling users to complete tasks they used to do in person or by using the telephone, such as online investing, paying bills, and buying everything from music to clothing to groceries. And speaking of groceries, let's use a grocery site as an example of a self-service site that obviously should be earning affiliate revenue.

Peapod, a leading Internet grocer, is a great example of a merchant that should also become an affiliate. Peapod offers their affiliates a program that pays $15 when a referred visitor from their sites places his or her first Peapod order, and an additional $15 when the customer places his or her third order. While it's commendable that Peapod sees the value in using affiliates to increase its user base, it could also benefit from including a few affiliate links itself. The site lists numerous online partners and sponsors, but there's still room for an affiliate link or two. For example: Say you typically include a few somewhat expensive bottles of wine on your grocery list, but this trip you add a corkscrew to your list. Well, Peapod doesn't sell wine accessories like the Screw Pull (a very cool, expensive corkscrew). It should, given its record of your (and no doubt others') repeated purchases of fine wine. Peapod could

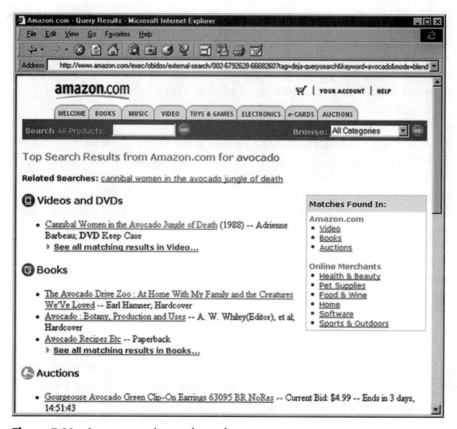

**Figure 3.11**   Amazon.com's search results.

add an affiliate link to, say, wine.com and earn an 8 percent referral commission on the sale of that $150 Screw Pull—after all, $12 is not too shabby for adding a single line of HTML.

## Make Your Affiliate Choice Count

Whether your Web site is a mega-portal that measures 1,000,000 pageviews a day or a one-person operation you're developing in your free time, and that has seen only a few hundred folks, whom you've met online while playing multiuser adventure games, it's very important that you make your choice of affiliate programs count—literally and figuratively. For example, let's say you own BuyFancyWine.com; well, you're not going to see your traffic increase and your revenue skyrocket by adding a link to a merchant offering AA batteries in bulk. The batteries could cost $.35 a gross and none of your visitors will care. They come for the wine—and maybe some chocolate—but definitely not for a bucket of AAs. Nor will your site income increase if you join an online car retailer whose program pays per click for referred visitors. It will send a mixed message, and that's distracting to visitors. Are you so hungry for that one visitor's $3 dollar commission that you're willing to throw irrelevant affiliate banner ads into prime real estate on your site? Your visitors might think so.

Spend the time to make thoughtful decisions. Try some things, watch your reports, and make modifications. The results can be very significant, whether you're a college student who can really use another $200 or a large, high-volume site struggling to make payroll.

Web sites should save their expensive real estate for affiliate links that supplement their own offerings. Otherwise, it just looks like another irrelevant banner ad.

## Summary

Whether yours is a hobbyist site that measures 100 unique visitors a month or a high-volume site that sees more than a million, there's an affiliate opportunity awaiting you. Make meaningful choices by joining programs that provide the highest earning potential for your site and the best value to your visitors.

Now that you're familiar with the four main types of affiliate programs and the appropriate affiliate opportunities for specific types of Web sites, you're ready to begin surveying the broad variety of affiliate programs available to you. Your goal is to identify those that will best meet the unique needs of your Web site. Chapter 4, "Joining the Right Program(s)," offers advice for finding and choosing the right programs.

# 4

# Joining the Right Program(s)

There are four steps to joining an affiliate program:

1. Choose the right type of program(s) to join.

2. Find the right affiliate program provider(s).

3. Sign up.

4. Add your links.

Chapter 3 provided guidelines for choosing the right type of program. This chapter explains how to find the right programs to join, how to sign up with those programs, and finally, how to get started.

The first three chapters no doubt excited you about the possibilities affiliation holds for your business, and you may be tempted to leap before you look. But it's important that you take your time and do the necessary research before you select an affiliate program or programs to join. Affiliates who have learned the hard way will tell you how frustrating it is, after having spent a good amount of time placing links and promoting their sites, to find out that an affiliate program is not an effective match.

# Basic Guidelines

A recent survey (summer 1999) by Refer-It.com indicates that 20 percent of affiliates join only one affiliate program and 41 percent join five or more programs. The benefits to joining more than one affiliate program include:

**Enabling comparison.** For example, placing links to multiple booksellers on your Society for Technical Communicators site.

**Cross-selling.** For example, placing a link to a phone card on your cellular phone accessories site.

**Offering distinctive and original recommendations for diverse market segments.** For example, placing a link to MD Healthline's Viagra page on your Corvette Central Web site.

Whether you decide to be loyal to a single affiliate program or opt to join 20 programs that offer relevant content to your Web site, here are key guidelines to follow for choosing the right affiliate program or programs:

- Consider the stability of the provider company and its program.

- Read the affiliate agreement in its entirety; look for loopholes in the compensation structure, exclusivity clauses, sales quotas, or other language that limits your options.

- Find out how well established the program is. Ask how many affiliates are already signed up with the program. A large affiliate base is a good indication that a program pays well and provides excellent customer service. Conversely, if the program has been around for a year and has only 50 affiliates, it might not be a very effective program.

- Get references; that is, find out the names of affiliates of the program. Are they happy with the program? You can get this information via Web sites about affiliate programs, and from newsgroups, mailing lists, chat rooms, and affiliate-related newsletters.

- Get details on the program's commission policies. Ask how much to they pay, or how much store credit, frequent flyer miles, or other goodies they offer. Do the program providers seem stingy or overly generous? Either may be cause for concern. Compare the commission offerings to similar affiliates. Remember that program providers reserve the right to change their commission schedule, in particular to correct for overly generous commissions. Find out how frequently the program pays. What is the minimum payment made (i.e., payout threshold)? Ask what happens if you don't meet this amount during a given payment period?

- Determine whether their tracking tools are dependable. Does the program provide an online tracking and/or similar reporting tool that enables you to pop in at will to see how effective your affiliate links are? You'll need to do this to determine whether you're promoting the right products/services in the right place, so it's imperative that you can easily and frequently access reports.

- Ask yourself: Are you passionate about (or a least interested in) or knowledgeable about the provider merchant's products or services? Are the products or services relevant to your site's visitors?

- Find out whether the program has a privacy policy. Would you feel comfortable buying something from them?

## Program Reputation and Online Ratings

When reviewing a merchant's affiliate program, it's essential that you feel confident that the company: offers the right products or services for the right price, is well positioned to handle customer service issues, has the means to deliver the product or service in a timely matter, and is financially stable enough to ensure that you receive your commission on time every time. It's also important that the program-provider company makes it easy for you to grab the links, banners, and HTML code necessary to create your links to their site. These key items demonstrate the merchant's commitment to its affiliate program and to you, the affiliate.

While a merchant's commission structure is very important, good, timely customer service is just as important. Shoppers will only put up with poor customer service if they have no other choice, and as you know, the Web, good or bad, offers a plethora of options. So make sure the merchant whose program you're considering has a well-defined customer service policy. A small commission from one satisfied customer is worth more to you than a large commission from a dissatisfied customer, because the former will become your repeat customer. The point is: Don't let merchants entice you with offers of high commissions if they don't have the means necessary to fill orders dependably. Not only will you alienate any visitors you refer to the merchant, but those merchants might not even bother to pay you.

Though having a creative product selection is important, we recommend that you consider joining well-established programs of experienced online merchants like Amazon.com and eToys when possible. Otherwise, as noted in the guidelines at the beginning of the chapter, be sure to spend some time researching the merchant's stability using newsgroups, mailing lists, and online forums to determine whether the merchant is a keeper or not. A good place to start is the appendix of this book where you'll find a review of 50 of the top affiliate programs available today. Also, visit one of the great online resources mentioned later in this chapter that rate different affiliate programs.

Refer-It, for example, rates programs based on several criteria, including commission rate, ease of implementation, responsiveness, reporting capabilities, clarity of the terms and conditions, and availability of free content.

## Affiliate Agreements

According to a recent survey by Refer-It, a whopping 26 percent of affiliates do not even read affiliate agreements before they join an affiliate program! An affiliate agreement is a formal business document, and as such, it is critical that you read every word of it—for each program that you join. You can even find a few program agreements will include clever wording that may result in your not getting paid your share of revenue. Other unscrupulous programs will charge you a percentage fee of the commissions you earn through *their* program; worse yet are those that charge you to participate in the program.

**NOTE** You'll also hear affiliate agreements referred to as affiliate terms, affiliate conditions, and associate terms.

If you don't feel comfortable with the wording of the agreement, do not join the program. It's as simple as that. There are many great affiliate programs from which to choose. You can and should be selective.

Follow theses tips when reviewing an affiliate agreement:

**Read the entire agreement.** Yes, they can be very long and not the least bit interesting, but you must treat it as you would any legal contract.

**Determine whether the program requires you to pay any fees.** If so, beware. Affiliates should never pay to sell products or services for merchants unless there is some justifiable reason, such as exclusivity, training, or an inventory purchase. And for any of these "justifiable reasons," double beware—there are a lot of scams and unrealistic promises being perpetrated on the Net.

**Make sure the agreement specifies how often you will be paid.** Monthly and quarterly payments are pretty common.

**Ask whether you must earn a minimum amount before you will receive a check.** If so, first make sure that amount is clearly spelled out; second, ensure that if you don't meet the quota for the assigned period the amount you did earn will be carried over to the next revenue period. For instance, let's say that you must earn a minimum of $50 before you are paid every month. If you only earn $30 in April, make sure that $30 will apply toward your May earnings. This is important, as you'll find some programs that roll back to zero at the beginning of each pay period, meaning, conceivably, that you might never see a dime.

**IN ENGLISH PLEASE**

The payment portion of an affiliate agreement can be really confusing, depending on how it is written. Here's an example:

*When the total commissions due to you (based on Section 6, above) exceed one hundred dollars ($100) for each of books, magazines, gift certificates, music, videos, and software, we will send a commission check for the applicable commission (less any taxes required to be withheld under applicable law) and a statement of activity to you. Such commission checks and statements of activity will be sent approximately thirty (30) days after the end of each three-month anniversary of the date hereof.*

The plain English version goes like this: You must earn at least $100 every three months to receive a check.

Note the ambiguity in the original: You might easily interpret it to mean you must earn $500 ($100 for each product category) before getting paid. In any case, whenever you're not sure of the precise meaning of the language in an affiliate agreement, check the FAQ or ask. And be sure to print out all relevant documents as they appear when you sign them for your records, because they can—and do—change on the merchant's site.

**Ask about any restrictions concerning your participation in other programs.** For instance, as of this writing, Barnes & Noble has the following restriction in its Affiliate Network Operating Agreement:

*Subject to the terms and conditions set forth below, we shall be the exclusive bookseller on your site. You agree that you will not (directly or indirectly) allow any other person or entity to sell books on your site or link their site to yours in connection with the sale of books.*

Now, if you intend only to sell a few books at Barnes & Noble, this restriction shouldn't keep you from agreeing to the terms. But if your goal is to enable your visitors to do some comparison-shopping for a particular book, you'll have to pass, as Barnes & Nobles insists on being your exclusive bookseller partner.

One more point to keep in mind regarding a restriction clause: If you disregard such a clause and link to one or more of the program merchant's competitors, that merchant will be perfectly justified in denying you payment. That said, be aware that in practice, few merchants bother to enforce such policies because it would not be cost-effective. Nevertheless, it's probably wiser to go with a less restrictive merchant than it is to knowingly violate an agreement you've signed.

**Ask if you have the option to co-brand your affiliate pages.** Remember, co-branding enables you to add your logo and formatting to a storefront, eShelf, or other type of virtual store.

**Be sure you know which products or services qualify for commissions or other incentives.** For example, if someone makes a purchase after following a link on your Web site, do you receive a commission for gift certificates, shipping costs, gift-wrapping, and so on, which your referral may have ordered instead of or in addition to the product you're promoting? (In most circumstances, you do not.) What about sales items or special orders? If your visitor adds an item to the merchant's shopping cart for purchase at a later date, will you get the credit when the final sale is made? These are important questions because they can substantially affect your bottom line. The argument might be made that not being paid a commission on these items is justifiable because merchants don't make any money from them, but that's not the case. In fact, certain companies make *all* of their money from "accessory" services and delivery charges. For example, we recently shopped online for a computer monitor and noticed a huge difference in delivery charges at two different merchant sites. Surely it should cost approximately the same price for two different companies to ship a monitor from Texas to California, right? Wrong. One charged less than $30 and the other was over $60, using the same mailing service. When you're earning a percentage of the total cost, a $60 delivery charge isn't small potatoes.

**TIP** If gift certificates do not qualify for commissions with the program you join, be sure to emphasize the actual product you're promoting (as opposed to the merchant's entire product line) to ensure that your efforts pay off for you.

**Find out whether you are required to use the links and/or banners provided by the program or if you can create your own.** Also, determine whether you are obliged to use specific product descriptions provided by the program. Understandably, merchants are concerned that their affiliates might inaccurately alter product information content (perhaps making false claims). Still, you're better off with the most flexible programs. You know best what to put on your site.

**Ask if you'll be restricted in the way you promote your affiliate link.** For example, some programs do not permit you to post your affiliate link in a noncommercial newsgroup, nor to cross-post it to multiple newsgroups. You can, however, usually post to newsgroups that specifically welcome commercial postings, which is proper netiquette anyway.

Make sure the program merchant will notify you regarding any changes made to program terms and conditions, commissions, commission schedules, or payment procedures. All affiliate agreements should include a clause to this effect. Merchants should agree either to send you an e-mail notifying you about changes or to post the changes clearly on their Web site. Merchants must limit their liability for any loss of revenue, profits, or data, so don't over-react to this aspect of these agreements. True, sometimes it's difficult to know if errors made in tracking earnings are intentional, but you can't afford to be too cynical; remember, quality merchants are interested in keeping their affili-ates happy and in avoiding publicity pitfalls. Merchants also generally specify that they reserve the right to reject orders that do not comply with any require-ments that they have established on their site.

> **NOTE** Some affiliate programs update their agreements quite frequently, so try to keep abreast of changes that may affect your site or business.

## How Long and How Many?

To accurately determine the effectiveness of an affiliate program, you will need to know three important numbers:

- How long the program has been operational.
- How many affiliates have signed up.
- How many of those affiliates are active—that is, how many have actually placed links on their Web sites.

While it's not very difficult to find the answer to the first two, the third is more of a challenge, for two reasons: First, as many merchants will complain, people will sign up for their programs, then never place a link on their site. Second, merchants go to a great effort to determine the number of their active affiliates, and they're not eager to share this information, for obvious com-petitive reasons. Similarly, though it would be useful information to have, it is difficult to find out how many important affiliates a merchant has; that is, how many of its affiliates are generating significant sales.

Given this lack of data, you'll have to rely on your judgment, coupled with your knowledge of the first two numbers: how long and how many. There are a few good resources that you can use to determine the date on which an affil-iate program was launched and how many affiliates are signed up with that program:

- Some merchants put the number of affiliates in their program on their Web site.
- Many merchants sign up with an *affiliate solutions provider (ASP)*, a com-pany whose services include managing affiliate programs. If the program uses an ASP you can sometimes get the number of affiliates in the pro-gram from there.

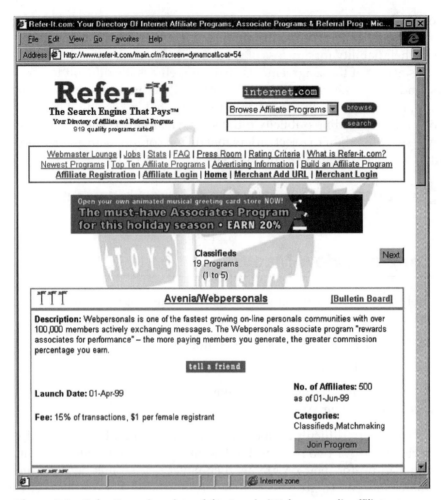

**Figure 4.1** Refer-It.com's review of the Avenia/Webpersonal's affiliate program.

- Free online affiliate directories, such as Refer-It.com, provide this type of information for each affiliate program they review and rank. Figure 4.1 shows an example of the information you can gather about Avenia/ Webpersonals' affiliate program, using Refer-It.com's affiliate directory.

## How Much Will You Make?

Sounds like a no-brainer to find out how much money you'll make from the program(s) you're considering joining. Well, we state the obvious, because it's not always as easy as it sounds. For instance, as of this writing, under the terms of the Barnes & Noble (www.bn.com) affiliate program, you can earn a 7 percent commission for *every* book sold as a result of your referral. In contrast, under the conditions of the Amazon program, you can earn 15 percent, but only on books not specified as "special order" or "deeply discounted." Clearly, if the book you were promoting were a special order title at Amazon .com, you'd earn more using Barnes & Noble. So do your homework.

But let's take this example a step further. Remember that earlier we noted that Barnes & Noble wants to be your sole bookseller, so you could lose money if you promote many different books on your site. If you don't like either scenario, you might want to try Powell's Books program (www.powells.com). Less well known, Powell's currently offers a 10 percent commission on *all* books sold as a result of affiliate referrals. But of course you must first ask yourself how your visitors might react to a new, less popular merchant. If your customers trust your judgment, however, no doubt they will feel comfortable buying from Powell's. Naturally, don't refer any merchant that you would not shop at yourself.

## How Much Should You Make?

According to a survey conducted by ClickQuick (www.clickquick.com), 70 percent of affiliates earn between $50 and $249 in U.S. dollars per month (with the majority promoting multiple programs). That said, a significant number (8 percent) of them earn $500 or more per month. (Refer to this book's companion Web site at www.affiliateselling.com for additional current survey statistics on affiliate earnings.)

## Repeat Business

Most business owners will tell you that a business cannot survive on one-time consumers—unless of course you're selling an island in the Pacific. Rather, business owners have to spend a great deal of time and money attracting new customers while maintaining their existing customer base. Your site will be no exception. Ironically, however, you earn affiliate revenues for doing the exact opposite: sending your visitors elsewhere—perhaps permanently. One of the most common complaints voiced by the affiliates of successful merchants, such as eToys or Cooking.com, is that after they refer a visitor and earn their $2 to $3 commission, the customer either remembers the program merchant's address (how hard is it to learn eToys.com?) or, simply, bookmarks it. Thereafter, when that visitor wants to buy a new toy, he or she will go directly to eToys rather than using your affiliate site as an entry point. Bye-bye commission.

Fortunately, there are some merchants that recognize that their killer brand could end up killing your business, and they've put together programs that help to solve this problem for their affiliates. One such program (typically offered by merchants whose services are paid for on a monthly or yearly basis—

credit card companies, Internet service providers, phone card companies, and the like) might offer residual earnings to affiliates that refer customers with whom the merchant establishes an ongoing relationship. As an affiliate with one of these programs, you make money every time a sales transaction occurs between the merchant and the person you referred, which, for a credit card company would mean every single month. Programs with residual earnings can turn a basic affiliate program into an exceptional ongoing revenue stream.

As merchants compete more and more aggressively to attract affiliates, you need to keep your eyes open for residual income opportunities. Recently, certain online merchants have made headlines by promising to fix a given customer's prices *for life*. Why? To establish long-term, loyal customers. In a similar fashion, expect to see the merchants most aggressive at building their affiliate networks to offer such long-term rewards for their affiliates. For instance, imagine how conscientious you'd be in promoting products for a merchant that promised you a lifetime commission on all of your referrals' future purchases, even if their future purchases were not made via your affiliate links.

## Commission Tracking Methods

Tracking your affiliate traffic and sales is important because it enables you to gauge the effectiveness of the average program, specific products, and even the placement of products on your site. It also enables affiliates who use multiple affiliate programs to compare the results from each program, as well as against other traditional advertising methods. An important factor to consider when choosing an affiliate program is whether the program offers a way for you to track your sales, commissions, number of items sold, and click-through rate. Merchants provide a variety of different tracking tools. Some provide real-time, online reports that you can access any time you feel like it (but beware: checking can become addictive!). Others simply send you an e-mail either each time you refer a new customer or at some predefined interval (usually weekly, monthly, or quarterly).

### How Merchants Track Affiliates

When you join an affiliate program, you will be assigned a unique affiliate ID, which will be used by the program-provider merchant to track your referrals and, subsequently, to pay you.

The program merchant will also provide you with a specially formatted URL that includes your affiliate ID and that links your visitors to the merchant's site. Every time a visitor follows one of your links to the merchant's site, this unique URL tells the merchant which product or page to display, as well as which affiliate sent the customer. Some programs offer many different types of banners and links from which to choose (merchant logos, text-only, search boxes, etc.); others simply spit out a few lines of HTML code for you copy and paste into your Web page.

## How Affiliates Keep Track of Traffic and Revenues

As just described, some affiliate programs will send you a detailed report via e-mail that describes the activity they've recorded from your Web site. Other programs provide you with access to online revenue tracking tools that generate reports, graphs, and more, which you can use as frequently as you'd like.

Whether your report is distributed to you on a weekly, monthly, or quarterly basis, or made continuously available for real-time reporting at a Web site, you should expect to see the following statistics:

- Number of items ordered, completed (online forms), downloaded, bid, and so on
- Qualified purchase amount (amount upon which your commissions revenue will be based)
- Referral fees/points you have earned
- Click-throughs (hits), which represent the number of times each of your visitors clicked on your link to the item/page
- Number of visitors you sent to the merchant

**NOTE** A *visitor* is a person who clicks on a link from your site, and is counted as 1 visitor, regardless of the number of different product pages he or she clicks on at the merchant's site.

Affiliate solutions providers, such as BeFree (www.befree.com) and Commission Junction (www.cj.com), enable you to sign up with multiple merchants and provide you with highly sophisticated tools that you can use to generate many different types of reports for each of your affiliate accounts. Figure 4.2 shows a page at Reporting.net, BeFree's Affiliate Information Center. Here, the affiliate can click on any one of the merchant banners to view that merchant's respective report. He or she can use this to identify top-selling items, see a day-to-day breakdown of shipped sales, and more. Cross-Commerce, which gives affiliates access to hundreds of merchants' products with a single sign-up and approval, aggregates reports across all of your program merchants into a single interface. This feature makes it easy to see what's working, what's not, and which products and merchants are most effective for you.

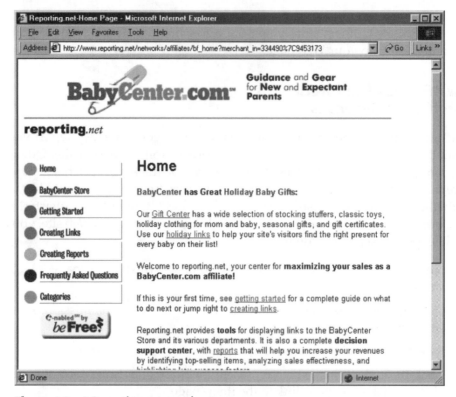

**Figure 4.2**   A Reporting.net merchant page.

---

**PROTECT YOURSELF**

Because merchants (or their affiliate solutions providers) use your affiliate link to track the revenue you earn, it's very important that you take care when cutting and pasting your link and/or affiliate ID into the HTML for your Web site. Incorrectly creating the HTML link is the most common cause of errors in unreported sales. If you make an error when you cut and paste your affiliate ID, though the merchant might see that your site was the referring site, your affiliate ID will not be passed along with the referral, meaning the commission will not be calculated or attributed to you. Once an error like this has been made, the merchant will probably never notice, and hence be unable to correct it for you.

As a spot-check against this occurring, periodically "redirect" pages to track hits generated by your affiliate. How? Just change the HTML for your affiliate link so that when a visitor clicks on the link, a hit is registered on another page *on your site* before it continues to its destination on the merchant's site. The user won't notice, and you'll be able to better track the amount of traffic you're sending to the merchant.

# Smart Merchandising

As you consider which program or programs to join, your primary focus should be on your site's purpose and your visitors' expectations—in other words, you should be focusing on product merchandising. Ask yourself what your users expect to see when they access your site from its key entry points. Too many affiliates make the mistake of "polluting" their sites with irrelevant banner ads that distract from their content. Not what you want. Worse, some affiliates fail to provide any content at all; they simply plaster ads all over their pages and hope someone will happen upon their site and buy something. Such sites are practically guaranteed to fail at reaching any long-term revenue goals. Visitors will not return to a site that has nothing to offer but a slew of unrelated ads.

How many affiliate programs should you join? According to a survey conducted by ClickQuick (www.clickquick.com), the majority of affiliates utilize between five and nine affiliate programs (only 4 percent promote more than nine).

Make your affiliate links count. Use common sense; the links should *add value* to a valuable piece of Web real estate. If, say, your site is targeted toward software junkies, add links to Egghead.com and Beyond.com. If your site caters to auto enthusiasts, add links to carprices.com and thecarline.com; and add a link to Amazon's top-selling books about cars; or maybe even add a link on your minivan page to BabyCenter.com, which sells car seats. But, don't add a link to cheap computer memory (unless you know something about your target audience that other auto affinity sites don't). You get the picture; sell in context. Make it worth your and your visitors' time; don't annoy them with ads they're already probably ignoring on more generalized sites. Take advantage of the fact that you know not only about your site's topic, but also about your visitor—and your merchant's future customer.

# The Gotchas

We've said it before and we'll say it again: Always read the affiliate agreement *in its entirety* before joining an affiliate program. Then go through it again, because even during a thorough first read, you could miss some important details. We call these the "gotchas." This section highlights a number of gotchas you want to avoid. (For details on specific programs, refer to the appendix and this book's site, www.affiliateselling.com.)

## Define Revenue

Ask: How does the program define revenue? Most affiliate programs offer a percentage of the total revenue (not including taxes) generated by your site's visitors (commission-based programs). But recall that some programs pay commissions based only on the dollar amount of the items purchased, excluding gift-wrapping and shipping. Keep that fact in mind when evaluating programs whose products sell well during major gift-giving holidays.

Beware of other programs that pay only a percentage of the "profit" on a sale. Depending on how such merchants calculate profits, this could leave you in a low- or no-commission situation. For instance, merchants occasionally offer sale products at below cost. These so-called loss-leaders do indeed cause the merchant to lose, but they also attract customers who, in theory, are more likely to buy additional profitable items during the same visit or to return repeatedly. Over the long term, loss-leaders are profitable for the program-provider merchants, but not for you, who will not earn a commission on such items.

Calculating what's profitable is particularly tricky in the case of original manufacturers (or, for instance, a software developer) that fold into the equation research and development, operating costs, and overhead. In such cases, the manufacturer could claim, for example, that the first thousand units sold were not profitable, but that the next unit was. Be advised: Steer clear of any programs that calculate your commission in so ambiguous a fashion. In summary, profit-based commission calculations are rare among affiliate programs, but forewarned is forearmed.

## Mind Your Ps and Qs

Again, the vast majority of miscalculated affiliate earnings result from errors made by the affiliates themselves when copying and pasting their program merchants' links into the HTML code at their own Web site; and it's not that easy to tell when you do this incorrectly, because the link will appear to work even if all or part of your affiliate ID is missing. The best way to prevent making this costly mistake yourself is to verify that you are copying the entire contents of the link. In particular, be on the lookout for programs that provide you with a line of code where you are instructed to replace the words "Affilite ID" with the actual ID they supply to you. Neglecting to replace this temporary code with your ID will result in nonpayment of earned commissions. Even after you correct this error, it may be impossible for the merchant (or program provider) to remunerate you for your past earnings.

## The Check's in the Mail

Make sure you know when to expect your first and subsequent checks. The most efficient affiliate programs pay promptly, usually a few days after the end of each period during which commissions were calculated. In stark contrast are the programs that seem to take forever to pay you, in some cases, upward of 90 days after the end of each payment period. That's 2.3 Internet years, during which time anything can happen: Investors may pull out; funding could run out; technology breakthroughs could render the merchant's site obsolete; Microsoft might buy the company—you name it. The bottom line: Look out for programs that specify they will hold onto your earnings for weeks or months before sending you a check. Chances are these programs are disorganized, strapped for cash, or intentionally delaying payment to earn money on the *float* (the interest *they* earn while *your* money is in *their* bank).

## Back at 'Ya

Beware of returns! Those of you who have worked in retail know that you can only earn a commission on completed sales, and only after the customer has decided to keep the product purchased. Of course, it's important to choose a program merchant with a reasonable return policy (read: good customer service); just make sure it's not too lenient for your liking, such as one that has a 90-day return policy (during which time, your commissions are held in limbo).

Remember, if a customer returns the purchased goods within the time allotted by the merchant, the merchant must: a) cancel the commission, b) deduct the appropriate referral fee from your payment, or c) send you a bill for the referral fee. (As of this writing, for example, Amazon will bill you if the product that generated the referral fee is returned and if you don't have adequate earnings in "the bank" to cover the referral fee for the return.)

**NOTE** You should only be sent a bill if you do not earn enough during the next payment cycle to cover the cost of the return.

## Only the Purple One Counts

Keep your eye out for affiliate programs that will pay you a commission *only* on the specific item to which your site links, and/or only if the visitor completes the sale immediately (during the same user session), as opposed to dumping the item in a shopping cart for later purchase. Here are a few examples: You place a link on your site to Tinky Winky Teletubbie (the purple one). If your visitor decides to buy all four colors of Teletubbies, you'll only get credit for the purple Tinky Winky. Worse, if the shopper puts the purple Tinky Winky into his or her shopping cart and leaves it in there for three days (is that legal?), you won't see a dime.

We recommend you look for programs that will pay a commission for all of the toys (or whatever) your visitors purchase during their initial (single) visit to the merchant's site. A few programs will even pay you a commission on all the toys that visitor purchases during a given period of time, from the date of the initial visit. Needless to say, these are, by far, some of the best affiliate opportunities available. (See the appendix of this book for commission-calculated policies for actual affiliate programs.)

## The Cookie Factor

Many affiliate programs track your referral activity to their site using *cookies*. A cookie is a block of data stored by a Web server on a client system, used to identify users and to enable the customization of Web content. When a user returns to the same Web site, the browser sends a copy of the cookie back to the server. Cookies are widely used—and, yes, they're safe; a cookie can't read data off your hard disk or read cookie files created by other sites.

Inside the cookie on the shopper's hard drive the merchant encodes details about your referral for future reference, when that visitor makes a purchase or returns to the site at a later date. Sound like a Big Brother thing? It's really not. The primary purpose of a cookie is to save the customer time. For instance, if it weren't for cookies, customers couldn't use shopping carts online. The technology of cookies is what enables shoppers to choose items from multiple pages of the merchant's site, to be purchased during the current session or at a later time. If it weren't for cookies, shoppers would have to purchase everything they wanted item by item. Can you imagine?

Though cookies are safe, there are a few problems associated with their use. For one, many Web surfers are increasingly concerned about their privacy online, so they customize their browser applications to refuse to accept cookies from the Web sites they visit. Consequently, if a number of your visitors have their cookie setting set to "Disable all cookie use," it could cost you your commission on their purchases. Why? Because if these users follow your link and shop around a while before buying the item to which you pointed them, there is no way for the merchants that use cookies to track those users' entry point to the site; hence it's impossible to reward you with a commission. Only if those users follow your link and immediately purchase the item you're promoting—and don't go to any other page—will you make the commission. One final caution about cookies: They are saved in browsers, such as Internet Explorer, as temporary Internet files, which users can delete at will. You can't do anything to prevent your visitors disabling or tossing their cookies, so to speak. And it's not a good idea to require users to enable their cookies to use your site. But the good news is that very few people disable their cookies and not all affiliate programs use them. If you're concerned about cookies, all you can do is to read the program's affiliate agreement to see if and how they use cookies.

## Beware of Resets

As we warned you in Chapter 2, "Types of Programs," few crafty affiliate programs will reset your earned commission to $0 at the end of every pay period (month or quarter). Translated this means that if you do not meet the threshold earnings set by these programs before the end of the pay period, you will lose all of your accumulated earnings. Our advice? Although these programs tend to pay higher commissions, avoid joining them unless you are confident you can afford to take the risk—that is, you're certain you'll earn enough each pay period. Obviously, large sites with heavy traffic need not worry. With this policy, it's the small, low traffic, personal homepages that the merchants are trying to discourage from becoming their affiliates.

## Expect Changes

We close this section with perhaps the most important-to-know-about gotcha: a line of text that is present in some form in every affiliate agreement:

> We may change our policies and program operating procedures at any time.

Hopefully, your relationship with your affiliate program providers will be an ongoing one. You can make sure it's a happy relationship if you remember to reexamine the details of your changeable contract on a regular basis.

# Affiliate Reviewers and Directories

There are hundreds of places online you can visit to find out what "the word on the street" is on most affiliate programs. Those described in this section comprise only a fraction of the number of great resources available to you. Currently, these are the top 10 sites that offer information on generating revenue through affiliate selling. Though all of these will undoubtedly continue to play a key role in educating Web site owners about affiliate programs, we also recommend that you visit this book's companion site at www.affiliateselling.com for an up-to-date list of other great sites that offer information about affiliate programs.

## Associate-It

Associate-It (www.associate-it.com) provides an extensive affiliate (associate) directory, program reviews, discussion forums, a free newsletter—as well as the Associates Mall, to which you can add a link to your own affiliated Web site (see Figure 4.3). You can use Associate-It to find programs based on categories that are relevant to your Web site, then read the reviews and ratings of these programs by other associates already enrolled in them. With Associate-It, you can find out how many affiliates are signed up with a given program, view the commission structure, and get a report of the top ranked associate programs based on popularity and user rating. Finally, be sure to visit Associate-It's discussion board to get answers to any questions you have about joining—or even building—affiliate programs.

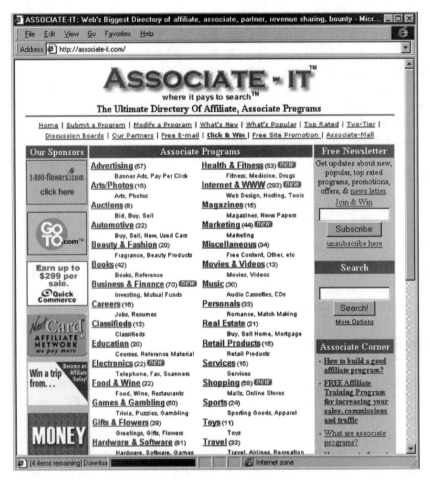

**Figure 4.3**    Associate-It, an affiliate directory and more.

## Associate Programs Directory

As of this writing, the Associate Programs Directory (www.associateprograms
.com) is perhaps the most comprehensive resource available for finding and
reviewing affiliate programs, containing more than 2,000 affiliate programs
listed in its directory. (By the time you're reading this book, we anticipate that
this number will have doubled.) Even if you don't use the Associate Programs
Directory for its exhaustive list of detailed program reviews, at least subscribe to its free monthly newsletter, which was started by Allan Gardyne in
April 1998. This publication is a must-have for both new and experienced affiliates. In fact, if you have the time, we recommend that you start with the first
issue and read as many of the archived newsletters as you can, *before* you join
any program, especially the more obscure ones floating around cyberspace.

The newsletter archive can be found at www.associateprograms.com/search/newsletter.shtml.

Figure 4.4 shows a review for Wine-related affiliate programs on the Associate Programs Directory. As you can see, currently there are seven program reviews for this category. If you have a Wine-related site, you ought to be able to find one that would add value to your Web site's content.

## BeFree

BeFree (www.befree.com) is an affiliate solutions provider with an extensive list of well-respected merchants that, as of this writing, have a combined 1,987,857 affiliates. You can use BeFree to review merchant offerings, view tips about affiliate selling, and apply to multiple affiliate programs simultaneously (see Figure 4.5). You can also go to the site's Decision Support Center, where

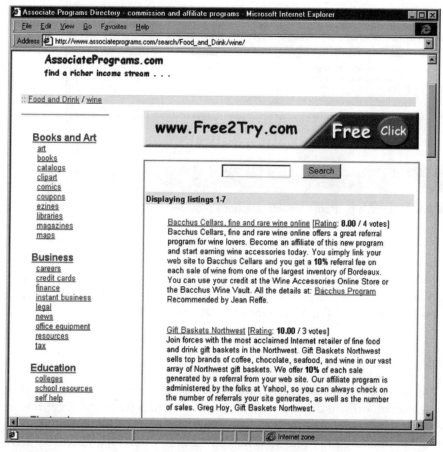

**Figure 4.4**   Associate Programs, a formidable affiliate directory.

**Figure 4.5**  BeFree, a premiere affiliate solutions provider.

you can access reports that can assist you in increasing your revenues by identifying top-selling items, analyzing sales effectiveness, and highlighting key success factors. Learn more about BeFree in Chapter 7, "Adding Links to Your Site," and Chapter 11, "For Merchants: Building a Program."

## CashPile

CashPile (www.cashpile.com) is another major affiliate program directory, but unlike the other affiliate directories listed in this section (with the exception of BeFree), you can use CashPile's AutoSubmitter to join multiple affiliate programs by completing only one affiliate application. Currently, however, there aren't a lot of affiliate programs available on the site to join using this method, so until then, you are better off using the category search tools provided here to find appropriate programs to join. Like the other affiliate program directories, CashPile reviews and rates programs.

Figure 4.6 shows an example of CashPile's AutoSubmitter Automotive category listings. Though the service in general is pretty useful, we have to point out that it's hard to find information on any poorly rated affiliate programs. Furthermore, the reviews use site design as a deciding factor for assigning high ratings. Certainly, site design is very important from both usability and credibility standpoints, but affiliates would be better served here if greater emphasis were placed on the programs' success rate, customer service response time, and so on. In summary, we recommend using this service to find program details, such as commission payout and number of affiliates, but suggest going elsewhere for affiliate reviews until those here become more quantitative and substantive

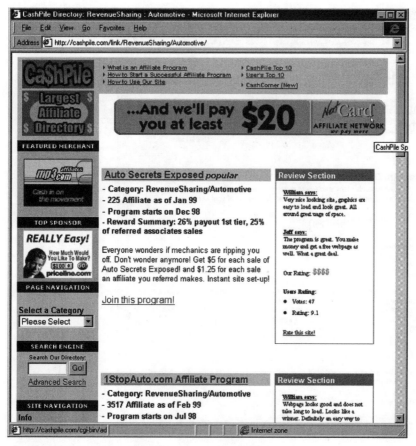

**Figure 4.6** CashPile's automotive program listings.

## ClickTrade

ClickTrade (clicktrade.linkexchange.com), a LinkExchange service and affiliate solutions provider, allows you to search for affiliate programs by category, keyword, description, and name; view their commission structure; and join the program. (ClickTrade also offers services for merchants, such as information about setting up affiliate programs for e-tailing sites.) Figure 4.7 shows the results of a search for music-related affiliate programs. You can easily decipher how much you'll earn, how many affiliates have joined, and how to implement each program with your site. Learn more about ClickTrade in Chapter 7.

## ClickQuick

ClickQuick (www.clickquick.com) offers extensive reviews of affiliate programs, a free biweekly newsletter, a discussion board, and the ability to promote your

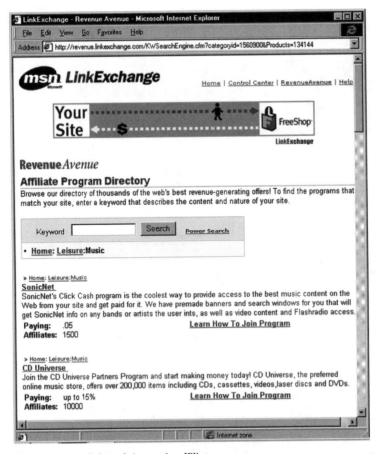

**Figure 4.7** ClickTrade's music affiliate programs.

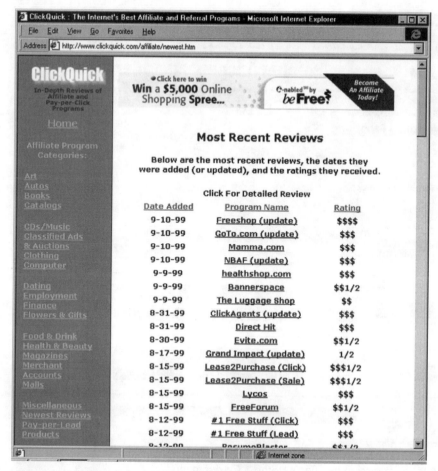

**Figure 4.8**    ClickQuick's Most Recent Reviews page.

site on ClickQuick.com. Its most beneficial offerings include a list of programs categorized by popularity and a list of the most recently added and reviewed affiliate programs. Figure 4.8 shows ClickQuick's Most Recent Reviews page.

## Commission Junction

Commission Junction (www.cj.com) is an affiliate solutions provider that offers affiliates access to more than 130 Web merchants in all major categories via a single user ID and password. Once you sign up to use Commission Junction's Web site, you'll have access to information about merchant programs, success stories, and instructions for joining programs (or starting programs). After you join an affiliate program using Commission Junction, you can get tips for placing your links, and access high-end reporting/tracking tools. And be sure to take

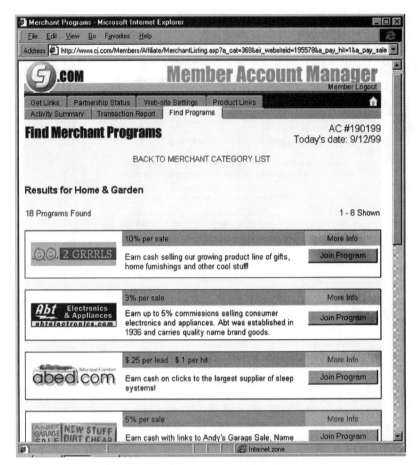

**Figure 4.9**   Commission Junction's Home & Garden page.

a few minutes to read a few postings in the Affiliate Corner message board, where other affiliates share strategies, warnings, kudos, and gripes Figure 4.9 shows Commission Junction's Home & Garden Merchant Programs page. Learn more about Commission Junction in Chapter 7.

## LinkShare

LinkShare (www.linkshare.com) is an affiliate solutions provider that offers affiliates access to more than 250 Web merchants in all major categories via a single username and password. Membership is free, and the service is easy to use; plus, you can get reports on all of your programs from one centralized location (though LinkShare's individual reports do not combine data across merchants, as do those of merchandise aggregators like CrossCommerce.com).

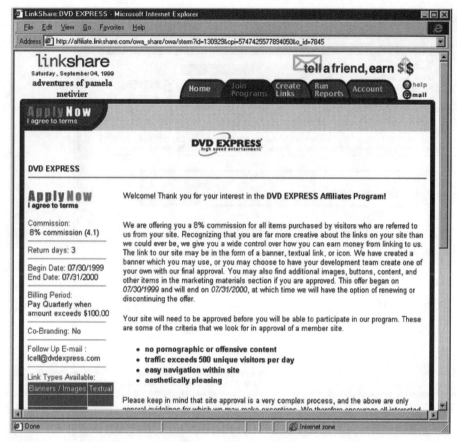

**Figure 4.10**  DVD Express, a LinkShare affiliate program.

LinkShare also provides affiliate program reviews, articles about affiliate selling, case studies, and more. Learn more about LinkShare in Chapter 7.

Figure 4.10 provides an example of one of LinkShare's affiliate program review pages, for DVD Express. Notice the information includes such program details as the commission rate (8 percent in this case), the commission payout schedule, and whether the program provides co-branded shopping environments.

## Refer-It

Refer-It (www.referit.com) is described as "The Search Engine That Pays." As of this writing, Refer-It has reviewed and rated more than 900 affiliate programs. You can easily search for and display details about all 900-plus programs for free on Refer-It's Web site. You can also view a list of the top 10

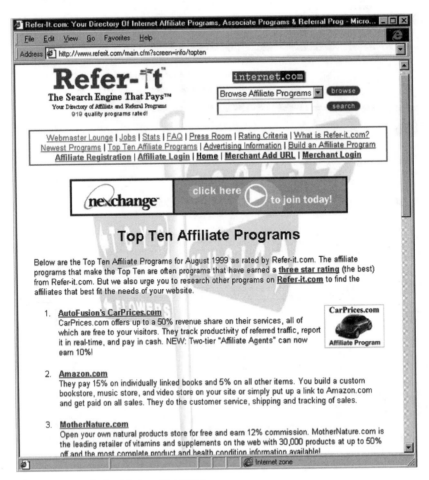

**Figure 4.11**    Refer-It's top 10 affiliate programs.

affiliate programs, register to join reviewed programs, add a link to your own affiliate program (if you have one), and subscribe to receive updates about the programs reviewed. As you can see in Figure 4.11, Refer-It makes it easy to find highly rated, effective affiliate programs.

## Sitecash.com

Sitecash.com is arguably one of the best sources of information for new affiliates. Not only does it offer a list of programs that have been reviewed in exhaustive detail, it also serves as an excellent affiliate guide. Figure 4.12 shows sitecash .com's review for AShoppingGuide. Notice the details provided about maximum earning potential. It's hard to find a better source for in-your-face, honest affiliate program reviews.

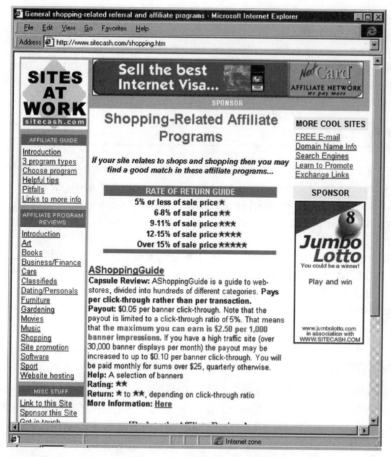

**Figure 4.12**    Sitecash.com's AShoppingGuide review.

## Other Great Sources for Information

Other great sources for information about affiliate programs include:

**Newsletters.** Refer-It.com, Associate-It.com, ClickQuick.com, and Associate Programs all provide free e-mail newsletters. Go to this book's companion Web site (www.affiliateselling.com) for a current list of affiliate-related newsletters, and sign up to start receiving your weekly or biweekly online publications now.

**Mailing lists.** SmartProfit Weekly, Affiliate Programs, Win the Affiliate Game (smart_affiliates), and AffiliateZone Digest (which currently has more 540 members) are all mailing lists available via eGroups (www.egroups.com). A word to the wise: Mailing lists can get overwhelming, so review the different lists, then choose only one or two. This book's companion Web site (www.affiliateselling.com) has a current list of affiliate-related mailing lists.

**Newsgroups.** Take a peek at alt.business, alt.business.home, alt.business .multi-level, and alt.html to find some threads about succeeding with affiliate programs. And refer to this book's companion Web site (www .affiliateselling.com) for a current list of affiliate-related newsgroups, along with instructions for posting to them.

# How to Join

As an affiliate, your only responsibilities are to create and promote *your* Web page(s). It is the merchant's job to maintain the hardware and programming requirements for the program; provide customer support; perform credit card processing/approvals, shipping and billing, cancelations, returns; and take care of customer service activities.

Merchants should also supply you with the graphics (banner ads), text (if required), and HTML code to generate the link to their product or service, as well as sales/click-though tracking tools. And note, some programs require you to measure a specific number of pageviews so they can weed out the low-traffic, personal homepage sites.

## The Basic Steps

There are three paths you can take to join an affiliate program. First, you can join directly from the merchant's site, which may be required when merchants have designed and built their own affiliate programs, which they alone host and facilitate (such as Amazon's Associates Program). Second, you can join by signing on with an affiliate solutions provider, such as BeFree or Commission Junction, which is a service merchants use to administer their affiliate programs. (If merchants use an affiliate solutions provider to run their programs for them, you can go to either the merchant's site or to the affiliate solutions provider's site to join.) Third, you can join from an affiliate directory like Associate-It.com or Refer-It.com.

Chapter 7 gives detailed instructions for joining affiliate programs and adding their links to your Web site.

# Doing It Right

Doing it right begins with researching and evaluating all of your options, and this chapter was designed to help you begin that process. The most successful affiliates are successful because they diligently monitor the ongoing operation of their sites, as a full-fledged business, as though it were a business, or as a labor of love.

Successful site creation and management is the result of a lot of hard work, to build, among other things, a site that visitors are truly interested in visiting; one to which they are likely to return and tell their friends about. To achieve this level of success, affiliates must constantly experiment and observe to determine what works and what doesn't. This applies not only to editorial content and site functionality, but to affiliate links to products and services as well. Experimenting with product links is particularly important, in that what you choose to include and/or eliminate will affect both how much your visitors like and use your site and how much money you will make. Clearly, taking the time to do it right will pay for itself many times over.

## Summary

Before you join an affiliate program, you have to make sure you're completely comfortable and confident with the offering. The affiliate agreement should answer all of your questions. If it doesn't, check the program's FAQ or write to the Webmaster for details. And if you don't want to do all of the homework yourself, check out one of the many online affiliate directories available whose ratings/reviews will serve as a great starting point for finding the best programs.

Later in the book, we'll discuss the nitty-gritty details of placing products on your site in ways designed to maximize your results. Before doing so, however, in the next chapter, for those of you who don't already have a site, we explain how to quickly and easily create a free Web site from scratch. We also reveal how you can earn affiliate revenue even if you don't have a Web site.

PART

Two

# Making Money

# Don't Have a Web Site?

Think you can't participate in the affiliate game because you don't have a Web site? Think again. You actually have a number of options. You can:

- Create a free Web page using a service like GeoCities or Tripod, which provide easy-to-use site building tools, with affiliate program opportunities built in.

- Use e-mail-based affiliate marketing.

- Just clip it! Use Clip2.com to create bundles of affiliate links that you can package with relevant content links and share with others.

This chapter explains how to set up a free Web page using Yahoo! GeoCities and Tripod, how to use e-mail-based affiliate links, and how to share your affiliate links via a self-perpetuating clip on Clip2.com. This book's companion Web site at www.affiliateselling.com contains a list of Web companies that offer free Web page development services and virtual store tools.

## Create a Free Web Page

GeoCities and Tripod are just two of the many Web services that offer free Web pages to their registered users. As of this writing, you get 6 MB (megabytes) of free disk space from GeoCities, and 11 MB from Tripod (and if you purchase a Tripod Premium Membership for an additional $3 a month, you get 22 MB of disk space). How can these services afford to give away free Web pages? Well, they realize that giving up some disk space on their massive servers isn't a high price to pay for the real money maker—*pageviews*, each of which is a place to place an ad that will hopefully be seen by someone. The more page-views a site has, the more ads it can sell to advertisers.

To that end, these free home page companies provide some pretty power-ful tools for building Web sites, which include HTML editors, color palettes, and prebuilt plug-in features for enabling guestbooks, chat centers, message boards, and more. More important to the topic of this book is that they make affiliate selling really easy by forming partnerships with some of the best mer-chants online and by making it a snap to place those merchants' affiliate links on your new Web site.

# Yahoo! GeoCities

Yahoo! GeoCities (admittedly an awkward name that is the result of the for-mer acquiring the latter), www.geocities.com, is the most popular provider of free home pages today. In fact, more than 3 million people have created a free Web page using GeoCities. Yahoo! GeoCities' affiliate program, called Pages That Pay, enables anyone with a Web page—whether you build your site on GeoCities or with any other Web page provider—to add affiliate links to their Web page. (Note: For the purposes of this section, we assume that you *don't* currently have a Web site.)

## GeoCities Pages That Pay

Before we begin to offer you some tips for getting started creating your own GeoCities home page so that you can place affiliate links, we should explain how the GeoCities' Pages That Pay program works.

With GeoCities' Pages That Pay, you can earn commissions up to 15 percent when your visitors buy products that you advertise on your Web site. In fact, as long as your visitors click on a merchant's link on your page and make any purchase on that site, you'll get paid. For example, if you have a link to the book *Green Eggs and Ham* at Barnes & Noble and one of your visitors clicks on it, then buys *Art for Dummies* instead, you'll still get your 7 percent com-mission from Barnes & Noble.

GeoCities Pages That Pay gives you access to a broad range of well-known merchants, such as egghead.com, reel.com, and tickets.com. And you only have to sign up for one affiliate program, Pages That Pay, to use any or all of the affiliate links on GeoCities' merchant list. (For a complete list of par-ticipating merchants, go to www.geocities.yahoo.com/pagesthatpay/ptp_merch_center.html.)

Joining Pages That Pay is pretty simple, but before you do so, you must decide what you're passionate about or what you think you can make a lot of money selling, then create content to support it. Our Point: It may take only 10 minutes to create a brand new Web site, but don't start until you know what your goals are. (Hint: If you skipped the first four chapters of this book, we recommend you take some time to read them.)

To begin the process of determining what you'll put on your Web page, ask yourself:

- Do you want to create a Web site because you've always wanted one and you didn't know HTML well enough to build it?

- Are you finally getting around to building a Web site for your offline company?

- Are you creating a Web site because you're excited about the opportunity to make money by jumping on the affiliate bandwagon? (The more likely scenario since you're reading this book.)

All of these reasons are good, but recognize from the get-go why you're creating a Web page.

To start our discussion let's assume first that you want to build a Web site because you've got the entrepreneurial bug and you're excited about the potential inherent with becoming an affiliate for your favorite e-merchants. (You don't want to be left out of the next big Web wave.) Let's also assume you've given some serious thought to what you'd like to sell and what you're qualified to recommend. And you've finally decided you can build a site that will bring value to your visitors and, in turn, make some money for you.

Let's say you're a Nerf gun guru, for example. You're obsessed with Nerf weapons and your knowledge is quite well recognized in the Nerf community. So, you decide to share your knowledge via a Web page that points to—you guessed it—everything related to Nerf weapons. You know that if you build it, fellow Nerf aficionados will drop by for Nerf weapon reviews and to make their purchases through your affiliate links. After all, you're the Nerf guru. So let's get started creating a page that pays.

Creating a page that pays using the GeoCities Page That Pays program is a straightforward process. You must, first, register with Yahoo! GeoCities; second, build your Web page(s) (remember, we're assuming you don't have one already); and, third, add some affiliate links. In the upcoming subsections, we provide some basic instructions for each of these steps using the fictional Joe Affiliate.

**NOTE** Keep in mind that Web tools change almost daily, so be sure to read the instructions provided by Yahoo! GeoCities before you begin.

## Registering with GeoCities

1. As of this writing, these are the basic steps Joe must follow to get hooked up with Yahoo! GeoCities: Register with Yahoo! GeoCities by going to http://geocities.yahoo.com/home/ and clicking the Get a Free Home Page link. Complete the registration form.

2. Add some personal profile information to his account so he can share his interests with others (this is optional). Click Continue to Yahoo! GeoCities to start building his Web page.

3. Choose one of the *themed communities* (called Neighborhoods) that interests him. Joe's Web page will be added to the community he chooses (e.g., Silicon Valley, Area51, The Tropics, or Hollywood).

4. Answer the questions regarding what his home page will be about (e.g., games), and then choose a topic that best describes his page. If Joe needs help building his page, he can indicate that he'd like to have a "community leader" contact him by e-mail. Joe takes note of the offer to receive an e-mail that describes how to use Pages That Pay to earn commissions from his Web site. He doesn't have to select Yes now; he just has to remember where to go to add affiliate links, which is the next procedure we guide you through in the following section.

After Joe's completed these four steps, GeoCities displays a page (like the sample page shown in Figure 5.1) that shows his Yahoo! GeoCities ID, e-mail address, and the URL (Internet address) for his new Web page.

## Build Your Future Revenue Stream

One quick glance at Figure 5.1 shows you what Joe Affiliate needs to do next: Build his page. So Joe clicks the "Build your page now!" link, and he's taken to the GeoCities home page. There he must click "Build a Page" again in order to display the different options for generating his page. (We probably would have taken him directly to the Build Pages page rather than dumping him at the front door, but we're sure they have a good reason for adding an additional step.) Joe is presented with more than 35 PageBuilder templates from which he can design his page quickly—and he doesn't have to know HTML. He can also choose to use the Advanced Editor tool to build a page using more complex tools that allow for greater customization and more control over the details.

Joe wants to create a site targeted toward online games aficionados, so he chooses the Hobby Time PageBuilder template; from there he can just point and click to build his site. All Joe has to do is click on the item he wants to change (each customizable piece is displayed in a blue box) and make his alterations. He can add images, change text, add form fields, include fun games, and more. (At the time of this writing, however, he couldn't add affiliate links

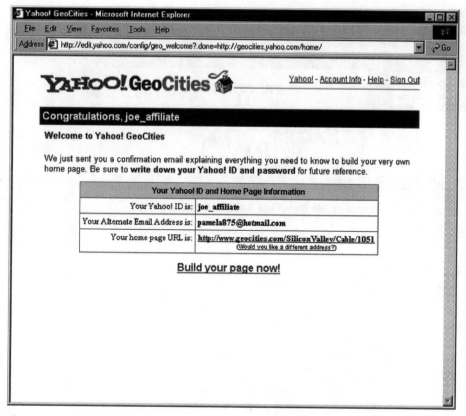

**Figure 5.1**  Future site of Joe Affiliate's page that pays.

while he was building his home page. Rather, he had to save and close his home page and return to the Yahoo! GeoCities' home page to find the Pages That Pay add-on.)

## Join the Pages That Pay Affiliate Program

After Joe spends a few hours building a killer Web site and adding some great content about online games, he is ready to start earning some money. So he returns to the Yahoo! GeoCities home page and clicks the Pages That Pay—Join Now! link under the Cool Home Page Add-Ons heading. He promptly—and thoroughly—reads the affiliate agreement and signs (GeoCities makes this step easy by automatically filling in most of the fields based on the information Joe provided when he signed up with Yahoo! GeoCities a few hours earlier). When he submits his request to join, he is presented with the Pick Merchants page shown in Figure 5.2.

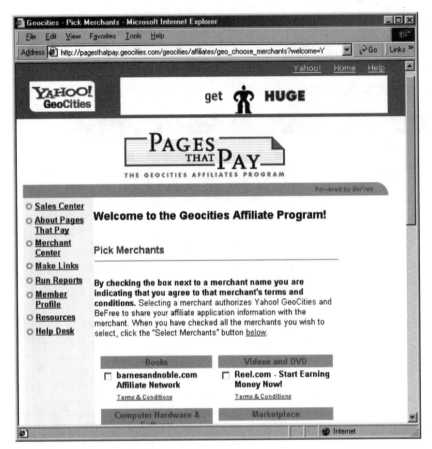

**Figure 5.2**   The Pick Merchants page.

Joe selects three merchants that offer products relevant to online games (the topic of Joe's page), promise great customer service, and are likely to be well known to his target audience. The merchants Joe chose to promote on his GeoCities Web page are shown in Figure 5.3.

Pages That Pay next presents Joe with numerous different banner ads from which he can choose. He picks the link type he wants for his egghead.com banner (shown in Figure 5.4).

**NOTE** You can add either text-based or banner affiliate links to each merchant's page. You can also link directly to a merchant's product, and, often, to a category of products, or to a search result. Different merchants provide different linking options, and Yahoo! GeoCities' Link Generator clearly displays them.

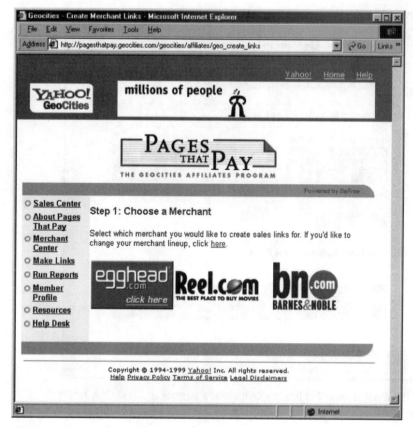

**Figure 5.3** Joe picks his merchants.

Finally, Joe clicks on the Make My Code button to have the GeoCities Link Generator activate the HTML code for the banner he selected to add to his Web page. This HTML code is shown in Figure 5.5.

When Joe clicks the Take This to PageBuilder button, the code is dropped into the hobby page he created. All he has to do now is to click on the banner ad and move it to a good location, as shown in Figure 5.6.

That's it! Joe is ready to start promoting his new page that pays, to get people to visit his site and start buying games. (See Chapter 10, "Increasing Hits and Selling More on Your Web Site," for some great ideas about promoting your affiliate site.)

## Running Reports

GeoCities' Pages That Pay feature provides you with reports for all your merchants with one easy-to-use tool. As of this writing, you can run daily sales

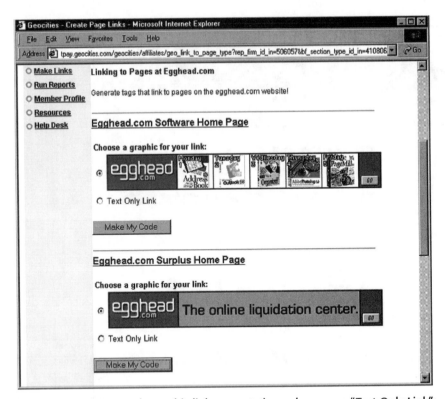

**Figure 5.4**   Joe must choose his link presentation: a banner or "Text Only Link"; which should it be?

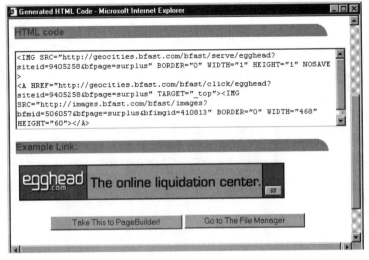

**Figure 5.5**   GeoCities' Link Generator activates HTML for Joe's egghead.com affiliate banner.

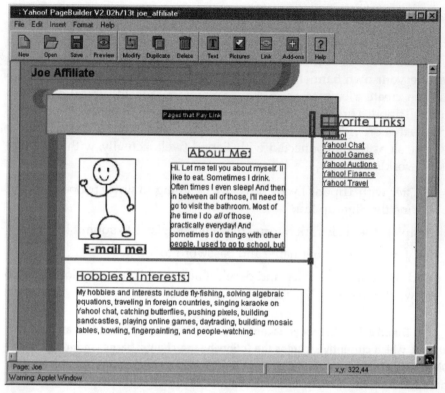

**Figure 5.6**   Placing the product link.

and traffic (product impressions and click-through rates) reports for a specific site, or, for affiliates with multiple sites, across all of your sites. The best part is that you will receive one paycheck from your GeoCities account.

**TIP**   Need help building your GeoCities page? Go to www.geocities.com/ features/Blueprint/ for an online tutorial.

# Tripod

Tripod's Homepage Studio makes it very easy for first-time builders to create a Web site. It also provides many tools to help members increase traffic to their sites. For example, you can make your own banner ads with the Tripod Banner Builder, then use the Smart Ads banner exchange program to display your banners across the Web, to drive traffic to your site. First things first, though. Let's learn how to build a Web site for your affiliate links using Tripod.

## Registering with Tripod

If you don't have a Web page and don't want to be one of the 3 million home page owners with "GeoCities" in your home page URL, or you are interested in creating your own banner ads and joining forces with other affiliates like yourself to create a banner ad exchange program, consider creating a Web site using Tripod. Tripod offers some interesting promotions tools, including Smart Ads that provide great assistance with promoting your Web site. Follow these basic steps to get connected with Tripod (well, actually, with the entire Lycos network):

1. Register with Tripod/Lycos Network by going to www.tripod.com and clicking the Sign-up link.

2. Complete the registration form, then click Register to submit it.

3. Use your new member name and password to log in.

4. Read the terms of service and deselect any e-mail subscriptions you do not want to receive. Then click Complete Sign-up.

**NOTE** Tripod asks whether you want to receive information about its affiliate program, which currently includes the following merchants: barnesandnoble.com, CDNOW, HeadHunter.net, and Chip Shot Golf. This is an interesting, but alarmingly small, selection. However, by the time you read this, no doubt many more merchants will have been added.

## Start Building Your Fortune

After you register, you'll be taken to your member page, where Tripod displays several easy-to-use Web site building tools. Beginners should use one of Tripod's QuickPage templates, while more experienced Web developers might want to try Tripod's freeform or filemanager tools. To describe the Tripod offerings, we'll assume you're either new to Web development or that you're really eager to get a page up so you can take your shot at the affiliate game. Again we'll use Joe Affiliate to take you through our beginners' scenario.

### Joe Affiliate, a Beginner's Scenario

Joe Affiliate, brand new to the Web and eager not to get left out of the affiliate game winnings, decides to build a Web page using Tripod's QuickPage feature, which requires absolutely no experience with HTML or Web design. QuickPage offers three different tools to build a page quickly:

- QuickStart, the one-minute page builder that enables Joe to select pre-packaged items to be displayed on his Web page

- QuickTopic, which enables Joe to build a page based on a specific topic such as a hobby or a personal/commercial Web site

- QuickDesign, which enables Joe to build a highly customizable Web site of any sort

**NOTE** We recommend QuickTopic or QuickDesign for greater control of the content that resides on your site. Remember, it's imperative that you add value (read: provide quality content) to attract visitors to your site.

For this scenario, we'll demonstrate how Joe might use the QuickTopic page. First, he clicks on the My Company QuickTopic template and he's prompted to type the URL for his site (this is actually just his URL extension; the complete URL will contain "www.tripod.com"). (Remember, your URL is very important, so keep it descriptive.) Joe chooses gadgets.html because he intends to build a site that provides reviews and recommendations (and, of course, product links) for gadgets like the Palm Pilot, digital cameras, and so on.

When he's prompted to enter a company name, he enters GadgetGateway because it sounds enticing and descriptive. When he's prompted for a logo, he decides to choose one from Tripod's logo library because he hasn't designed a logo yet, and besides, the selection is very professional. Conveniently, to his surprise, there's even a logo category called Gadgets.

Next he types in a special promotional message to his visitors, along with a description of his new company and contact info (like any good reseller would provide). At this point, Tripod displays a preview page that shows Joe what his page will look like. He clicks a Continue link to finish building his page.

## Earning Cash

At any time, Joe can go to Tripod.com, log in, and click the Buy/Sell link to find out how to add affiliate links to his site. Or he can go to http://www.tripod.com/buy_sell/index_earn.html. Unfortunately, as of this writing, Tripod does not fully integrate the affiliate program into its own free Web page service. This means that Joe must complete an application for each participating merchant in order to join its affiliate program. Furthermore:

- No centralized reporting tools are available.

- Joe can't receive one check from Tripod for all of the revenue he generates from multiple merchants.

- Joe must figure out how to place the special affiliate code provided by each merchant into his existing Web site.

Let's say that Joe joins barnesandnoble.com's affiliate program, which provides him with an affiliate link containing his special affiliate ID so he'll get paid. Joe follows these steps to add the affiliate link to his GadgetGateway page:

1. After he has obtained his affiliate link from barnesandnoble.com, he logs in to Tripod at www.tripod.com.

2. On the Welcome page he clicks the Edit link (shown in Figure 5.7) to edit his GadgetGateway page.

3. He checks the gadgetgateway.html page and chooses Edit with from the EDIT-options menu (shown in Figure 5.8).

4. A pop-up window displays his editing tool options. Joe chooses Quick-Page. The QuickPage editor is displayed.

5. Joe clicks Continue twice to advance to the Promotions page. There he copies the affiliate link barnesandnoble.com provided and pastes it into the Promotions text box, as shown in Figure 5.9. He adds some text (content) that describes the book he's promoting.

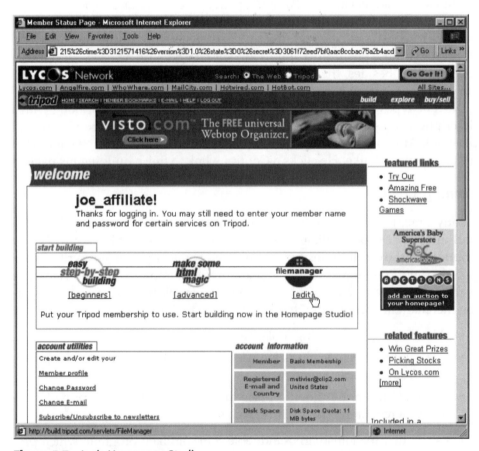

**Figure 5.7** Joe's Homepage Studio.

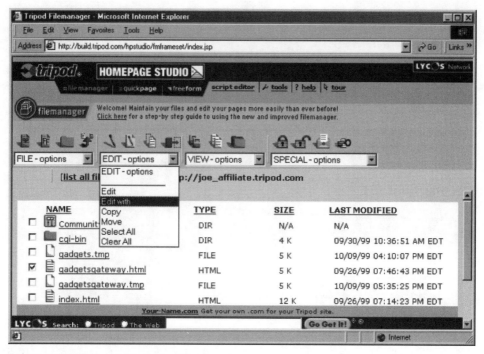

**Figure 5.8** Editing Joe's GadgetGateway home page.

Now Joe's ready to promote his new Tripod home page and return to www.barnesandnoble.com to track sales.

**NOTE** Keep in mind, Web services change frequently. To stay up to date with Tripod, go to its Help section at www.help.tripod.com.

## SmartAds Banner Exchange Program

Tripod's Banner Builder enables you to create a banner ad, which you can then exchange with other Tripod members to promote and, subsequently, increase traffic to your Tripod home page. Once you've created your banner, you simply submit it for display. Figure 5.10 shows an example of the Search Box Banner builder page. When you join the SmartAds Banner Exchange Program, you'll be given special HTML code to insert to your Web page so you can display ads belonging to other Tripod members. You can—and should—choose which types of banners you want to show on your Web page. Finally, you can use Tripod's reporting tools to determine which banners are the most effective, and design and target them accordingly.

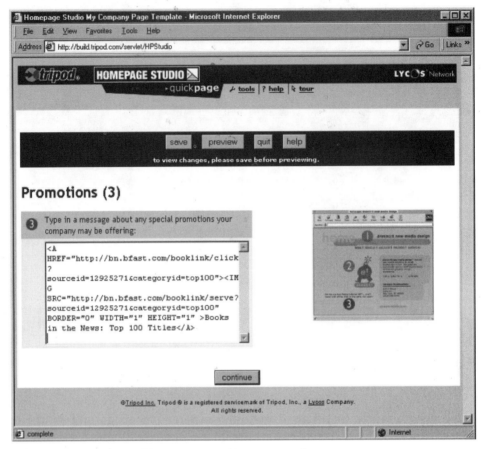

**Figure 5.9** Adding an affiliate to Joe's GadgetGateway home page.

The SmartAds Banner Exchange Program is a good way to promote your new affiliate site. For more ideas about promoting your site, refer to Chapter 9, "Designing Shelf Space and Picking Products."

## Builder Bucks

Tripod also offers its own affiliate program, Builder Bucks, that enables you to earn $1 for every 1,000 ad impressions served on your Web page ($.50 if you serve between 100 and 999 ad impressions per day). As a member of the Builder Bucks program, you have two options for serving ads on your page:

- You can use the typical Tripod-generated pop-up ad, which serves up an ad on your Web page every three times or so that your page is viewed.

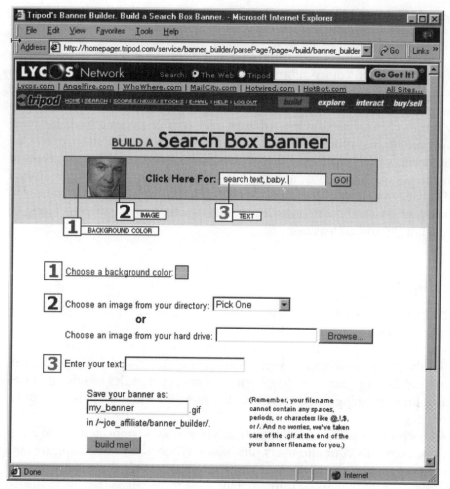

**Figure 5.10** Building your search box banner.

- You can embed an ad above the "fold" on your Web page (within the first nonscrolling region). Go to www.tripod.com/build/rewards/bucks.html for more information on Tripod's Builder Bucks program.

---

**MORE FREE WEB PAGE OFFERINGS**

**Many other Web communities offer free Web pages to their registered users. Refer to this book's companion Web site at www.affiliateselling.com for a list of Web sites offering free Web pages.**

# Don't Want a Web Site?

There are those among us who don't have a Web site and don't particularly want one either. If you're among them, you should know that there are other options for working with affiliate programs than creating a dynamic, well-conceived Web site, some of which are quite low-maintenance yet potentially lucrative. This section provides an overview of two methods for placing and promoting affiliate links without maintaining a Web site—ever. One is Clip2.com, which enables you to publish and share your favorite links to products, pages, downloads, and more without ever writing a single line of HTML. The other, Barnes & Noble's MyBNLink (built by BeFree), enables you to copy and paste affiliate links into e-mails, which you can pass along to friends, family, and colleagues.

## Just Clip It!

Clip2.com is a free service, and it's pretty easy to use. Briefly, it enables you to create and publish dynamic link collections (clips) for specific individuals or anyone and everyone on the Word Wide Web who might find them valuable or enjoyable. Clip2.com offers several tools that provide easy solutions for creating and publishing your best *clips*, which are simply bundles of links that you package for publishing to others, much the same way that a CD is a compilation of songs.

You can publish and share clips with anyone who is connected to the Internet. Clip2.com calls your clip users *subscribers*. When you make changes to the links within your clip (add another affiliated product link, for example), your subscribers see your changes immediately.

### How You Make Money with Clip2.com

Even if you have a Web site that contains affiliate links, you should consider extending your marketing reach by building clips that generate revenue. For example, if you're a major Star Wars fan, you might have a clip called "Star Wars" that contains links to: updated news about the next prequel, FAQs, and downloadable movie clips; and—of course—you'd include links to some great Star Wars products available online.

The links to the movie clips, and star bios, and so on, are called *content links;* the links to products, such as books, games, and so on, are considered affiliate *product links*. When you publish your Star Wars clip, you get additional exposure by dropping the clip into Clip2.com's directory, where anyone surfing the Web can find it and add it his or her own Clip2.com link collection. Just think: You can publish your affiliate links in a community environment where users are encouraged to share links with others. Then when someone subscribes to *your* clip, he or she is adding your revenue-generating links to his or her personal link collection. That's like being able to place your affiliate links on someone's Internet Explorer Favorites or Netscape Bookmarks list; in short, having others make money for you. How cool is that?

Figure 5.11 is an example of a Star Wars clip, whose publisher, Pamela Ratte, shares it with several other Clip2.com users. Her clip is dynamic, which means that when she adds or changes any links in it, they are automatically updated in her subscribers' clip collection—instantly. Notice that she added some affiliate links in the Books clip. Now, when one of the people sharing her Star Wars clip buys one of those books, she receives a commission from Barnes & Noble.

Perhaps the best part about Clip2.com is that you don't have to do much to promote your clips—Clip2.com does it for you. For example, the people

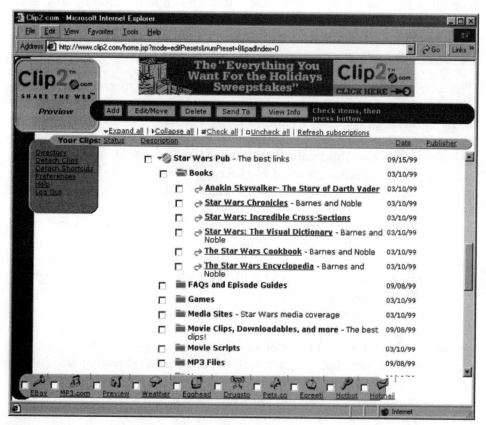

**Figure 5.11**  Pamela Ratte's Star Wars clip in Clip2.com.

subscribing to Pamela's Star Wars clip can share it with their family, friends, or colleagues using Clip2.com's pass-along feature; those people can then share it, and on and on. Additionally, Pamela can submit her clip to Clip2.com's directory where it can gain recognition through popular use. Essentially, Pamela can score new users without ever having to contact them directly (*and* she doesn't have to pay a dime). Thus, there's no limit to the amount of exposure her Star Wars clip can get, and therefore, no limit to the cash she can rake in just for sharing her clip *once*. It's impossible to get that sort of attention with search engines—especially without dedicating some serious time to building and promoting a cool Web site.

All that said, we do need to point out that even though Pamela could sustain a nice steady flow of revenue from her growing clip user base, she still must conscientiously maintain her clip to ensure that her clip's users (and subscribers) continue to find it valuable (and pass it along to more people). Remember, it's the value of the content (or links to content in Pamela's case) that drives repeat traffic; and repeat traffic is important even if your user base is continually growing—which, no doubt, is just fine with Pamela. After all, with all of the Star Wars merchandise out there—music, action figures, even toothpaste—she'll never run out of affiliate links to add!

## Get Niche-y with It

Clip2.com also can act as a great tool for creating many specialized clips targeted at narrow niches. This capability allows you to promote to radically different market segments. For instance, let's say you have a Web page specifically targeted at software usability professionals. But, in your personal time, you're a Nerf weapons guru, and your friends expect you to share links to Nerf stuff. However, adding your reviews of Nerf weapons and affiliated links to eToys might be distracting to your Web site's target audience. In fact, it could very well have a negative impact on your credibility with that crowd. The question is, do you really want to create another Web site just to sell Nerf weapons? Yeah, it might earn a nice commission, but face it, you don't have the time. Why not maintain your usability site, then build a dozen or so clips that represent your other interests. (You can even add a usability clip that drives traffic back to your site if you want to.)

With Clip2.com, your Web presence can consist of a collection of Web pieces that you find relevant, thereby making a Web site unnecessary. And you can choose to publish these different pieces for different types of folks. Figure 5.12 is an example of our Clip2.com account, which contains clips that are relevant to a wide range of viewers: usability information management professionals, Star Wars enthusiasts, marketing folks, and Nerf junkies. Notice the clip from our friend Jason, who plays music for us while we work. His clip lists the CDs he had been playing in our office, and provides us with an affiliate link to each

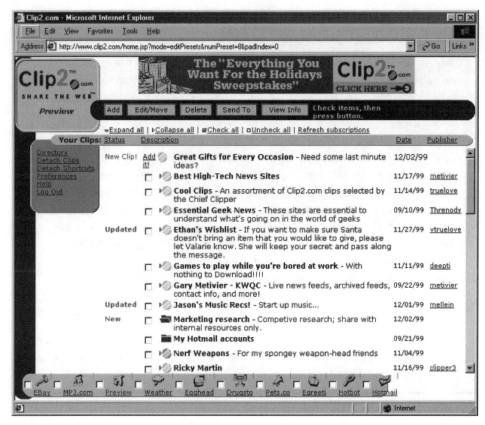

**Figure 5.12** A personal Clip2.com account with several niche-y clips.

CD at Amazon. If we like what we hear, we click on a one of the links and make a purchase (it helps to pay for Jason's extensive music collection).

## Getting Started

Getting started using Clip2.com is fairly straightforward. First, go to www .clip2.com and check out the clip directory. You can use any clip in the directory as often as you'd like, but you'll want to *subscribe* to your favorite clips—the ones you use frequently for work or entertainment or are likewise dependant upon for up-to-date information. When you subscribe, you're establishing a relationship with the publisher of a clip. Got a question about snow shoeing in Tahoe? Use Clip to send an e-mail to the publisher of your Snow Shoeing in Tahoe clip!

When you're ready to dive in and start creating clips, click the Join button to set up an account. (You don't have to have an account to use Clip2.com, but you need one if you want to publish and/or subscribe to clips.) Next, create a

**A REALLY FUN SCENARIO**

Okay, so we've convinced you that you want to organize your favorite links and subscribe to some great clips using Clip2.com, but you don't think you are really into publishing clips for other people. Think again. Consider this really fun scenario:

*I couldn't decide which of my clips to publish first—that is, until my sister asked me for my birthday wish list. So, I created a wish list that contained links to things I wanted for my birthday. This was an ideal opportunity for me to point her to the exact items, in the exact size and color, that I wanted for my birthday. She loved the idea of being able to click once to find out what I wanted, and click once more to go ahead and buy it for me. I made it really easy for her to shop for me. Then I got to thinking . . . how could this be even better? And the answer came: Make the links on my shopping lists and birthday wish lists affiliate links. So, when my sister buys me that new book for my birthday, not only do I get the exact item I wanted, but I earn a 15 percent commission from Amazon as well.*

People either love or hate this scenario. If you're one of those who hates it, you might also consider that you could donate any commissions you made in this way to your favorite charity.

clip and add your best content links to it (you can use one of their Import Links tools to get a head start by importing your browser-based bookmarks or favorites). Finally, add your affiliate links to the clip. For example, if you have a great "Tips for New Mothers" clip, you might want to add some BabyCenter products to that clip. To do so, copy the affiliate link's URL (for example, http://amazon.com/exec/obidos/ASIN/0201696967/affiliateselling) and paste it as a new link for that clip.

When you create a clip, Clip2.com provides you with a special hyperlink that points to a page where the links for that clip are shown. When someone visits that page, he or she can use your links and even save them in his or her own link collection for reuse. As we mentioned previously, users can, in turn, share your clip with others, who can also use your links and add them to *their* link collection, ad infinitum.

As you can see, Clip2.com offers clip publishers a very powerful marketing tool—free viral marketing. You can advertise your clip once and it will spread on its own. Or you can take the really simple route: place your clip in Clip2 .com's directory and let your would-be visitors find you. We also recommend that you place links to your clips on *relevant* newsgroups, message boards, or in chat rooms (only when it's suitable and permissible to do so). Chapter 10 describes various methods of announcing your clip (or site) to the Web without violating netiquette or otherwise getting yourself into trouble.

### Maintaining Your Clip

You can change your clip and its contents as frequently as you'd like; and you can use Clip2.com's reporting tools to find out how many people are using your published clips, how often they use them, and more. Read Clip2.com's FAQ for some great tips on building and maintaining clips that make money.

## E-Mail Marketing with MyBNLink

Barnes & Noble's MyBNLink program enables you to earn a 5 percent sales commission on every book, music item, or other product that you sell via e-mail-based marketing. And if you prefer, you can choose to donate your commission to one of five major charities. Whether you donate your proceeds to a charity or not, Barnes & Noble turns over 1 percent to First Book, a literacy organization that donates books to disadvantaged children.

Although potentially effective, e-mail marketing raises red flags all over the place (it's one of those "Oh no!" tools that—although potentially effective—you can't help getting excited about when you consider the onslaught of unsolicited emails that will may be borne from it). There is no doubt that e-mail is super-easy to pass along (in a few seconds you can forward something to everyone in your address book) and that it offers a simple, inexpensive method for spreading your marketing message. But unless it's sent exclusively to those who have agreed to receive it, it's spam, plain and simple. So while we can't help being excited about the possibility of making money by sending relevant affiliate links to interested recipients, we're painfully aware of the number of people who abuse this type of system. Fortunately, companies like Barnes & Noble, and its partner, BeFree, have very strict guidelines for their MyBNLink e-mail marketing program, and they have the brand power to police their members. But what about smaller, less ethical merchants? Will they enforce their e-mail marketing guidelines? Will they provide guidelines at all? That remains to be seen. Needless to say, if you're going to join an e-mail marketing program, we recommend that you join MyBNLink or a similar program backed by BeFree. You should have no trouble finding a relevant product(s) at Barnes & Noble's site (barnesandnoble.com) to include in your e-mail; let's face it, B&N has a book on everything for everyone you can think of. Furthermore, Barnes & Noble has a good reputation, which means you won't have to worry about handing off your recipients to an unscrupulous merchant. Last but not least, this is a great way to participate in affiliate selling online if you don't want to maintain a Web site.

## Getting Your MyBNLink

To get your MyBNLink, either go to BeFree (www.befree.com) to sign up to become a Barnes & Noble affiliate or go directly to Barnes and Noble's site (www .barnesandnoble.com) to sign up. After you sign up, you'll receive an e-mail from barnesandnoble.com, along with directions to go to mybnlink.reporting .net, where you can make some affiliate links. Figure 5.13 shows an example of MyBNLink's Make Links page (provided by BeFree's reporting.net).

Follow these steps to create affiliate links to distribute with e-mails.

1. From the Make Links page, choose the type of link you'd like to make, then click Make My Code. A page displays that contains the HTML code you'll need to add to your e-mail.

2. Copy the HTML code from this window and paste it into your e-mail message (or into a text editor, if you want to keep it handy on your computer).

3. Copy and use the line of text that mentions Barnes & Noble's terms of service in your e-mail as well. It's not required, but it's a good idea to let

**Figure 5.13**   Making links to include in e-mails.

your e-mail recipient(s) know that you're onboard with the rules for using affiliate links in e-mail. They'll need to know the rules, too, if they want to pass along your e-mail.

**NOTE** When you place a link in your e-mail, make sure that the link is placed on a separate line with no other text, to reduce the chance that a link might "break" at the end of a line of text.

Need some hints for including your affiliate link in an e-mail? See Figure 5.14 for an example.

## *Obey the No-Spamming Rules*

Joining MyBNLink is simple, but the restrictions are numerous (this is a good thing). Barnes & Noble wants to make sure that you adhere to all of its no-spamming rules, a sample of which are listed here:

**Figure 5.14**   Letter to Anthony, the rare-book fanatic.

- Don't send e-mails to more than 50 people at the same time.

- Make sure that those 50 people welcome your e-mail (in other words, friends, family, or colleagues).

- Don't post your link in a listserv, in a newsgroup, to a message board, or to a bulletin board.

- Don't mask your link or your identity.

- Don't set up a fake, temporary e-mail account using a service like Hotmail just so you can send out unsolicited mail.

Basically, if you know all the tricks, don't use them, because Barnes & Noble reserves the right to request to view all of your out-going MyBNLink mail. In fact, if you earn more than $250 in a given payment period (three months), B&N automatically requests to see all of your e-mail transactions that contain affiliate links. You are given a very powerful revenue-generating tool, and the company doesn't intend to let anyone abuse it or damage its good reputation. Recognize this tool as the opportunity it is: To create an effective viral strategy for getting your affiliate links viewed and shared by as many people as possible without impinging on the rights or wishes of others.

## Summary

We've described some great free tools for creating, presenting, and promoting your affiliate links whether or not you build and maintain a Web site. The next chapter explains additional ways you can take part in affiliate selling with or without your own Web site. But these alternatives have a different twist. That twist is the *virtual storefront*.

# 6
# Building a
# Virtual Storefront

Virtual storefronts are Web pages that contain product-related content (usually in the form of product reviews and descriptions), product links, and, sometimes, images of the products themselves. You don't have to be a credit-card-accepting, order-tracking, delivery-making e-merchant to have your own storefront. As an affiliate (a true reseller, in this case), you have a number of options for building a storefront, options whose "headaches"—product sourcing, customer service/support, inventory, fulfillment, and delivery—are managed by someone else because the storefronts are owned by someone else.

Some of the affiliate solutions provided, such as LinkShare (www.linkshare.com) and BeFree (www.befree.com), enable you to build a virtual storefront for each of its merchants that comes complete with a prefabricated Web page with product links, weekly specials, seasonal promotions, and more. Figure 6.1 shows an example of a BabyCenter storefront that we created using BeFree. First we joined BabyCenter's affiliate program via BeFree, clicked the Creating Links option on BabyCenter/BeFree's Reporting.net site, then copied the HTML and saved it in Notepad as an HTML file. It was incredibly easy and took less than two minutes. And if you know basic HTML, you can choose to customize the storefront; all we did was to add a title to the page. Learn the details about adding links through affiliate solution providers in Chapter 7, "Adding Links to Your Site."

We must point out, however, that though LinkShare and BeFree offer some very professional storefront building capabilities, they also limit you to

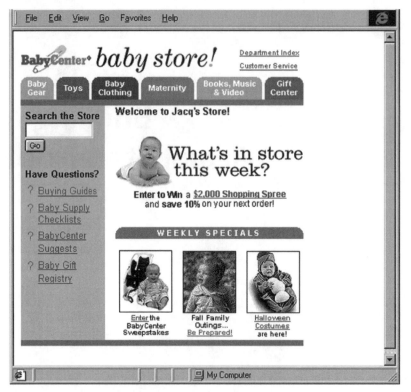

**Figure 6.1**  A customizable BabyCenter baby store.

single-merchant storefronts (unless you hack around and combine them). Fortunately, there are other Web companies whose sole purpose is to provide customizable storefronts that you can build in a matter of minutes and contain a number of affiliate links from different merchants. We chose three virtual storefront providers—Affinia, Nexchange, and VStore—to review in this chapter, but you can find a more complete list at this book's companion Web site at www.affiliateselling.com.

The key to building a virtual storefront that encourages repeat customers is to find a program in which the transaction takes place (or seems to take place) on the affiliate side (that is, within the storefront) rather than requiring a hand-off to the merchant before a purchase can occur. After all, do you want your visitors to click on a product link that takes them to a merchant's site and leaves them there? No. You want them to bookmark *your* storefront and use it to make all of their future purchases *through you*. Programs provided by VStore and Nexchange, for example, enable affiliates to accept a product order, process the credit card transaction, and display an order confirmation page—all without requiring their visitor to leave their storefront. It's important that *your* storefront appear to fulfill *your* customers' orders, as opposed to going directly to a merchant site, if you want them to come back.

# Affinia

Using the Affinia free Web service anyone can create a dynamic, customized storefront (a virtual shopping environment) in about five minutes. You can use Affinia to provide your Web site visitors with a shopping environment that offers products specifically relevant to them.

Your Affinia storefront is stored on Affinia's Web server, so all you have to do is add a link to your storefront from a page on your existing Web site. Or you can set up a storefront that is not a part of *any* site at all; that is, your storefront can be your Web site. Just be aware that it's much more difficult to succeed with an orphan storefront because you will have to provide some additional value to persuade people to visit. And let's face it: It's difficult enough to get attention for a Web site that contains tons of content; it would be virtually impossible to get noticed if you offered nothing whatsoever.

Affinia boasts more than 1,000 merchants, but unfortunately you can't find out who they are when you start. The Affinia emphasis is on the product being placed, not on merchant co-branding opportunities. The process works like this: You select the types of products you'd like to add to your storefront and Affinia presents you with a list of available products from participating merchants. Admittedly, this is a little frustrating if you're interested in promoting your favorite e-merchant, but what Affinia doesn't mention (as of this writing) is that you can search by the merchant's name to find products made available as affiliated products. It doesn't matter how you find the products for your storefront; just as long as you choose the right types of products, which means either they're relevant to your existing site or to the theme you've chosen for your stand-alone storefront.

Another heads-up: Using Affinia, you can customize some design variables (colors, fonts, etc.), but you will probably not be able to closely match the storefront to your site. This makes Affinia a poor option for strongly branded commercial sites; conversely, its simplicity makes it a good choice for individuals trying to earn extra income.

## Making Money

How much money can you make? Each of Affinia's merchants sets a fee for its products, and Affinia splits that fee 50/50 with you, the storefront owner. Your share is typically anywhere between $.03 and $.05 per click-through for each merchant. Keep in mind as you select products that you can make the same amount of money whether the shopper buys or not, and regardless of the price of the item.

## The Shopping Experience

Here's how the Affinia storefront shopping environment is experienced by your visitors:

1. Your customer clicks on a link to your Affinia storefront from your existing Web site, your Clip2.com clip, your e-mail signature line, or wherever else you've promoted the link. He or she is taken to your storefront that is hosted by Affinia.

2. Your visitor pokes around your storefront, reading—we assume—its well-written, enticing content, and of course finds a product he or she wants to purchase. The customer clicks the Go to Merchant Page to Buy This Product button next to it.

3. Affinia launches a new browser window that contains the merchant's product page. The customer enters his or her mailing information, billing information, and so on, to place the order on the merchant's site. (From this point on, the merchant "owns" the customer, and all purchases are private transactions between the customer and the merchant.)

4. After the customer finishes making the purchase, he or she closes the browser and returns (hopefully) to the browser window containing your storefront. He or she can then continue to shop from your storefront, opening new windows when it's time to buy.

To repeat: The good part about this scenario is that the transaction becomes the sole responsibility of the merchant. However, that's also the bad part, bad because the transaction is the sole responsibility of the merchant so your visitors can never really become your customers. Rather, they're simply your referrals, who become your merchant's customers. This is significant—especially if your intent is to offer this storefront as an additional service offered by your existing content site. You don't want your customers to side-step you when it's time to make a similar purchase. Worse, you don't want to appear as though you—egad!—can't afford to host your own store for your visitors.

The bottom line here? If your intent is to add e-commerce to your already awesome personal home page in order to make some extra money in a fun, creative way, then Affinia is a good choice. After all, it's easy to find relevant products from any one or more of its 1,000 online merchants.

Okay, that's the Affinia overview; now let's go through the process of joining the program step by step.

## Step 1: Sign Up

As mentioned, when you sign up with Affinia, a storefront is created for you that Affinia maintains and hosts. Your job is to choose products to display on your storefront and to promote them. As a member of Affinia, you earn a flat click-through referral fee (as opposed to a percentage of the sale) every time one of your visitors clicks on a link in your storefront that leads to a participating merchant's site.

Affinia pays referral fees to members once every quarter. If, at the end of any quarter, you do not have at least $25 in accumulated referral fees, Affinia will hold your payment until your referral fees are equal to or greater than $25, at which point they will send you a payment at the next quarter.

To sign up for an Affinia storefront, go to www.affinia.com and do the following:

1. Click on the Build Your Own Storefront link.
2. Enter your e-mail address and choose a login name and password.
3. Read the membership agreement, then click I Accept.
4. Click Continue to begin creating your storefront.

## Step 2: Build Your Storefront

First you need to pick a name for your storefront. Consider which products or services you'd like to sell and choose a suitable name based on that decision. For example, Mark's Store is not intuitive, but Mark's Movies and Videos is. Figure 6.2 is an example of the Create Your Storefront page.

After you've chosen a name for your storefront, type in a keyword that will be used to select products for your storefront, then select the types of products (in this case, movies and videos) you want to sell. Affinia displays a sample list of products that match your keyword entries for the product type you selected, as shown in Figure 6.3. Notice that there were 250 products that matched our keyword search "Cohen Brothers, Hollywood" and product categories "Books and Magazines" and "Food and Drink." You can: add all products that directly match the keyword(s) to your storefront; add all products that generally match your keyword(s); add only the products you approve; or reenter your keywords and start the search over. Keeping in mind that your storefront will be more successful if you are selective about the products you're selling on it (i.e., create a thematic storefront), we recommend using the product approval method, which means you'll essentially be building your storefront from scratch—especially if you receive 250 product matches as we did. (For more great ideas on building your storefront, read Affinia's "9 Steps to Build a Great Storefront.")

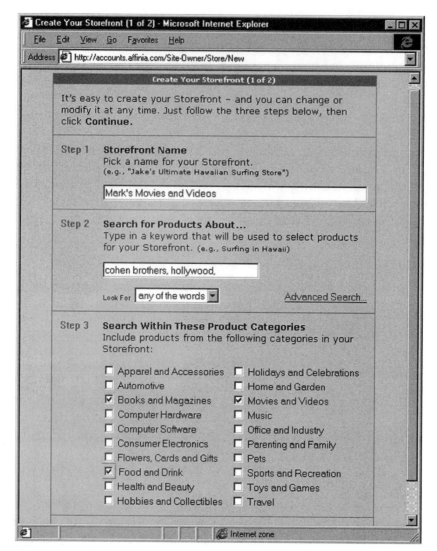

**Figure 6.2**   Name your Affinia storefront.

### Building from Scratch

If you decide to build a storefront from scratch, choose the Build a Storefront from Scratch option on Affinia's second Create Your Storefront page. You'll start with an empty storefront, to which you add products simply by clicking the Modify Your Storefront option, followed by clicking the Add button in the Storefront Products portion of your storefront. You'll see the page display shown in Figure 6.4. Notice that we've deselected the items we don't want to sell.

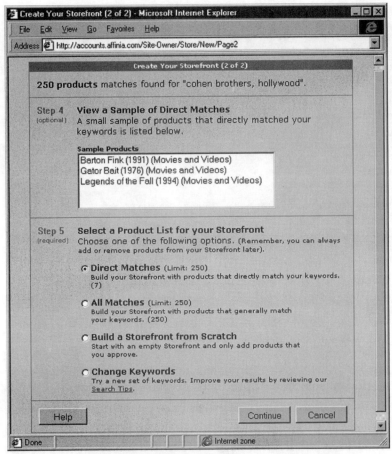

**Figure 6.3** Wow! We found 250 matches to our keywords.

## Step 3: Customize Your Storefront

Affinia makes it easy to create a storefront, then enables you to place your site's logo in a fairly prominent place on the page (the often-sought co-branding spot). This sort of co-branding should make your shoppers feel comfortable when they leave your Web site (assuming you have one) and end up on a page hosted by Affinia. If, however, you don't have a logo, simply put, there's not a whole lot you can do to clearly identify your storefront. Some alternatives are: add a background color or wallpaper image; change the colors; toss in some animated GIFs. In short, you'll have to be pretty creative to make your cookie-cutter storefront stand out. At the very least, you should:

- Choose a unique color palette to give your site a distinctive look and feel.
- Come up with a good storefront greeting that grabs attention.

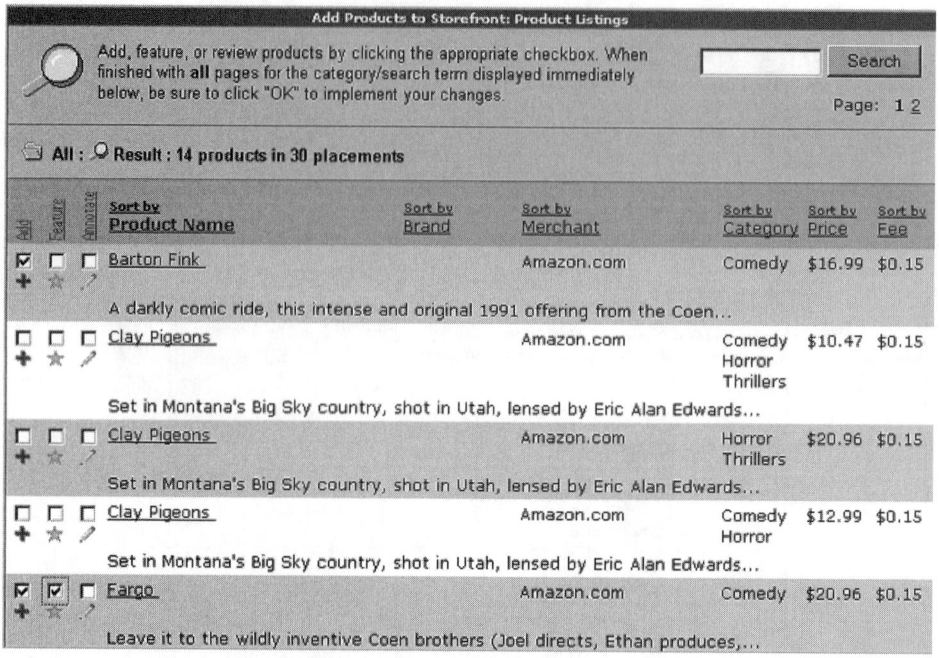

**Figure 6.4**   Affinia's Add Products to Storefront page.

- Choose a relevant selection of products, or make sure your selection is thematic.

Figure 6.5 shows an example of Mark's Affinia storefront. Mark didn't have a logo, so he used the default page header. It's a nice storefront, but without a "parent" Web page with killer content directing visitors to his storefront, he might not see a check from Affinia any time soon. If he's a popular fellow, he might make a few dollars from friends, family, and colleagues who respect his opinions about the movie business. But to make a significant amount of money, he really needs a Web site from which heavy traffic can be drawn in to make a purchase.

## Step 4: Mind Those Reports, and Tweak as Needed

Good affiliate sites require constant promotion and tweaking. Good affiliate solutions providers like Affinia offer reports that enable you to, first, track the success of your promotion, then tweak and act on those results. Affinia's online reporting tools let you view activity (performance) and revenue reports. When you run a revenue report, you can define the period (starting date and ending date), granularity (daily or monthly), and reporting format (display on

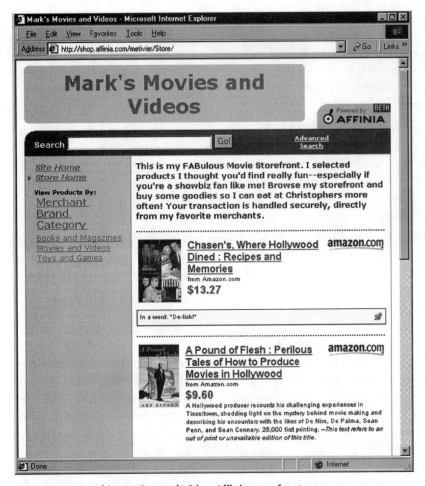

**Figure 6.5**   Mark's Movies and Video Affinia storefront.

screen or save as a file that can be imported into Excel). The report displays the
following:

- Date
- Store name (you can have many storefronts)
- Distinct visitors (number of new visitors)
- Product viewed
- Click-throughs
- Percentage click-through
- Average click fee amount
- Total revenue

Affiliates like Mark should review the statistical information provided by Affinia regularly to track buying patterns and to ensure he's allotting enough shelf space to the right products. The Storefront page, shown in Figure 6.6, is where Mark can tweak the look and feel of his storefront, as well as rearrange or add to his storefront product offerings. The following list briefly describes the options available on this page:

**Category summary on the Welcome tab.** Provides information that will help you optimize your product offerings. It's important that you understand the data in these reports so you can use it to make good decisions about which products to include and how they should be presented in your storefront. Great product placement spells value to your visitors and more revenue potential for you.

**Activity and Revenue Reports.** Allow you to view in detail either the overall performance of your storefront(s) or the performance of individual products, product categories, and product subcategories. Use this information to make decisions about adding, removing, or featuring (highlighting) specific products.

**Account Management Reports.** Contain information about merchants that have recently changed their referral fees. (Don't forget: Merchants can change their referral fees as often as they like. In fact, they *should* change them as needed to remain competitive.) Review the Account Management Report area frequently to stay on top of your earning potential. If you find that one of your average-selling products' commission has increased, you might want to feature that product more prominently on your storefront to take advantage of the higher visibility in the future. On the flip side, if you find that another product is generating a lower commission rate, you might want to remove that product to make room for another more profitable item.

**Store Content Reports.** Enable you to view information about the products in your store, as well as a list of top-selling product categories. This will help you decide which different types of products you should consider packaging in your storefront.

**Charts feature.** Shows you three different charts (as of this writing). The first shows the number of times your visitors view additional information about a product. The second shows how many times your visitors have clicked through to a merchant's site. The third chart shows the amount of revenue you have earned.

## Step 5: Promote and Revisit

Chapter 10, "Increasing Hits and Selling More on Your Web Site," contains a number of great ideas for promoting your affiliate site; and be sure to review

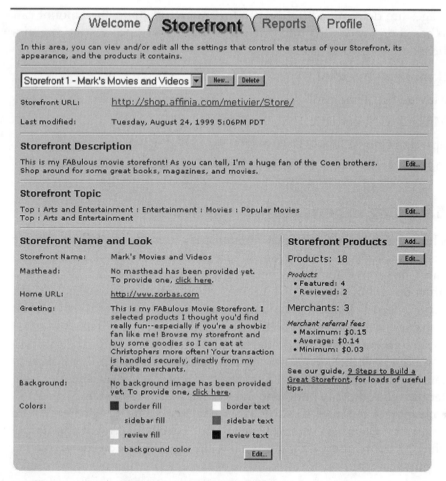

**Figure 6.6** Mark's Affinia Storefront page settings.

Affinia's tips for promoting your storefront at www.affinia.com/site-owners/ promote.html. There you'll find good grassroots marketing ideas, such as adding the URL to your storefront to every e-mail you send; featuring your storefront prominently on your existing site; and more.

# VStore

VStore enables you to create in minutes a customized virtual storefront for free. VStore calls its affiliates "partners," and gives them a percentage of every sale made on their storefront (VStore keeps a small percentage as a fee for providing the service). VStore commissions range from 5 percent to 25 percent.

Percentages are determined by the product merchants, and the amount can change based on availability and pricing. As of this writing, VStore commissions break out as follows:

- Books: 5 to 20 percent
- Movies: 5 to 25 percent
- Music: 5 to 15 percent
- Sporting Goods: 10 to 25 percent
- Other miscellaneous products (electronics and games): 5 to 25 percent

## The Shopping Experience

Here's how the VStore shopping environment is experienced by your visitors: Your customer clicks on a link to your VStore storefront from your existing Web site, your Clip2.com ClipZine, or your e-mail signature line, and he or she is taken to your storefront hosted by VStore, which ideally reflects the look and feel of your referring Web site (if you have one, of course). Your visitor browses your storefront, checking out its well-written, enticing content (including product descriptions and prices), and hopefully finds a product he or she wants to purchase from your site. At that point, the customer clicks the Buy button to complete the transaction. Figure 6.7 shows an example of a page shoppers will see after they click the Buy button on Jake's DreamCast storefront.

The customer continues to shop, dropping items into his or her VStore shopping cart. When the customer is ready to "check out," he or she simply clicks the Checkout button. If the customer is already a VStore customer (having made a purchase from *any* VStore), all he or she does is enter his or her e-mail address and password to sign in and complete the purchase. New customers must click the Continue button to open a VStore account, which they can use at any VStore storefront. At no point do your customers have to leave your site to complete their order.

## Getting Started

There are five steps to building your own VStore:

1. Select a store type.
2. Create an account with VStore.
3. Choose a design for your store.
4. Customize your storefront by naming it, adding a tagline, and selecting products that create a theme.
5. Tell VStore where to send your commissions check.

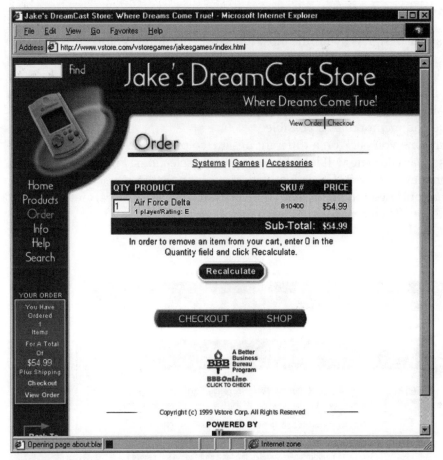

**Figure 6.7**    Visitors buy directly from Jake's DreamCast site!

### Select a Store Type

With VStore's service, you can select from a wide range of store types: Superstores (for books, movies, sports), Sports & Outdoors (from baseball to camping), Books, Music, Movies, Video Games, Electronics, and—our favorite—Themes (such as Aviation, DreamCast, or the Elvis Store). Each store type offers a different range of commission percentages, so if you're interested in more than one type of store (but you don't want to build more than one), compare their commission structures.

### Create an Account

Setting up an account consists of entering your full name, e-mail address, and password for access. It's very straightforward, and takes about 10 seconds to complete.

## *Choose a Design*

Choosing a design is by far the most fun aspect of joining VStore. If you expect to use your existing site (assuming you have one) as a gateway to your storefront, when you choose your overall design, color palette, and font for your store, make sure that you match it as closely as possible to the look and feel of your site. If you don't have a Web site, try to establish a look and feel that is as unique and memorable as possible.

Each time you click on a different design, color palette, or font, VStore previews what your site will look like using those selections. First select a design, and preview it. Like it? Great. Now select a color palette for that design. Finally, select a font. Keep in mind that you can customize your storefront later, so if you're not 100 percent satisfied with the preview page, don't worry. Figure 6.8

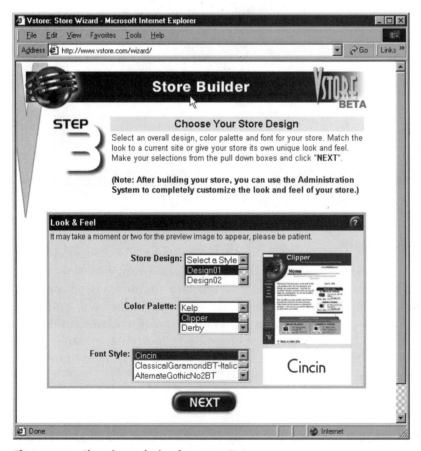

**Figure 6.8**   Choosing a design for your VStore.

shows the Choose Your Store Design page. Notice that we chose Design01, the Clipper color palette, and the Cincin font style.

## Customize Your VStore

VStore automatically "stocks" your virtual store based on the store type you selected. If you don't agree with all the default selections, you can customize your product offerings by deselecting products, as shown in Figure 6.9. If you don't see the product(s) you want to sell, use the link VStore has placed a Merchandising Request Form on Choose Your Store Design page to request it.

You can further customize your VStore by changing its name, the default slogan (tagline), and welcome message for your visitors. VStore also chooses a default domain name and store directory name for you, both of which you can

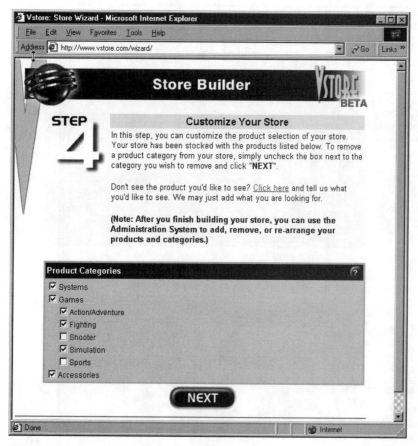

**Figure 6.9**   Choosing your product offerings.

also change, as we did in Figure 6.10. Finally, you can add a return link to your VStore to point your visitors back to your Web site.

### Get Paid

The final step in creating your virtual store is to tell VStore where to send your commission checks. Fill in the required contact information, including your name, address, and phone number(s). Be sure to read the Terms and Conditions agreement. As a VStore partner, you get paid on a quarterly basis. However, you can generate monthly sales reports and up-to-date

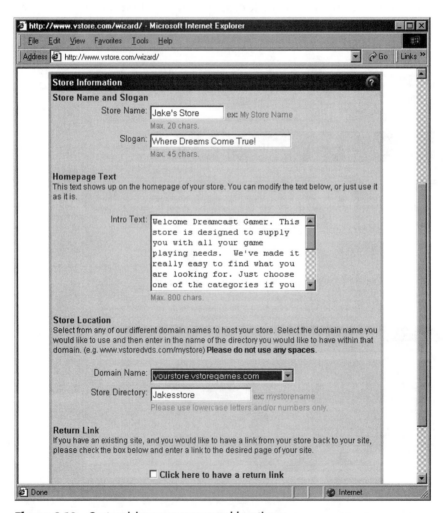

**Figure 6.10** Customizing your name and location.

commission reports at any time by logging in to VStore's Store Administration section.

## VStore Maintenance

VStore offers several tools you can use to promote your new VStore, including personalized business cards, e-mail announcements to friends and potential customers, and tips for registering with search engines.

As noted, you can change the look and feel of your VStore as often as you'd like; change the text and hyperlinks on your storefront; and—in the near future—upload images and customized HTML to create a seamless connection from your existing site to your VStore storefront. Figure 6.11 shows VStore's Products & Categories tab on the VStore Administration page. You can tweak the text, fonts, product listing, and more, as often as you want.

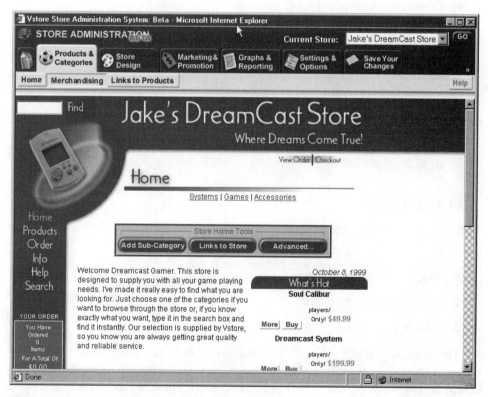

**Figure 6.11**   Jake tweaks the products in his storefront.

You can also view a Sales and Commissions report by clicking the Graphs & Reporting tab in the VStore Administration "department," so you can see what's selling and what's not.

# Nexchange

The Nexchange program comes with a wizard application that lets you design and generate storefronts that you can embed in your existing Web site. You can sell a single product, a category of products, or an entire product line, using one or more embedded storefronts; and you can earn anywhere between 10 and 20 percent commissions on sales made from a storefront that appears to be seamlessly integrated to your own site. First, you create an image that points to your storefront (such as a Buy It Now! button). When your visitor decides to make a purchase (and clicks the Buy It Now! button), Nexchange retrieves the latest product information and presents it to your user in the style of *your* site. Nexchange's features let you:

- Design the look and feel of your online storefront.
- Choose from a wide variety of brand-name products to sell.
- Create individual stores to add to your Web site.
- Choose products, create stores, track your results, and manage your account within a single environment.
- Create as many stores as you like.
- Generate your own custom reports based on timeframe, products sold, or individual stores.

## Getting Started

Adding a Nexchange storefront to your existing Web site is a simple three-step process:

1. Register with Nexchange.
2. Design your storefront.
3. Create your online store.

The process—designing and choosing products for your new Nexchange storefront—takes about 20 minutes. However, with the Nexchange program, you must be approved by *each* merchant whose products you want to sell *before* you can generate the code for your storefront. And be aware that you can be declined by a merchant after you've invested time in preparing your storefront.

### Register with Nexchange

To register with Nexchange, follow these steps:

1. Go to Nexchange (www.nexchange.com) and click the Build Your Own Online Store link.

2. Complete the registration form.

3. Read the Terms and Conditions, then click I Accept.

4. Enter a username and password (twice), then click Submit.

The HOST MANAGER page displays, as shown in Figure 6.12. Now, it's time to design and build your storefront.

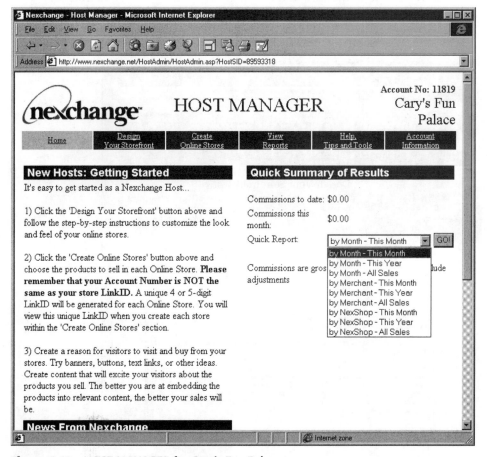

**Figure 6.12** HOST MANAGER for Cary's Fun Palace.

### *Design Your Storefront*

Designing your Nexchange storefront consists of copying the HTML for your images, text, and links from your existing Web site and pasting it into a text window. This enables Nexchange to present your storefront using the same layout, to ensure that your storefront looks as much like your Web site as possible.

1. Click Design Your Storefront.

2. Enter the URL for your Web site (containing the text, links, and images that you want to use on your new storefront).

3. Paste the HTML code for the text, images, and links that you want to appear on the top and left side of your storefront into the text window provided; click Continue. Figure 6.13 shows an example of HTML code for Cary's Fun Palace site.

4. Click Validate to have Nexchange test the links and images for your new storefront, to make sure that they are "live" and point to the correct places.

5. Click Save.

**Figure 6.13** The HTML code for the text, links, and images for Cary's Fun Palace.

Your storefront design is complete, and you're ready to create your online store.

## Create Your Online Store

When you first create your online Nexchange store, you must choose some products to sell. You can choose a catalog, to offer your customers a broad selection; a product category, to offer a range of products for that catalog; or a specific product. The instructions that follow describe how to create your storefront entry page using a specific product.

1. Click the Search for a Product to Sell! button. The Search or Select Catalogs page displays, as shown in Figure 6.14.

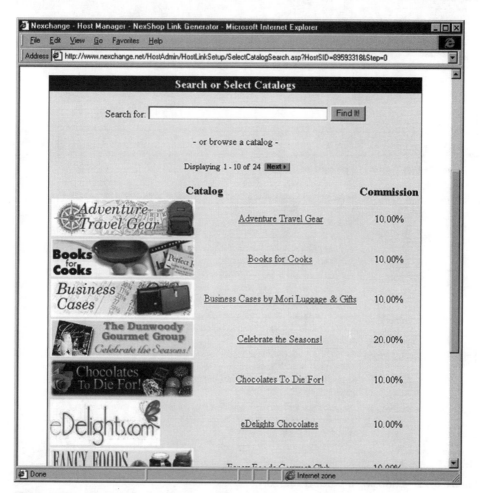

**Figure 6.14**  Choosing a catalog of products to sell on your site.

2. Click on the merchant whose products you'd like to sell on your site. The Merchant Store Catalog for that merchant displays, as shown in Figure 6.15.

3. Click a category name to display products for that category. A list of products for that category displays, as shown in Figure 6.16.

4. Choose the product you want to sell; click Click Here! to create your entry point for your online store.

5. Enter the URL to which you want your visitors to be returned after they finish shopping.

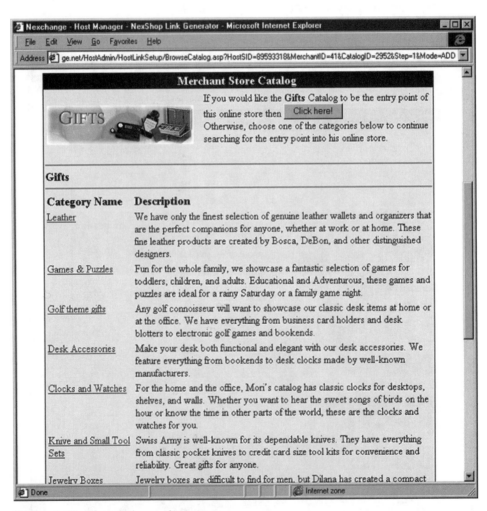

**Figure 6.15**   Choosing a product category.

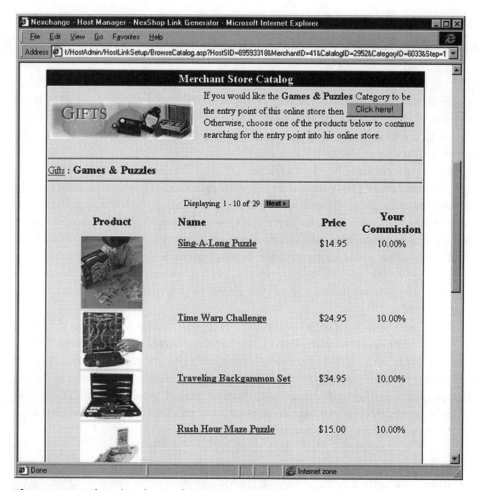

**Figure 6.16**  Choosing the product you want to sell.

6. Enter a name for your online store so that Nexchange can generate the HTML link to your new online store. (This is used only within your HOST MANAGER page.) Click Continue. If this is the first time you've used a particular merchant, a page displays notifying you that the merchant will review your request to add its product links as your storefront.

7. Once you have been approved by the merchant, copy and paste the HTML text link into your Web site source code.

8. Create a banner to drive users to your new storefront using Nexchange's Image Library (www.nexchange.com/imagelibrary). If you don't want to use one of the banner images provided, you can use an image or text link of your own.

# Is a Virtual Storefront
# Right for You?

Affiliate selling works best when highly relevant products are placed within the context of high-quality content. Therefore, make sure to choose a storefront provider that gives you the flexibility you need to meet your personal or business objectives. If you can't add and update content frequently and easily, keep looking.

If you're promoting products for an existing Web site, make sure that you give your customers easy access to relevant products. This means they should not have to click more than a few times to get from your home page to your product links. Moreover, your storefront should look as similar as possible to your existing content site, which should contain many in-context links to your storefront. If the storefront provider doesn't provide a suitable, ready-made design, customize one by tweaking the HTML code directly. If the service doesn't allow you to tweak the HTML code, find a different service that lets you to do so.

Finally, as a self-appointed topic expert, it's important that you maintain credibility with your visitors (see Chapter 10, "Increasing Hits and Selling More on Your Web Site"). If you're doing nothing more than passing your visitors along to a merchant's product page where the final sale is made, ask yourself whether that gives you enough brand power to maintain your visitor's perception of you as the master of your domain. It's possible; after all, if you're pushing high-priced items, it might be important to your visitors that their sales take place on a well-known and trusted e-commerce site where they will feel comfortable giving their credit card information. Furthermore, it might appear to your customers that you have a meaningful partnership with that company. On the other hand, if you're serious about building revenue on the Web, we say, shoot for the stars and convince your visitors that you're worthy of handling their transactions; in this case, forgo the merchant hand-off and build your own virtual store using VStore, Nexchange, or another service that facilitates transactions within your branded environment.

## Summary

If you're interested in creating affiliate partnerships with a plethora of category-killer merchants and in passing your visitors along for a few cents per click-through, try Affinia. If you're interested in acting as a true e-merchant reseller for a particular merchant, build a virtual storefront at BeFree or LinkShare.

If you're interested in adding a co-branded one-stop storefront to your Web site's current offerings, try VStore or Nexchange.

If you're not a commercial content site that requires tight control, you can't lose with any of these. If you are, probably you'll want to exercise tighter control by deploying "buy" links directly from your own site's pages, rather than using a virtual storefront service. The next chapter provides detailed instructions for generating links and placing them on your Web site.

# 7

# Adding Links
# to Your Site

Adding affiliate links to your site is easy—especially if you know HTML. But as we've cautioned throughout the book so far, before you join an affiliate program(s), you must first determine which products to display, which merchants you want to link to, and how many programs you want to join. From there, you can go about finding the appropriate affiliate links. As you've learned already, certain merchants require you to join their affiliate programs by completing an application on their sites (e.g., Amazon and Beyond.com), while others use a third-party service referred to as an affiliate solutions provider that enables you to join their affiliate program either from the merchant or the ASP site. In the latter case, the affiliate solution provider handles the implementation and maintenance of the merchant's affiliate program, and offers additional services to you, as described later in this chapter.

**NOTE** If you're not sure which affiliate program(s) you want to join, we recommend you visit a major merchandising aggregator, such as CrossCommerce, or an affiliate solution provider, such as BeFree, Commission Junction, or LinkShare, to review and sign up to join multiple affiliate programs from a single source.

# The Build-It-from-Scratch Guys

Many merchants use affiliate solutions providers to design, implement, and maintain their affiliate programs, but there are a few big-name e-merchants with the branding and the know-how to design and run their own programs directly from their site. (Adding affiliation to an existing e-commerce site isn't rocket science—see Chapter 11, "For Merchants: Building a Program.")

Why should you care how a merchant chooses to run its affiliate program? Simply, because that decision can affect you, the affiliate, in a few important ways. For starters (as of this writing), merchants that build and run their own affiliate programs typically don't provide affiliates with online commission tracking tools. You have to depend on their monthly or quarterly e-mail-based statements. This delays your access to the information you need to shuffle your product offerings, remove products that aren't earning you a commission, and so on. There's also no centralized place where you can go to run commission reports, create links, review and join other programs, compare program results, and so on. In contrast, affiliate solutions providers offer all these capabilities. Furthermore, in the case of individually run programs, you have to go to each merchant's site to create links; they don't want you to become an affiliate of their competitors.

However, if you're planning to join only one or two affiliate programs, or you're simply interested in an affiliate program offered by a single merchant, don't let the aforementioned restrictions of a direct program dissuade you from joining them. Some of them comprise the biggest and most well-organized programs on the Web today, and they usually have a dedicated staff to assist you with your affiliate needs. It's easy to add affiliate links, no matter where you go to create them.

Most affiliate programs that require you to apply directly from the merchant's site operate as described in the following paragraphs, with only slight variations.

**NOTE** Remember to adhere to the instructions provided by each merchant for creating your links correctly. As previously mentioned, the most common mistake affiliates make is in this process. We repeat, if your link is missing any part of the program-provider's HTML code, you won't get paid, and it's next to impossible for merchants to correct mistracked commissions.

The first step is to go to the merchant's site and find a link to its affiliate program (keep in mind that some call them partner programs or associates programs). Review the affiliate agreement thoroughly.

Complete the affiliate application. Typically, the merchant will send you an e-mail that indicates whether you've been accepted into the program. Some merchants automatically approve of every applicant, while others take the time to ensure that your site is suitable for their target audience (no pornography and so forth); still others spend considerably more time to verify that your content is relevant or that you can be counted on to direct a significant number of customers their way.

If you're accepted, the e-mail will usually contain information for getting started (adding and promoting links). This e-mail might also contain your unique affiliate ID (it might look something like this: AF-00061484VS) or your affiliate ID embedded in a string of HTML code, like this:

```
http://www.merchant.com/booklink/click?sourceid=AF-00061484VS&categoryid=gifts
```

Save this e-mail so you can access this information easily and as often as needed. (However, it's usually available on a special page on the merchant's Web site.)

**NOTE** You may find programs that: 1) Ask you to provide the number of unique visitors you receive at your site each month. If you know, tell them; if you don't, leave the field blank. 2) Ask how many pageviews are logged on your site each month. 3) Require you to have a certain number of new visitors each month to ensure that you will be directing a certain volume of traffic to them.

After you've received your e-mail from the merchant (we'll assume you've been accepted), return to the merchant's site to get the HTML code for your affiliate links, if you didn't receive it in the e-mail. You'll need to add this to the HTML code for your Web site or as a link in your Clip2.com clip.

When you go to the merchant's site to create your links, often you'll be presented with a variety of linking methods, which might include:

- A link to the merchant's front door
- A link to a specific category of products (e.g., New Age music)
- A link to an individual product (e.g., Enya's Watermark)
- HTML code used to create a search box that your visitors can use to search the merchant's site from your Web site

Browse the category or individual product page to find the appropriate URL (Web address) for the product or products you want to promote. Copy the URL by highlighting (selecting) it and clicking Edit >Copy from your browser's drop-down menu. See Figure 7.1 for an example.

**Figure 7.1** Copying the product URL to create your affiliate link.

To add the URL as an affiliate link to your existing Web site, open the source code for the page on which you want to include the affiliate link and paste the URL in the appropriate location. Remember to add your affiliate ID to the URL as directed by the merchant. Figure 7.2 shows what the HTML code looks like when we added an affiliate link to *Increasing Hits and Selling More on Your Web Site* on our Web page. Notice that we removed the query information "qid%3D939591916," which resulted from performing a search from the URL. (Note: You can leave it in if you're uncomfortable editing your URL.) Figure 7.3 shows an example of what our visitors will see when they click on this book's affiliate link on our Web page.

Program merchants should provide recommendations, linking instructions, and an FAQ on the portion of their Web site dedicated to their affiliate program. If you have any questions about joining, linking to products, or receiving your commissions, review these areas. If you don't find the information you need, ask via e-mail. If you can't find an e-mail address or fail to get a response in a timely manner, join a different program. Life's too short. The merchants you want to do business with will provide excellent service to their affiliates.

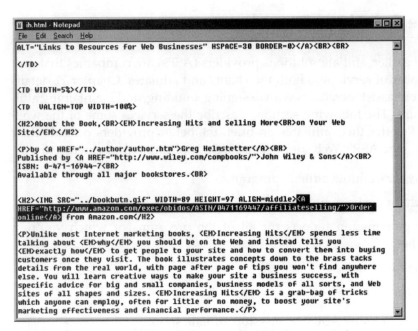

**Figure 7.2** Adding an affiliate link to your Web site's HTML code.

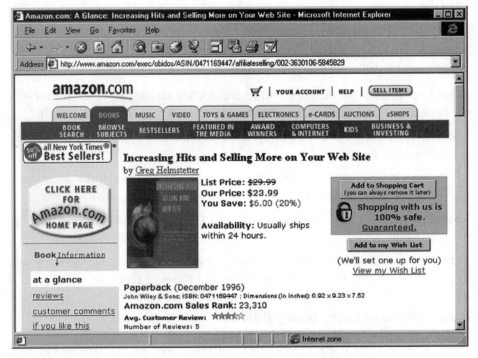

**Figure 7.3** What your visitors see when they click on your link.

# Affiliate Solutions Providers

As defined earlier, affiliate solutions providers (ASPs) are companies that provide a number of services to both merchants and affiliates. Chapter 11 details how ASPs can assist merchants with designing, building, and maintaining affiliate programs. The following sections describe the services some of the well-known ASPs offer their affiliates. In brief, the better providers provide their affiliates (via the ASP's Web site) with a single application they can use to:

- Apply for multiple affiliate programs.
- Search for participating merchants.
- View commission reports for all of the programs of which you're a member.
- Request assistance.
- And more.

Essentially, a quality ASP is a one-stop affiliate shop.

## BeFree

BeFree (www.befree.com), one the most popular affiliate solutions providers, currently offers more than 1,750,000 affiliates the ultimate in one-stop affiliate shopping. As of this writing, free affiliate services include the following:

**FastApp.** A tool that enables you to complete a single application that will be sent to any merchant in whose program you request membership.

**Merchant catalog.** Lets you review the affiliate offerings for over 100 BeFree merchants.

**Flexible linking options.** Enable you to create affiliate links in textual, image, or e-mail formats.

**Storefronts.** Lets you build a storefront in which to feature your product selections.

**Online reporting.** Provides you with access to reporting.net, BeFree's tool that enables you to generate more than 15 types of reports.

### Adding Affiliate Links Using BeFree

As just stated, when you join BeFree, you have to complete only one application to apply to all of BeFree's program merchants. Follow these steps to join BeFree and add affiliate links to one or more of its merchants:

1. Go to BeFree (www.befree.com) and click the Affiliates option.

2. Click the Affiliates Sign Up Now! button.

3. Fill in your contact and mailing information so merchants will know where to send your checks.

4. Request a username and password to establish an account. You'll use this information to apply to all affiliate programs on BeFree's merchant list.

5. Provide your tax ID/Social Security numbers. (You're accountable for the applicable taxes on this income.)

6. Choose one or more affiliate programs from the merchant list on the application page to which you'd like to submit an application (you can always join individual merchant programs later). Figure 7.4 shows a sample from the sign-up page depicting a portion of BeFree's merchant list.

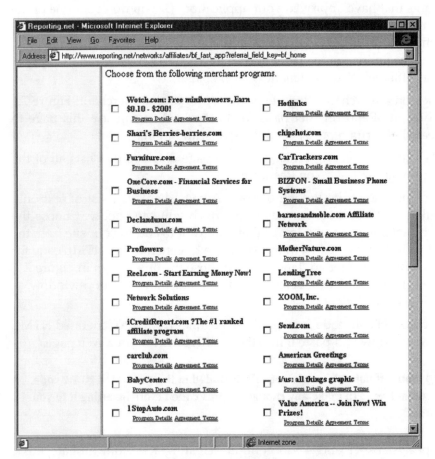

**Figure 7.4**   Picking programs offered by BeFree merchants.

**NOTE** Click the Learn More link for information about merchant commission structures, billing cycles, and more. Click the Agreement Terms link to read the agreement before applying.

7. Click the Apply button to submit your application. You'll receive a confirmation page that your applications have been sent to the various merchants. You'll also receive a confirmation via e-mail explaining how to begin adding links and earning commissions. Individual merchants will also notify you via e-mail whether you've been accepted into its affiliate program. Some merchants will respond immediately; others can take a week or longer.

8. Once you've received your confirmation e-mail from BeFree, and you've been accepted into at least one affiliate program, go to www.reporting.net and log in using the username and password you chose in step 4. The Your Merchant Partners page displays with the logos for each of the merchants that have approved your application. (If you don't see one of the merchant's logos to which you applied, it's either because your application hasn't been processed yet or because your application was denied. You'll be notified of the latter via e-mail.) Figure 7.5 shows an example of Jane Affiliate's Your Merchant Partners page.

9. Click on a merchant's logo to create a link to that merchant. Figure 7.6 shows the Reporting.net page for Reel.com. You can use this page to create links, run reports, get linking tips, and more.

10. Click on the Creating Links option. A page displays that lists all of the pages you can link to on Reel.com.

11. Click on one of the linking options. A page displays a list of text-only affiliate links and banner ads from which you can choose. Choose the text-only link or banner image that you want to add to your site from the list provided; then click Make My Code to generate the HTML code for this affiliate banner ad. Jane Affiliate chose the one shown in Figure 7.7. The HTML code for the selected banner ad displays in a pop-window, as shown in Figure 7.8.

12. Copy the HTML code for the selected banner from the Generated HTML Code window and paste it into the HTML code for your Web page.

**NOTE** Your affiliate ID is automatically included in the generated HTML code, so you do not need to make any changes to this code before inserting it to your own code.

13. Repeat steps 11 and 12 to continue creating Reel.com affiliate links. Return to Reporting.net to create links for any other programs. You can create and remove affiliate links as often as you'd like.

**Figure 7.5**    Jane Affiliate's Your Merchant Partners page at BeFree.

**Figure 7.6**    Reel.com's Reporting.net page enables you to create links, run reports, get great tips, and more.

**Figure 7.7** Jane Affiliate's choice? A banner for *The Matrix*.

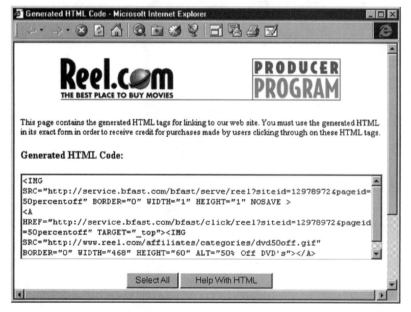

**Figure 7.8** Generated HTML code for *The Matrix* banner (no tweaking required).

14. After you've spent a few days promoting your site, return to Reporting .net and click on the logo for the merchant for which you'd like to run a report. On the merchant's Reporting.net page, click on the Create Reports option. A page displays listing all of the reports available for the selected merchant. As you can see in Figure 7.9, Jane Affiliate can run the following reports to check the performance of *all* of her affiliate links: Revenue (Detail), Top 10 Best Sellers, Sales (Daily), Traffic, and Revenue (Summary). She can also track the performance for affiliate links to a specific merchant using the following reports: Sales, Traffic, Top 10 Best Sellers, and Page Link (Impressions). Learn more about running reports from www.reporting.net.

## Commission Junction

Commission Junction (www.cj.com), is a rapidly growing affiliate solutions provider that currently offers affiliates a great one-stop shop with access to more

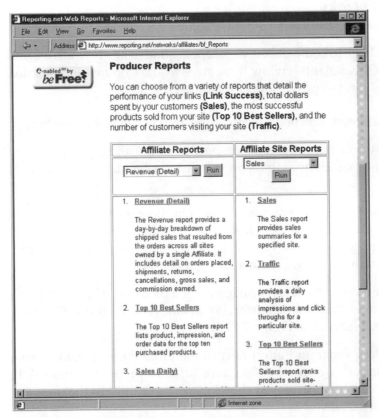

**Figure 7.9** Jane Affiliate checks the performance of her affiliate links.

than 160 merchants. Though, as of this writing, its merchant list is not as dense with top-tier e-merchants as that of BeFree, Commission Junction offers an interesting combination of free affiliate services, which include the following:

**Two-tier programs.** Enable you to earn $1 for each new affiliate you send to Commission Junction, plus 5 percent of the earnings made by those affiliates.

**Reporting tools.** Let you access reports for all of your affiliate programs using a single username and password.

**Your CJ virtual store.** Offers a co-branded virtual storefront hosted by Commission Junction.

**One check once a month.** Receive a single check from Commission Junction for *all* affiliate earnings on the fifteenth of every month (as long as you meet the $25 minimum).

## Adding Affiliate Links Using Commission Junction

Like BeFree, you have to complete only one application to apply to all of Commission Junction's merchants. Follow these steps to join Commission Junction and add affiliate links to one or more of their merchants:

1. Go to Commission Junction (www.cj.com) and click the Join Now button.

2. Complete the General Information portion of the affiliate application; click Next to continue (after you've read the Service Agreement, of course).

3. Complete the page that requests information about the Web site to which you'll add your affiliate links; click Next to continue. The Find Merchant Programs page displays a directory containing links to merchant programs for each category, as shown in Figure 7.10.

4. Browse the merchant category directory for a merchant. Click on a product category to choose a merchant. When Jane Affiliate chose Electronic Toys, the page shown in Figure 7.11 displayed.

5. Click the Join Program button next to the program you want to join. Jane Affiliate chose to join Kaesona's affiliate program. Figure 7.12 shows the page that displayed showing the types of links that Jane can add to her Web site.

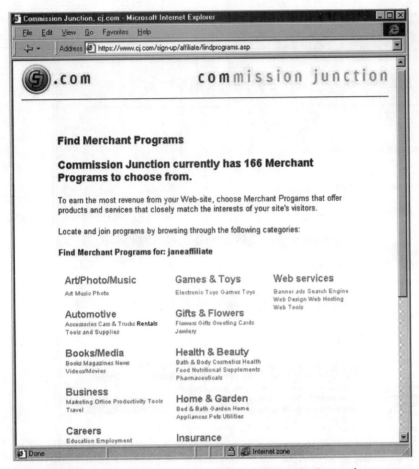

**Figure 7.10**   Find a merchant using Commission Junction's merchant category directory.

6. Copy the HTML code displayed in the window below the banner or text link that you want to add, and paste it into the HTML code for your Web site.

**NOTE**   Your affiliate ID is automatically included in the generated HTML code; you do not need to make any changes to this code before adding it to your own code.

7. Click the Find Other Programs link to continue joining programs; or click I'm Finished Placing My Links and return to the Commission Junction Member area.

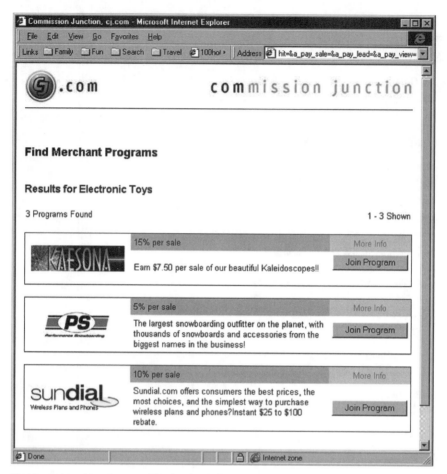

**Figure 7.11** Merchants with electronic toys.

8. From the Member area (shown in Figure 7.13), you can run reports, add affiliate links, join more programs, and do other related activities.

## LinkShare

The LinkShare Network (www.linkshare.com) offers its hundreds of thousands of affiliates the opportunity to choose from more than 350 available affiliate programs. As of this writing, free affiliate services include the following:

**Single sign-up.** Sign up once to access more than 350 affiliate programs, listed by categories.

**Four linking options.** Create textual/e-mail links, banner ads, individual product links, or even a virtual storefront.

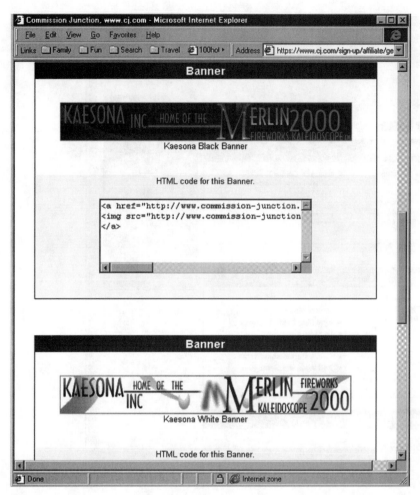

**Figure 7.12**   Kaesona's affiliate links.

**Affiliate news.** Read case studies, marketing tips, and the latest news about affiliate marketing.

**Online reports.** Generate 11 different types of reports, aggregated or by merchant; view information about your top performing products or links, click-throughs and impression ratios, and more.

**Multiple site maintenance and reporting.** If you have multiple Web sites, you can add or update all of them from the same LinkShare account.

**Follow-up mail.** Send a customized thank-you note via e-mail to customers who have made a purchase on a participating merchant site after being referred by your site.

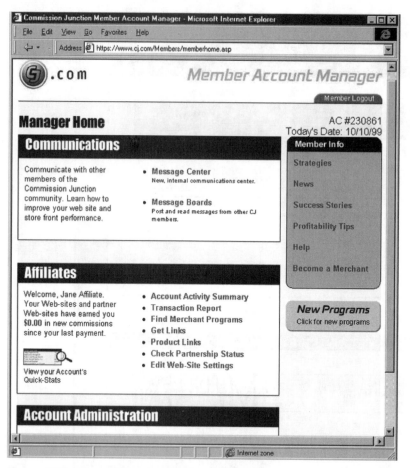

**Figure 7.13** Commission Junction's Member area.

## Adding Affiliate Links Using LinkShare

Like BeFree and Commission Junction, you complete just one application to apply to all of LinkShare's merchants. Follow these steps to join the LinkShare network and to add affiliate links to one or more of its merchants:

1. Go to LinkShare (www.linkshare.com) and click the Become an Affiliate link.

2. Complete the Primary Contact Information portion of the affiliate application; click Accept to continue (after you've read the Participation Terms, of course). You'll receive a confirmation page notifying you whether you've been accepted into the LinkShare network.

3. Complete the Account Specifications form; click Accept. (Note: Though you do not have to complete all of the fields on this page, some of the

information you supply, such as the number of unique visitors your site receives monthly, will be reviewed by merchants whose programs you're applying to. Although there's no guarantee you'll be accepted, to ensure that you'll be considered, complete all of the fields on this page. You'll receive an e-mail confirming your new LinkShare username and password.)

4. Click Continue to access your LinkShare Welcome page. Figure 7.14 shows Jane Affiliate's LinkShare page.

5. Click Join Programs. A page displays a list of program categories, as shown in Figure 7.15.

6. Choose a category by clicking on it. A page displays a list of merchants that offer affiliate programs associated with the categories you select. After Jane Affiliate chose Wine, the page shown in Figure 7.16 displayed.

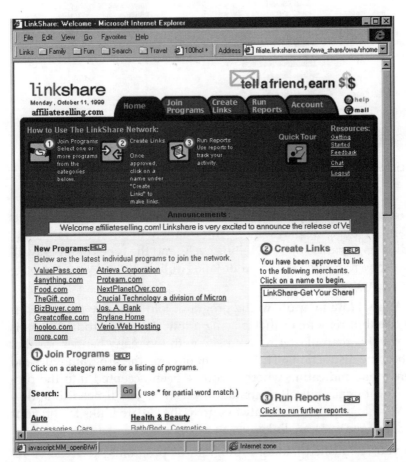

**Figure 7.14**   Jane Affiliate's LinkShare page.

**Figure 7.15** LinkShare's program category listings.

7. Click on one of the merchant's logos to view more information about its program. A page displays more information about that merchant, including its commission rate, billing cycle, and the types of links available, as shown in Figure 7.17. After Jane Affiliate chose Wine, the page shown in Figure 7.17 displayed.

8. Click Apply Now to apply to the program. Join as many programs as you'd like, but remember that placing a few strategic product links is more effective than plastering your site with too many banner ads that often become distractions. The merchant offering the program will send you an e-mail indicating whether you've been accepted into the program. This e-mail will often contain the HTML you'll need to add to your Web site; if not, you can always go to the Create Links tab on your LinkShare page to create links.

9. When you've finished joining a program or programs, and you've received an acceptance e-mail from at least one merchant, click the Create

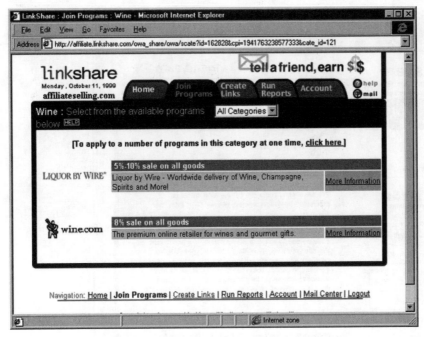

**Figure 7.16** Wine-related affiliate programs listed by merchant.

Links tab on your LinkShare page to create links for the programs to which you've been accepted. A page displays those programs.

10. Click on one of the merchants to generate an affiliate link for your site. The Create Links page displays a listing of the types of affiliate links you can create, as shown in Figure 7.18.

11. Click on one of the available link types to generate the HTML code for your Web site.

**NOTE** If you choose the product-specific link type, LinkShare will launch the merchant's Web site in a second frame (as shown in Figure 7.18). You must then locate the product you want to sell and copy its URL into the Linking URL field; then copy the appropriate image URL in the Image URL field in LinkShare's frame. Finally, add some custom text, then click Generate Code to access your code.

12. Copy and paste the code into that for your Web page.

13. Repeat steps 10 through 12 to add more affiliate links.

After you've spent a few days promoting your site, return to LinkShare and click on the Run Reports tab to run one of 11 different reports. Learn more about running reports from LinkShare's Help pages.

**Figure 7.17**   Further information about affiliate program merchants.

## CrossCommerce.com: The Merchandising Portal

Affiliates interested in a high-end, one-stop solution should take a close look at CrossCommerce.com. Though the CrossCommerce services are aimed primarily at the higher-volume traffic sites, this provider offers a rich set of features that are available for free to anybody. This list summarizes CrossCommerce's features:

- Single-application registration, and automatic access to millions of products from hundreds of merchants

- Aggregated product selection (search across all merchants with one search form)

- Aggregated traffic and sales reports (across all merchants)

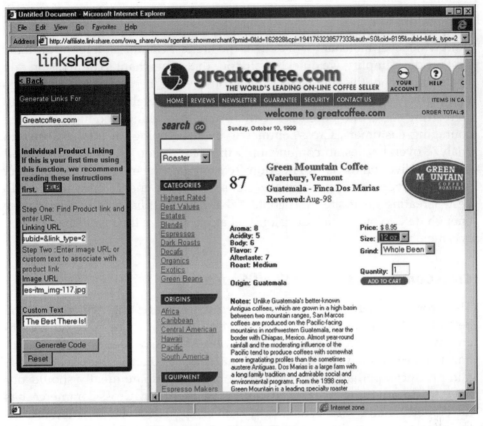

**Figure 7.18**   Generating affiliate links for GreatCoffee.com.

- Product selection optimization and commission-maximization (across all merchants)
- Real-time product prices visible to your site's visitors
- Integration of dynamic content within your existing site's content
- Customizable look and feel, to mesh seamlessly with your site
- Best of all, dynamic, automated selection, refresh, and rotation of products

CrossCommerce has built its business on the premise that a merchant-built affiliate program favors the merchant that built it, rather than the affiliate who can either take it or leave it. By gathering millions of products from hundreds of merchants (including many that are competitors), CrossCommerce can serve as an affiliate advocate, doing whatever it takes to help affiliates make more money.

For instance, if an affiliate wants to show products related to a given category, CrossCommerce is interested in helping that affiliate get the products from whichever merchant will deliver the highest commission to the affiliate. Lest we oversimplify, we quickly point out that a merchant's commission rate to affiliates is not the only factor worth considering, because some merchants that offer a higher commission might perform miserably when it comes to converting clicks into purchases. Others may price things too high, thus discouraging customers. CrossCommerce, by developing an infrastructure to analyze overall sales, in conjunction with commission rates, has positioned itself to deliver on its central mission: To automate the merchant and product selection processes so that affiliates can spend more energy on what they do best—creating great sites and content. No single affiliate could ever gather enough data to make such decisions, let alone analyze the results before they became obsolete.

### CrossCommerce's Virtual Shelf Space

The CrossCommerce approach gets even more interesting. "Shopping" the best deals for affiliates would not be very useful if there were no way to automatically update an affiliate's links once they have been cut-and-pasted. For instance, if a new merchant were suddenly to offer a great deal on certain products, perhaps for two weeks only, the affiliate ideally should not have to do anything to take advantage of the offer. CrossCommerce has developed a method for dynamically delivering product information to affiliate sites. Similar to the way banner ad syndicators automatically select and serve up ad GIFs to their affiliates, CrossCommerce serves up product information (HTML and images) based on criteria that you, the affiliate, define. You can:

- Choose to hand-pick a particular product that never changes.
- Choose to hand-pick a group of products that are rotated randomly or according to whatever time interval you stipulate ("automated product refresh").
- Define criteria (such as "highest commission-generating book about jewelry") and let CrossCommerce continually refine the exact mix of products that will make you the most money. Such refinements include rotating in brand-new products (to see how they perform), which will eventually lead to identifying products that sell well, for instance, to certain visitors at a certain hour of the day. Such sophisticated solutions may or may not be available by the time you read this, but the important thing to note is that you can define a virtual shelf space, plop it down on your site, and forget about it on a day-to-day basis.

More impressive is that the CrossCommerce architecture allows you to create these shelf spaces with a one-time cut-and-paste of HTML; later, you or your staff can modify the shelf contents without ever touching the code again. Your designer, for example, could visit the CrossCommerce service site (called the *Merchandising Portal*) and change all of your shelf spaces from one background color to another in just a couple of clicks, no new cut-and-paste required. Even better, your e-commerce manager could visit CrossCommerce and change a particular shelf's product, or the criteria that govern how products are selected for dynamic display. Again, no new cut-and-paste and no work required from your Web production team.

Naturally, such a flexible technology gives you an amazing array of options. That means that, even though products might be served automatically on any given day, you will want to keep abreast of things at a higher level. To that end, CrossCommerce's provides a suite of reports that give you at-a-glance insight into which items are selling well—not only on your site, but across the entire Web. You can track high-level Web trends and make more intelligent decisions about your editorial vision and business strategy, specifically the road map you want to follow as you take your site content into the future.

### The Product Selection Process

As stated, CrossCommerce allows you to paste into your site a virtual shelf space that can pull either products that you've selected or products selected by CrossCommerce according to criteria that you define. Visit the CrossCommerce site to see all of the options. For the purpose of this discussion, we're going to walk you through the simple process of placing a hand-picked (by you) product onto your site, including a real-time price (see the sidebar *Real-Time Pricing Information*).

### Registering as a CrossCommerce.com Affiliate

CrossCommerce's sign-up process is quick and painless; you can get started by providing only minimal information such as your name, e-mail address, username, and password. The other information required for you to get paid (address, tax information, and so on) can wait until later. This means you can get started experimenting and playing with the service immediately. To that end, CrossCommerce grants a conditional acceptance automatically; your site is evaluated later to confirm that you are not in violation of the user agreement (by displaying pornography or racist content, for example).

CrossCommerce boasts that you can have products on your page in 10 minutes, which is truly possible, though you'll probably want to take more time to

## REAL-TIME PRICING INFORMATION

One of the noteworthy aspects of CrossCommerce.com is that it allows you, the affiliate, to display current, real-time products and prices on your site through an easy-to-use Virtual Shelf Space mechanism. In essence, you tell CrossCommerce which product(s) you want to "put on the shelf," and CrossCommerce serves up the product image (if you so desire) and HTML, refreshed each time a visitor comes to your page that hosts the shelf space. Thus, the prices shown accurately reflect the prices at the merchant site. (Affinia and VStore also display prices, but on storefront pages that they host, not on your site's native pages. BeFree hints that it's working on dynamic content, but details were not available at the time of this writing.)

Is it important to show a price? In a word, YES! Do not underestimate how important this capability is. No doubt you've had the annoying experience of walking into, say, a car dealership that didn't display prices. It's frustrating to have to ask a salesperson every time you're just curious, especially for high-end automobiles that you have no intention of buying. To generalize, customers are willing to do some work to learn a price, only *after* they have decided that they might buy the product in question! That goes directly against the grain of impulse shopping and what we're calling "serendipitous shopping." With these, you see an item you never considered buying (or didn't realize you needed until you saw it) and at the same time, you see that it's in your price range or that it's a good value. These two realizations should occur *in the same instant* to overcome your natural resistance to buying something you hadn't anticipated buying. If you were slightly interested in an item, and didn't know its price, you probably would be less likely to click through to see how much it is because you haven't really made a decision to "find out more." However, if you see the price at the same moment you begin to consider buying, and find it reasonable (or a great bargain), you are much more likely to click through.

Why don't all affiliate programs offer pricing? The short answer is: primitive technology. Merchants would love to have prices appear on affiliate sites, but only if they can guarantee that those prices are accurate. As we've said before, the only thing worse than no pricing is incorrect pricing. Unfortunately, most affiliate programs were built using 1994-era static HTML links, so there's not much they can do without retooling from the ground up, or moving their affiliate program operations over to a third-party provider that has the technology to deliver prices in real time.

explore the various options, particularly the nifty Customize Styles screen, which we'll describe momentarily.

### Begin Building a Virtual Shelf Space: Select Products

To add products to your site, you create what CrossCommerce calls a *virtual shelf space* (abbreviated at V-shelf on-screen), into which product content will be delivered dynamically. (An option is available for creating static text links of the type used in most affiliate programs. It is useful for making a mid-paragraph word become an underlined link that points to a product on a merchant site.) As stated, the products may be either hand-picked by you or automatically by CrossCommerce according to criteria that you define. Here though we demonstrate only how to use the hand-pick option, don't forget about the automated option, which uses an interface only slightly different from the one we discuss.

1. To begin the shelf building process, you first conduct what amounts to a keyword search with some added parameters, such as which product categories to "shop" from and how to sort the results: for example, highest or lowest price, highest margin, best-selling, or no preference (see Figure 7.19).

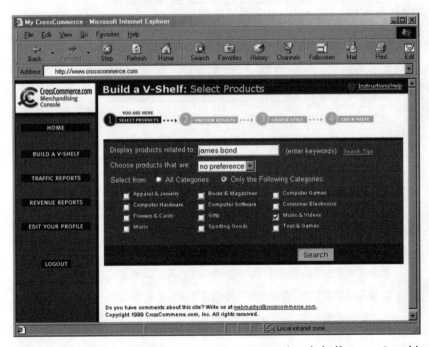

**Figure 7.19** Step 1 of building a CrossCommerce virtual shelf space: Searching for products using keywords.

2. Make your selections and click on the button labeled Search.

3. Preview your results. You will next see the results of your search in the form of a table comprising up to 100 products that match your query (see Figure 7.20). If there are more than 100 matching products, you can scroll through the results, 100 at a time, selecting multiple products as you go. As of this writing, you may select from 1 to 10 products for each shelf. To display more, simply create multiple shelves; there is no limit to how many shelves you add to a page.

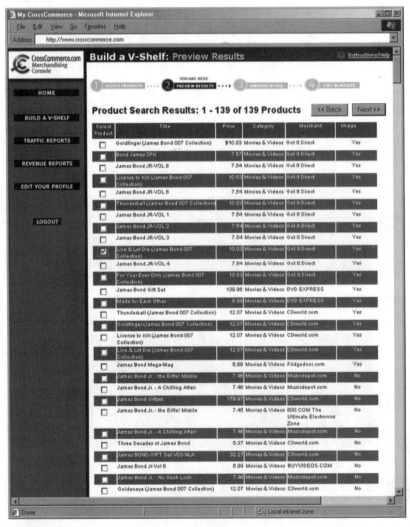

**Figure 7.20** Step 3 of building a CrossCommerce virtual shelf space: Selecting products you'd like to display.

4. Check the box next to the name of a product to select it; click the Next >> button.

5. Choose your style. The resulting virtual shelf is shown at the bottom of Figure 7.21. Above the shelf is a console you use to modify the display styles of the shelf contents. Notice the array of options.

6. Customize any of the following:

   ■ Dimensions of the shelf (making it tall and narrow, short and wide, or the size of an entire page, for instance).

   ■ Layout format (either vertical or horizontal).

**Figure 7.21**   Step 5 of building a CrossCommerce virtual shelf space: Customizing the style of your shelf to blend seamlessly with your site's look and feel.

- Whether to include images.

- For each text element (product name, merchant, price, and description), choose: to display the element; which typeface to use and in what size; bold and/or italics; and color (from a drop-down box of browser-safe colors, or your own hex value). Note, at any point, you may update the shelf preview to see your changes by clicking on the button labeled Preview Below.

> **TIP** If scrollbars appear at the edge of the shelf, simply make the shelf's height or width larger until the scrollbars disappear. Make the background color the same as that of your page. This will make the shelf blend seamlessly with your site. No border will appear around the shelf when it is pasted into your site.

7. Give your shelf a name, something meaningful that will remind you of its contents or its location on your site. When reading your reports, this will help you to later understand which spots on your site are performing the best or need to be changed.

8. When you are satisfied with your selection of display styles and have given your shelf a name, click the button labeled Create eShelf. Cross-Commerce then generates some code, composed in three parts, to add to your site:

   **Code Block 1.** Must be added one time (only) to any page with a Cross-Commerce virtual shelf space. Place it in the header of your page's HTML (someplace between <HEAD> and </HEAD>). This code makes your shelves viewable to users with different browsers.

> **TIP** Even after you have pasted the shelf code into your site, you can change its height and width at any time by manually editing the pasted code (labeled Height and Width).

> **WARNING** Do not change any other part of the code, or the shelf will not display properly and you won't get paid.

   **Code Block 2.** Add to the actual location where you'd like the shelf to appear on your page, such as in the cell of a table.

**Disclaimer.** CrossCommerce's User Agreement requires you to add a disclaimer link on any page that displays products served by Cross-Commerce. The link may be small and appear at the bottom your page. It could read "Disclaimer" or "Terms of Use," and it can link either to a page of yours containing legal verbiage (provided by CrossCommerce) or to a page with the same verbiage hosted by CrossCommerce.

9. Cut and paste your HTML code, as shown in Figure 7.22. Look at Figure 7.23, which shows how this shelf looks once it has been added to an affiliate site. Notice the seamless integration: It appears as though it's another element of the affiliate's content.

10. Kick back and watch commissions roll in. Naturally, this will happen only if you've got traffic coming to your site and if you've selected products of interest to your visitors. The point is, once you've pasted the code, the product price will be updated with no effort on your part. And if you opt to use CrossCommerce's dynamic product selection option (not demonstrated here), even the products themselves will be refreshed with no work on your part.

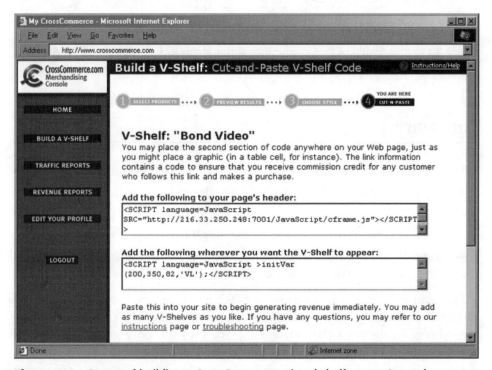

**Figure 7.22** Step 9 of building a CrossCommerce virtual shelf space: Cut and paste two sections of code and a disclaimer link into your HTML.

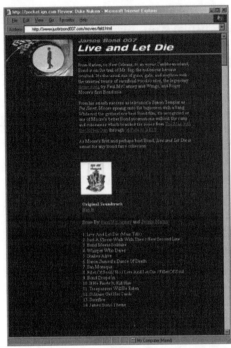

Before          After

**Figure 7.23** The Results: A CrossCommerce virtual shelf stocked with James Bond movies has been added to this sample James Bond fan site.

## Summary

You have three primary options for obtaining affiliate links:

- You can go directly to a program-provider merchant site.
- You can search for and access individual merchants though an affiliate solutions provider (BeFree, Commission Junction, or LinkShare).
- You can pull products from many merchants simultaneously and in real time through CrossCommerce.com.

In this and the previous two chapters we have explored several of the best programs for adding affiliate-based e-commerce to your site and how to create those links. In the next chapter, we'll delve into the nitty-gritty business of deciding which products to place and where to place them.

# 8

# Planning Your Implementation

Chapter 5, "Don't Have a Web Site?," and Chapter 6, "Building a Virtual Storefront," described the more important, widely known, or novel starting points for building your affiliation-based site that are currently available. The operative phrase here is "currently available," because the number of options for becoming an affiliate is increasing faster than site owners can keep up. This trend will continue, so expect your alternatives to expand at a mind-numbing pace.

**NOTE** Lists of additional programs and resources can be found in this book's appendix and at the book's companion Web site, www.affiliateselling.com.

Now that you've learned about some of the options available to you, it's time to start thinking about which of them you might want to implement. But before you decide what you want to do, it will help to ask why you want to become involved in affiliate selling.

## The Big Picture

Why are you interested in affiliated selling? As discussed in the first chapter, some people are looking to add e-commerce as a supplement to advertising revenues on their large, established commercial sites. Others with amateur (though not necessarily amateurish) sites that draw traffic are asking "why not?" Still others are thinking of building a large-scale, affiliate-revenue-focused site from the ground up, essentially starting a new business venture. And there are a host of others—fans who want to show support for their favorite musical artist or favorite charity; nonprofit organizations that are trying to raise money; future entrepreneurs who want to test their ideas. The list goes on.

Fortunately, regardless of your specific objectives, there is a program or combination of programs to suit your needs. (We can say this with confidence now that virtually every product category is at least partially represented by one or more online merchants that offer or participate in affiliate programs.) There is no one-size-fits-all approach, so let's delve into the possibilities, according to different types of sites with their respective agendas.

# Established Sites

This section assumes that you already have a Web site and that you are considering adding affiliate selling to that site. To begin, recognize that crafting an affiliate-based merchandising plan is not necessarily a complex task. However, it can become complex if you have a lot of factors to consider, as is usually the case with adding affiliation to preexisting sites. Simply put, you must decide how prominent a role you want your affiliate links to play. Do you intend them to be a marginal add-on to your existing pages? A fundamental redesign of your UI, editorial mission, and positioning? A mixture of the two?

The question becomes more complex still when many people will be involved. This is typically the case for large-scale established sites, particularly when affiliate revenue expectations conflict with someone else's objectives. We would hazard a guess that probably few staff members at large sites have not resorted to heated debate and, finally, compromise when trying to decide how to best utilize Web real estate.

Planning also becomes more complicated when the site is only one element of a company. To help you understand the various issues, we structured this chapter somewhat like an interview, asking basic questions to get you thinking about your particular situation. Some of these questions are intended simply to introduce the broader issues; others are intended to lead to specific suggestions/recommendations, depending on how you answer the questions.

## What is the role your site plays in your organization?

How many employees work at your organization? Of those, how many are currently devoted to developing and maintaining the Web site, its content, and functionality (your answer should also include outside developers, contractors, design firms, and so forth)? How many people work in other aspects of your Web-based operations? Put another way, what percentage of your organization's employees are involved with your Web operation? In a *pure-play* Web company (one with no non-Web operations), this will be a high factor, from 50 to 100 percent. This figure is an important consideration for traditional firms with significant non-Web operations; for example, companies in which only 5 percent of the employees are devoted to Web operations.

Other ways of determining your site's relative role in the organization include discovering what percentage of your company's operating expenses is being spent on the Web, or what percentage of the company's revenue is dependent upon or is amplified by its Web operations. And depending on the organization, centralized decision-making, interdivisional conflicts (across profit-and-loss lines), and good old political/power struggles can, unfortunately, be major factors in the plan to move forward with affiliate program participation—as well as with any major strategic initiative undertaken by your Web team.

If your site is primarily an offshoot of your firm's structure, then affiliated selling might be more difficult to integrate meaningfully. That is, if the site exists to support some other objective, then affiliate links would need to continue supporting that objective, rather than generating a new goal for the site.

If, on the other hand, yours is a pure-play site, then the site is its own reason for being. The difficulty in this case is that everybody in your company cares—and, thus, has an opinion—about exactly what should be included on the site, where, why, and how.

## How complex (bureaucratic) is your organization?

How many people must approve a change in even a minor alteration in site verbiage? How many must approve the addition of a new high-level navigational feature? How many must approve (or how many levels up must the designer go to get approval for) a major site facelift? How many people must approve a major business decision such as whether to include affiliate links? Even if the *idea* has been given a green light, some firms can expect future iterations (translation: delays) when it comes to actual implementation. Generally, the fewer people involved in making any of these decisions, the better. One of the advantages of affiliate programs is that you can repeatedly change what you display (as well as where and how) to maximize results. Those of you running an operation with small staffs in flat organizations have a considerable advantage (albeit with smaller operating budgets) that should be maximized.

> **NOTE** If any of the bureaucratic questions require the intervention of a lawyer, forget it, it's all over. Well, not really; but book your vacation to the Bahamas now to get the best fare; your lawyers will want to pore over the affiliate agreements far longer than Web-time businesspeople will be able to tolerate. The major frustration for attorneys will be that these cookie-cutter affiliate agreements are almost always written in "take it or leave it" language, meaning no negotiation; you either click the "I Accept" button on an online form or you don't. True, affiliates regarded by merchants as more important or valuable might be able to negotiate a better commission, but you don't need an attorney to push for a better cut; you would probably only get such a concession *after* you've demonstrated exceptionally high sales volume. In other words, you would have already signed the agreement before attempting to negotiate a better deal.

If you require the sign-off of many people (or of one lawyer) on each and every affiliate agreement you're considering, be sure to factor this delay into your plan. We recommend that you spend more time evaluating programs yourself and then narrowing the list down before you turn it over to the powers that be. Unfortunately for major e-merchants, a number of affiliates sign up and then fail to deliver a single visitor. This is partly the result of affiliates using trial and error to explore and see what works. Experimentation, unrelated to serious business, is okay if you're not involved with a serious business. And, even if you are involved with a serious business, experimentation is still a good thing. Unfortunately, your own internal processes may hamstring your ability to experiment and try out new creative ideas as they come to you.

To help alleviate this problem, you might consider signing up with a number of programs purely for evaluational purposes. Once you've done some evaluation and testing, you can go back and confirm that everything is good-to-go with your company's management.

Also be aware that, in larger organizations, other people in your company may have already been knocking on doors or rubbing elbows at happy hour with somebody in the company whose affiliate you'd like to become. As said before, affiliate agreements are one-size-fits-all, cookie-cutter agreements. If somebody on your team has a relationship or has begun talking about a more customized business deal with a particular merchant, then you'll want to proceed carefully. There's a trade-off to be made between highly flexible, seat-of-the-pants experimentation versus a slow and deliberate approach. A lot depends on the quality of communication in your organization. In some large companies, thanks to good communication and strong leadership, the left hand knows what the right is doing, whereas in some five-person companies one employee doesn't know what the person sitting next to him or her is doing.

Thus, communication (good or bad) is at least as important as is size in terms of an organization's ability to mobilize quickly and turn on a dime.

Whether you're driving company strategy or pasting HTML links (or both), make sure you're also communicating with and eliciting feedback from the others in your organization, even if that just means talking to the person sitting across the room from you.

## What is the scale of your site?

One small e-commerce site we know pulls in about $1,500 per month for its owner. Not much to get excited about, you say? Well, the owner has neither promoted the site nor changed a single word or pixel on the site in over two years! So we're talking $1,500 every month for doing nothing! Though the site is not large, it's focused on a very narrow topic, and users find it primarily through search engines. Could the owner make more money if he devoted more time to updating, expanding, and marketing the site? Almost certainly. But it's a hobby for him, one of many, and he makes better money doing other things.

Other hobbyist and personal sites are less static. Many, for instance, are updated whenever the owner gets the urge to create, or when time permits. But if there's a central theme to these sites it might be "when I feel like it," or "when I get to it."

In marked contrast, actual business sites obviously can't be so cavalier about when and how much to expand and update. The companies behind these sites pay employees to do whatever is necessary to make the sites productive. The central theme for these sites might be summarized as "we needed it yesterday" or "our competitors just launched, so we need to do it, too." Business sites are always looking for new ways to leverage their capabilities; they're looking for quick and inexpensive ways to add more and/or to go in new directions.

The wonder of affiliated selling is that it can work so well for all of these structures. Big or small, narrow or broadly focused, affiliate links are flexible to an almost infinite degree of granularity due to their capability to align single-product merchandising along single-topic content (actually, down to specific *words* within an article). In theory, any clever mix of product and content is possible. However—and it's a big however—such a wealth of possibility doesn't always translate to fast, cheap, or easy implementation. Scalability becomes a problem; that is, discovering how to achieve single-product effectiveness on huge sites or sites that change frequently. Consider some of the following parameters.

**What is the refresh rate at your site?** How frequently does your content change? Most sites have some static content (they call it "evergreen"). Other site content changes rarely, periodically, daily, multiple times per day, or dynamically in real time. If your content changes in some combination of these, figure out how much content falls into which category; for example: 30 percent daily, 50 percent periodically, 20 percent evergreen.

**What is the typical traffic volume?** How much traffic do you get? A million pageviews per month? A thousand? Two? How much of the traffic is composed of first-time visitors, as opposed to repeat or regular visitors? The answers to these questions will have implications not only for how frequently you decide to refresh and add to your content, but for how much money you can justify spending on alterations to your site.

**How "sticky" is your site?** *Stickiness*, in Web industry jargon, is the tendency for a service or feature to get users to stay longer, return frequently, and become loyal, that is, to continue using the site and not switch to a competitor. What percentage of your visitors are repeat visitors? What percentage are regular visitors? What do you mean by "regular"? That they drop by every few months? Weekly? Daily? Many times per day? Many sites have some of each category. If you are one of them, if you haven't already, break down these visitor categories; for example: 80 percent never return, 15 percent return once a month, 5 percent return several times per week. Naturally, your volume of traffic and frequency of repeat visits will comprise the most important drivers (other than your available resources) to the determination of how frequently to add to or refresh your site content. The key is to think of affiliate links as merchandising content, and evaluate it as such, as you would all other content, including how much to display, how to display it, and how often to update it.

## What is the scope of your site?

Scope, for the purpose of this discussion refers to what your site is all about: how it makes money, what it says or does, who it says it to or does it for, and so on. With that definition in mind, consider the following elements.

### What is the business model behind your site?

What is the current business model driving your strategic decisions related to your site? To support a brick-and-mortar company? To sell your own products directly? To sell subscriptions or downloads? To sell ad impressions? Or is there no revenue purpose whatsoever? In that case, what is the site's overriding purpose? To build brand awareness? To promote awareness of something else? To have fun?

Whatever your model (or mix of models), you must determine whether the addition of affiliate links will enhance your other revenue streams or non-revenue objectives. An enhancement might be, for example, to create a richer content environment that is devoted to the same targeted topic—remember, product information is a form of content. Or will such links detract from your focus or confuse your visitors? Is it safe to send your visitors to another site (the merchant's), even if you are earning income by doing so? Will short-term revenues kill your long-term prospects if you lose repeat visitors?

Another factor you can't afford to overlook is simple office politics. Is there, for example, a VP in your organization who will "put a price on your head" if your affiliate income starts making you the most important person in the company? We've seen it happen and things can get ugly. Or perhaps someone, after success of the affiliate program is assured, will take credit for another person's ambitious pet project, magically transforming it into his or her own—implying—or flat-out saying, "I've been planning this all along; thanks for helping implement *my* strategy. Now go away."

We are not encouraging you to think cynically; rather, we're suggesting that a sound, solid, defensible, sensible implementation will include being sensitive to all who will be affected by your affiliate business plan. That means communicating across functional lines and enlisting support. You may find that not everyone will be in favor of adding affiliated selling—in fact, in some cases, doing so would be a mistake. You may also be confronted by others who bristle at hearing the word "affiliate"; they do not want their companies associated with what they regard as home-grown amateur sites, even though it is those sites that have made affiliate selling an important aspect of e-commerce. (If you have a bristler in your midst, refer to this effort as "merchandising partnerships" and don't be surprised if the resistance simply disappears.)

## How broad is your content?

Is yours a one-topic site or one of the portals that seems to be trying to target everything in existence? Or maybe you think not in terms of subject matter, but of audience and market segments. In that case, is your target narrow or broad? Perhaps you've got a few related niche audiences. Or an umbrella site that has acquired a few different sites, narrow and broad, some relating to one another, some not. In this case, it's probably best to leave the decision as to whether or how to roll out an affiliate-based revenue model to the individual responsible for each site, rather than trying to implement one program across all properties simultaneously. (The exception would be where resources from one subsite can be leveraged across other subsites to cut costs and time-to-market. But never lose sight of the fact that each subsite will maintain its own set of considerations that might require a customized plan.)

If your site content is narrow in scope, you are a good candidate for the "few hand-picked merchants" approach. It works just like it sounds: You pick a few merchants one at a time and sign up to become an affiliate to each of them. The benefit of this approach is that you earn a higher commission dealing directly with the merchant than if you were to access that merchant's products through a third-party infomediary like Affinia, VStore, or CrossCommerce.com. If a single merchant can provide all of the products you think you'll ever need, then all of your reports will be in one place—at that merchant's site.

The drawbacks to this approach are first, by signing up with just one or two merchants, you are guaranteed to miss out on some products that have a great deal of potential at your site. Let's say you have a golf site. Keeping in mind that no single golf-related e-merchant carries every product related to golf, and that great Web merchandizing means targeting products at narrow market segments—sometimes to just one person in the case of dynamic sites powered by personalization engines—you need as many different products as possible. (It may sound like we're talking about an unthinkably high number, but a million products are not enough for highly granular targeting. To serve multiple categories well, tens of millions of products are required.)

The second drawback to the "few hand-picked merchants" approach it that it's not unreasonable to predict that a number of nongolf-related products will perform outstandingly at a golf site. We offer as an example the newer, smaller, lighter, yuppier Nokia cell phone du jour; not a golf product to be sure, but something every golfer seems to need. If affiliate revenues are just a side business for you, an incremental bonus only, obviously it's not essential that you try to capitalize on all or most of these opportunities. But if affiliate revenues are the foundation of your entire business model, you should definitely look into third-party solutions such as CrossCommerce.com to optimize your returns or to automate your product selection and refresh capabilities. You can always sign up with multiple programs and generate hybrids where appropriate; that is, you can hand-pick certain items direct from merchants (at a higher margin) while you use CrossCommerce.com or another third party to alert you to less-obvious big hits, which constantly change. As we pointed out in the previous chapter, a benefit of dealing exclusively with just one third-party provider is that all of your traffic and sales data (across potentially hundreds of different merchants) will be aggregated into one set of reports. This is invaluable if you are interested in constantly monitoring, tweaking, and improving.

If, on the other hand, your site is oriented at many audiences or a broad audience (such as college students or women), then forget about signing up with individual merchants, unless your volume is so great that you can negotiate special commission rates or custom integration. And even if you're big enough to command such cooperation, you'll want to sign up with a key merchant only in each of the major categories (books, music, gifts, etc.), then utilize a third party such as CrossCommerce.com to scoop up the microcategories in one motion. One-off business development deals don't scale well to the dozens, let alone the hundreds; they require a lot of time to create and even more time to manage once the bits and bytes are in place.

## How branded are you?

How strong is your brand? Are you a household name or a name no household ever heard of? If your brand is unknown, will it be enhanced by its association with a well-known merchant like Amazon.com? Conversely, do you fear that your well-known brand will be tarnished by associating with an unknown merchant?

Generally speaking, associating with strong brands will help you; associating with unknown brands won't hurt or help. Obviously, you take the greatest risk by associating with a merchant that has earned a bad reputation, for botching shipments, for failing to honor posted prices, or for killing all of the otters in Prince William Sound. Be vigilant, therefore, when signing up directly with merchants. We suggest you first find out how they rate in customer satisfaction according to BizRate.com. If you are operating through a third-party provider, make sure it deals only with reputable merchants, or that the program enables you to deselect products from merchants you'd rather not associate with. Fortunately, in general, because third-party providers have a vested interest in maintaining a high standard, they conduct due diligence so that you don't have to. If, however, you do receive complaints from customers whose transactions were handled poorly by a particular merchant, by all means pass the information along to the merchant *and* to the third-party provider. And be reasonable: Mistakes will happen, and a small number is understandable and acceptable. But if a particular merchant is causing more than its fair share of problems, eliminate the product links pointing to them.

Another common brand-related concern—in particular, to actual business sites (as opposed to hobbyists)—is what happens when the customer clicks through to the merchant. Some affiliates would like their customers to click through to a page hosted by the merchant but branded to look like it belongs to the affiliate. Some would even like their customers to believe they are buying directly from the affiliate. In the extreme, are those sites that want to conduct the transaction themselves and then pay the merchant what amounts to a wholesale price for the item. (This is more common among public companies that want to post higher top-line revenues to impress the financial markets.) In conducting transactions directly, these sites technically become retailers, rather than an affiliates. Fancy financial footwork aside, this scheme would legitimately enable the "affiliate" to control its brand and to hang onto the customer through the entire transaction; the visitor would never be linked to another site. Clearly this is a case of trying to have their cake and eat it, too.

(In Chapter 1, "Affiliate Selling: The Next Big Thing," we discussed a *hyper-enabled* affiliate world that, in the future will, indeed, let these companies have their cake and eat it too.)

If your company is one that would prefer to hang onto the customer from beginning to end, think through this so-called hyper-enablement strategy; many large sites will opt instead to build out their own internal e-commerce capabilities. How badly do you want your company logo on the packing slip in the box that arrives at your customer's house? Enough to give up a few percentage points and exclude products from distributors and merchants that do not provide such a service?

In the short-term, it will be the third parties (such as Nexchange and others), major distributors (like Ingram Micro) and lesser-known e-merchants that will provide affiliate brand-friendly services, including affiliate-side shopping carts and affiliate-branded fulfillment capabilities. The large, well-known e-merchants will resist any attempt to erode their brand share, and will offer, at best, co-branded shopping carts and, possibly (though less likely except for major affiliates), co-branded fulfillment. This resistance will pave the way for lesser-known distributors and e-merchants—whose brands are weak to begin with and therefore have nothing to lose and everything to gain—to move in and capture market share.

Furthermore, affiliates concerned about preserving their brands will naturally be best served in one of two ways. First, using direct merchant/affiliate links or e-commerce modules such as those provided by CrossCommerce.com, affiliates will want to place products directly on those pages that contain their native content. Second, most will want to build their own strongly branded mini- or megastores that are plugged directly into multiple merchant databases and be able to extract dynamic products and prices in real time. Currently, though such linkages are technically possible, they are labor-intensive. Building these so-called "one off" relationships is therefore out of reach for most affiliates, even those up to the technical task, due to limited technical resources on the merchant side. (They only have time to play with the biggest sites.)

A better solution (and one available to all at no charge) is to use a third party. Affiliates can design their own merchandising environments, in coordination with their own look-and-feel, and hosted at their own domains, simply by adding a combination of CrossCommerce virtual shelf spaces. Affiliates not up to the task of building complex pages can use templates provided by a third-party store builder. Ideally, these would allow complete control over look-and-feel. However, as of this writing, affiliate-based store builders such as VStore, and Affinia do not enable the design of stores to mimic the referring affiliate's site. From a branding perspective, this is a nonstarter because not only does it look to visitors as if they've left the affiliate's site, a glance at the URL confirms it. As of this writing, these services are oriented toward private individuals and smaller-scale sites, but this could change as the market evolves and these services enhance their product offerings.

# New Sites

This section looks at affiliation from the perspective of someone starting from scratch. Perhaps you've got an idea, perhaps not. We assume, however, that you have not yet built a site.

**NOTE** Even if you do already have a working site or one in production, this section may be helpful as a means of depicting a sort of ideal scenario; that is, affiliation without the constraints forced onto it by an existing site's business model, editorial scope, or design. You might find ideas here to help guide decisions and plans from this point forward. Indeed, few sites are ever finished being "under construction."

## What are your goals?

As with established sites, you need to ask yourself why you're building a site. Is it a serious business endeavor? Just a fun distraction from life's drudgery? A way of procrastinating writing your Ph.D. dissertation? (Don't laugh, that's how Yahoo! got started.) Maybe building a site is your way of justifying to yourself your dream of making big bucks through affiliate selling. Whatever your reason(s), your level of commitment will be a factor in its success. It's okay to admit it if your Web site is a hobby; and it's okay to dream of quitting your day job once your site takes off. What's not okay is not being honest with yourself about what you're trying to do. Those of you developing business plans or designing brand-new sites that have to make money (you know who you are, there in the VC-backed, Silicon Valley-style startups), no doubt these grand schemes have already been committed to paper or at least have been scrawled on a whiteboard next to the espresso machine. Affiliated selling is shaping up to be a legitimate business model for certain types of new Web-based companies like Epinions (which is new as of this writing), which lets users write their own reviews about any product or service. Affiliate links to reviewed products pay the company's bills.

Newbies must also decide what role affiliated selling will play in their business model. This decision can be stressful because it often impacts virtually every later decision, such as how to design your site, which partners to hook up with, and so on.

### Is affiliation your Raison d'Être?

Is affiliation the backbone of your business model? Will your business fold if affiliated sales don't produce? Do you have other ideas for making money, such as running banner ads or "OEM-ing" your technology to other sites for a hefty licensing fee or revenue share? (To OEM means to let another Web site use parts of your functionality.)

If you're building a site only to display affiliate links in one form or another, then you've got ultimate flexibility with respect to tweaking and optimizing *every* aspect of your site (architecture, look-and-feel, editorial scope, and scale) to make click-through and conversion rates as high as possible. This means, for example, that merchandising leads editorial decisions. In other words, if you find that a particular product is a hot seller, you can modify your editorial plan and start creating more pages and content related to that particular product.

## Is affiliation a supplement to other revenue?

On the other hand, if affiliate links will comprise just one of many revenue mechanisms (and not be the primary mechanism), you can't be as flexible about changing things to optimize your affiliate revenues. Each decision must be considered holistically as to how it will impact other aspects of your site and company. One point worth repeating is that (according to some reports) product links tend to be more profitable and more appreciated by and acceptable to users than banner ads. But banner ads are typically compensated on a per-impression (CPM) basis, whereas affiliate links are usually compensated via a commission when a sale occurs. This means that affiliate product link revenues, though potentially higher, are not guaranteed, whereas banner ad revenues are. Good product selection and presentation make all the difference. For those with the time and inclination to experiment and do things right, affiliation is probably the way to go.

## Will your site be big or small?

As with established sites, your desired or intended scale and scope will be one of the major determinants of the type of affiliate product plan you'll create. Stating the obvious, one person working from home can do only so much (though it can be substantial, not to mention impressive and profitable), whereas a 10-person Web production crew in a converted San Francisco warehouse can do a lot more, and a 100-person team can do even more. But along with scaled-up productivity comes scaled-up accountability, expectations, and costs. Big companies can do some neat things, but if they don't attract a big enough audience, or if they don't entice repeat visits, then everybody might be looking for a new job.

As of this writing, many big Web companies are just beginning to look at ways to integrate affiliate links into their sites. Needless to say, they have to be careful not to fix something that isn't broken. In contrast are yet-to-be-launched Web companies being planned from the ground up to focus on affiliate revenue models. The aforementioned Epinions is one example.

The data aren't in yet, but we strongly believe in the potential of affiliate revenue models—otherwise we wouldn't have written this book. We expect to see many big companies using affiliation in lots of ways, even subaffiliating, to allow their huge user base to line their own pockets by exploiting affiliation mechanisms. But we're also aware that companies of all sizes and kinds will continue to search for newer and better ways to leverage what they've got and make additional money in additional ways. That means that even those companies who focus sharply on affiliate revenues initially will eventually broaden the scope of their business models to make money in other ways whenever it makes sense to do so. Who knows, perhaps something will come along that outperforms affiliation. Constant change is what makes the Web so exciting.

# The Plan

Before launching headlong into any huge production effort, you should conduct some tests to find out what sort of implementation will work best at your site, given your objectives moving forward. You can put off making major decisions until after test results are in, but eventually, you'll need to answer all of the following questions. To help you with that task, we've attempted to steer you toward an appropriate action on a question-by-question basis. Naturally, you'll also have to consider these issues as interconnected parts of the whole.

## How many products will you place on the site?

If you're planning to place just one or a few products, look around for the best merchant for that product or for each product. We mean "best" in terms of the reputation of the merchant and the parameters of the affiliate agreement, in particular, the commission structure. The rationale for this approach is straightforward: If you only have to go through the effort once (or a few times), it makes sense to spend time hunting down the best deal in town. If, on the other hand, you are planning to stock many products, simply put, this strategy does not scale; you can't afford to spend the time it would take to search for the best merchant for each product.

To find the best merchant based on the criteria of reputation and affiliate terms, the quickest and easiest test is to visit the merchant(s) in question as if you were a customer. Do this after you've whittled down your list of potential merchants that carry your desired product(s). From which merchant would you be most likely to make a purchase? At which do you think you'd be tempted to buy additional items during that visit? Remember, some affiliate agreements pay you for products your visitors purchase during a single visit even if you hadn't linked to those products specifically. Again, because you are placing all of your eggs in one basket, carefully weigh all of these factors.

Most sites that refer to only one or a few products do so because their site content is specifically related to those products. An extreme example is an author's site dedicated solely to a book that he or she had written. On such sites, there is no real distinction between content and merchandising. As we've said repeatedly, on all sites, merchandising content is a subset of total site content, but on these product-specific sites, all content serves to sell a specific product. For that reason, the products rarely change on one-product sites (or on few-product sites). Changing a product would require an overhaul of much of the site's content and possibly depart from the site's overarching mission.

Sites that link to anywhere from a handful to a couple of dozen products are typically narrow-focus, special-interest sites; for example, related to topics such as backpacking, Southwest cooking, magic tricks, or a genre of music. The products might relate very closely to the content on a given page (such as reviewing a product and making it available via an affiliate link) or they might relate only generally. If this scenario describes your site, it might suffice to use just one or two good merchants to cover all desired product links. Let's take the backpacking site: There, you might only need to suggest a dozen or so products carried by REI.com. This strategy works for many hobbyist and non-profit organization sites that are trying only to make side income, as opposed to those sites attempting to fund an ongoing, full-time business concern.

For those sites with larger revenue requirements, using one or two merchants may not be adequate to cover the product requirements in such a way as to enable highly targeted products to appear in context with the site's content. Clearly, sites with more comprehensive business requirements must offer more in the way of content to appeal to a larger audience and to keep them coming back regularly. These true business sites provide links to many products, anywhere from 50 to thousands. This is not to say, however, that sites built and maintained by one person or a small group of people will not sometimes have equally aggressive revenue targets. We're talking in general terms here. At the low end of this scale, products are often less closely linked to other page content, or they may be separated into a dedicated "products" page. At the high end of this range (sites with hundreds or thousands of products), out of practical necessity, sites must build dedicated pages or entire shopping environments to display these thousands of links. In the latter case, the products may be selected by hand, but that would require brute-force effort, which is really unnecessary now that it's possible to invoke custom programming to quickly build kajillions of links. Where such sites may fail to add content value (too labor/space-intensive to write a kajillion book reviews) they do sometimes add organizational value by creating subsets of products that merchants have not adequately addressed on their sites. For instance, when Amazon.com first created its Associates Program, savvy Webpreneurs were quick to build their own "bookstores," featuring hundreds of links to books on nonmainstream topics such as conspiracy theory, or to fill niches like plastic injection molding. These are topics that even Amazon.com would be less likely or slow to target.

As you know by now, one common problem with these affiliate "stores" is that they fail to display pricing information. The reasoning is that prices can and do change frequently, and merchants don't want affiliates displaying outdated information. Until merchants provide real-time product data that is pushed to their affiliates, the preference is to use a third-party provider that shows prices updated in real time. Even if the margin is not quite as good as when dealing directly with a merchant, the ability to include prices might easily make up the difference, earning you more in total commissions because visitors are much more likely to buy when they can see prices while examining a product. You should, however, consider testing with and without price to find out for sure. Your results may vary because different sites draw different users with different degrees of price sensitivity. If you want hundreds of links on your site dynamically updated—the products change automatically over time—then you must use a third party like CrossCommmerce.com (again, until merchants provide such functionality). Another advantage to using a third party is that you can draw many products from many different merchants' product databases and have the service automatically show selections based on criteria such as "best-selling products," "lowest priced," "highest commission," and so on.

## How frequently will the products change?

Frequency of product refresh is an implementation factor that is similar in many ways to the how-many-products issue we just discussed. Whether you're picking a thousand products once or changing one product a thousand times, you have to do the same amount of work. Therefore, a number of our suggestions in the previous section apply to this topic as well.

To begin, if you don't expect your product selections to change frequently, we recommend that you hunt for the best deal with an individual merchant affiliate program. If, conversely, you expect to change products more frequently, then consider whether one or two merchants will provide all the products you need. If so, signing up with their programs would be simple; if not, weigh the pros and cons of signing up with several merchants versus a third-party provider. And don't forget: There's nothing to stop you from using both (unless a given merchant requires you to sign an exclusivity requirement, which is best avoided). You may opt to have the bulk of your products supplied by a third party, while having a couple of mainstay (rarely changing) or big-ticket (higher-commission) items be linked through direct affiliate programs.

If your site has products that must be (or should be) refreshed frequently, by all means, go with a service that automates this process, such as CrossCommerce.com. By using a feature such as CrossCommerce.com's Top Selling dynamic product selection, you can display Today's Hot Items (or whatever you'd like to call it) on your home page, while you or your whole team go skiing, comfortable in the knowledge that the products will be refreshed each day to reflect the true top-sellers.

## What impact will merchandising have on your management and production teams?

Merchandising—which we define here as placing products and related information on a Web site, along with undertaking the efforts to sell them—can be a major task. You need to determine whether your company is up to it. Do you have the warm bodies you need, both in production and management? Or, if you are the single person running a single-person site, either as a hobbyist or an aspiring entrepreneur, have you carefully considered the pros and cons of working alone? For starters, consider that everything stops happening the moment you stop working (con). A big pro, however, is that you don't have to get anybody's permission to do anything. CrossCommerce.com allows the serious do-it-yourselfer with a Web site to massively scale things up for no cost and little time, by adding many products that are selected automatically and updated frequently. (Well, not quite no cost; obviously the service takes a percentage, as do all the third-party services. But you never have to pay them anything.)

If you are part of a bigger company, you have both the need and the ability to test different approaches to determine what works best; the costs of sub-optimizing can be great, even spelling the difference between success and disaster. To allow for greater experimentation and flexibility, naturally you'll want to avoid signing exclusive agreements. Sounds like a no-brainer, we know, but exclusive deals sometimes sound tempting when they come attached to guaranteed revenue. But you also don't want to cut yourself off from options (see *The Future: A Hyper-Enabled World* in Chapter 1, "Affiliate Selling: The Next Big Thing").

Quick-and-easy e-commerce solutions do exist. To review from previous chapters: CrossCommerce.com targets the high-end market (but is useful to any Web site) with its context-sensitive product placement and automated refresh. Nexchange allows transactions to occur without the customer ever leaving affiliate sites—clearly an important benefit to large Web companies whose business models are built upon assumptions about stickiness and brand awareness. At the extreme end of the spectrum are expensive providers. Inktomi, for one, doesn't accept affiliates; it licenses (for a fee in the six-figure range) full-blown, turnkey comparison-shopping engines to portals.

Major Web companies, too, have unique problems that often must be addressed by their own internal resources. Some banner ad-supported sites, for instance, have an interest in placing affiliate product links in so-called remnant (unsold) real estate. This sort of problem is not adequately addressed by any merchant or third-party program, although one or more of these programs might be useful as part of an in-house solution. Another problem is that many larger sites are constructed and managed using expensive content management software (Vignette StoryServer, for example) and affiliate programs may have to be tweaked in order to work with that infrastructure. The option is to make changes to your systems, decisions which require more thorough financial modeling. And even when the numbers look good, big changes of any sort can be highly disruptive to an organization.

## Will you integrate product links with content tightly, loosely, or not at all?

If your Web site falls on the low end on the integration spectrum between merchandising and editorial content, you might simply create a link to your site's "store" that houses affiliate links to various products. If your site has a broad-based readership, as opposed to a narrow-focus audience, then the linked products don't necessarily have to be related to any topic in particular (think of the Yahoo! and Excite shopping areas, which house numerous product categories with no particular focus relating to the sites). On the high end of content-product integration, you might, for example, include feature articles about a specific product or category of products, say, fishing lures, and embed text hotlinks wherever a lure is mentioned in the body of the article. Those who consider their sites to fall in the middle of the integration spectrum might place topically related product links in the margins of a page devoted to that topic, without an exact match between the product and the page contents. Let's again use our fishing lures example; the page with the aforementioned article might have affiliate links in the margins pointing to Alaska fly-fishing vacation packages or to sunscreen/bug-repellent.

## Will your editorial plan, design, or navigational scheme require major alteration?

Perhaps the easiest way to integrate affiliate e-commerce to an existing site is to add product links to any unused space on your site, perhaps the right-hand margin of sites designed in a columnar (newspaper-style) format. Many sites design their pages to be 640 pixels wide in order to be viewable by "lowest common denominator" users. However, 85 percent of users have the capability to view Web pages at 800 pixels wide or higher. This means that those sites designed to 640 pixels (unless they use automatically expanding tables) have an unused, blank margin along the right side (or both sides if content is centered on the page).

Why not drop in related product links to these otherwise going-to-waste slots? There is no downside. Oh sure, you won't be able to "capture" those users who see only to 640 pixels, but you might get the others. Don't be one of those sites unwilling to devote resources to developing content that cannot be viewed by everyone. Affiliate links don't necessarily require a lot of work, as we've explained. CrossCommerce.com, for instance, provides hundreds of ready-made ministores designed to fit into narrow margins.

Unfortunately, if your site is being built from scratch, obviously, you do not have the luxury of dropping products into established Web pages. You may find it tempting therefore to start building a site that contains blank pages to which you can start adding products or ministores (because it's quick and easy), without substantive content. This might work if you are developing a true shopping environment, but you must do a good job of it, perhaps pulling together novel combinations of products that surfers can't find elsewhere in one place. But if you don't do a good job, or you don't add value in some other way—either with original content, functionality, or something else of interest to visitors—trust us, you won't fool anyone. A bunch of products is just a bunch of products. If you don't present them in a useful or creative format, the user is not likely to return.

Here are some examples of what we mean by useful and creative:

- Pull from multiple merchants to create the longest list of products possible devoted to a narrow niche. Such a list might not exist anywhere else on the Web and could be very valuable to customers interested in the category.

- Create a unique list of hard-to-find items.

- Generate a unique list of bizarre items.

- Put a new spin on an old category. For instance, you might pull together products from several golf e-tailers, but direct them to amateurs who are terrible at the game.

- Establish a whole new category. For example, things related to carrots. Sound dumb? You'd be surprised at the things customers fixate on. Pull together every potholder or soap dish on the Web shaped like a carrot or decorated with a carrot motif. Don't forget carrot-shaped refrigerator magnets. Carrot juice. (Maybe carrots aren't your thing, but Siberian Huskies are. You could pull from hundreds of merchants, doing keyword searches through a third-party provider like CrossCommerce.com, and pull up odd things related to huskies—a cigar clipper shaped like a husky, for instance—things that would rarely be found going through a pet site's affiliate program.) You get the idea.

Our point: It's okay to make your site overtly commercial, but be up-front about it. Don't try to pass your site off as something it's not; users will see right through your attempt. Review the basic criteria on a regular basis: Is there something at your site worth visiting? Does it offer something that makes you a little (or a lot) different from any other site out there? Are you making life easier or more interesting for your visitor? We're not saying you can't meet all these criteria with just a good selection of products, but we are saying it is usually better to offer more.

If your site isn't going to be just a "store," then focus on the content or functionality that makes your site attractive to visitors. For example, a useful Web-based calendar site or a site that offers free e-mail are valuable offerings. And at such sites, it's perfectly acceptable to be "sponsored" by affiliate links. Your users understand that you have to pay your bills, and will be more accepting of interesting product links placed into the margins than of annoying, slow-loading, animated banner ads. And we say again: Targeting products is better than selecting products randomly.

However, there are a number of things that everybody needs that are hard to target to any one consumer subset. Generic (nontargeted) Web-based service sites, like one that offers free e-mail, are natural places to present nontargeted products like auto insurance and cruise vacations. Nevertheless, we encourage you to always try to delineate among your users in an ongoing effort to target products and services to them as appropriately as possible. Your guiding principle should be to include items that they have an interest in seeing. If you are successful at accomplishing this, you will have achieved a win-win situation for yourself and your visitors.

The ideal mix of products and content (or functionality, in the case of Web-based services) probably will not become apparent immediately. You will have to experiment and continually refine your choices. In fact, in the Web world, it's almost always preferable to launch fast rather than being slow in order to get it perfect. As Guy Kawasaki of startup-enabler, Garage.com, says, "Don't worry. Be crappy," meaning that you can begin to improve from the moment you launch, until, incrementally, you get it right.

So don't fret too hard about whether you should have products along the left versus right, three products per page versus ten, prices in red versus blue, and so on. Just put something up. Maybe first show it to a small group of people if you've got concerns about diminishing other strong aspects of your site.

By improving gradually, you avoid dramatic (read: labor-intensive) reworking of your site. Said bluntly, don't spend a lot of time making lots of changes that may not stick after you gather some user feedback and traffic and commission data. Undertake "baby" implementations—that is, pepper your site with a few samples here and there, in a variety of shelf-space formats (we discuss this in Chapter 9, "Designing Shelf Space and Picking Products"). Watch the numbers to see what happens. You might even consider presenting the same product in different positions and formats, on different days, and watch to see whether a particular style-layout combination generates significantly higher click-through. Only after you hit on a formula that works for your site should you commit to a wholesale site redesign to multiply your test results across many pages.

There is also nothing wrong with standardizing on an interface format that includes multiple approaches to displaying product links. Just remember to be consistent enough so that your site easy to navigate, particularly for new visitors. It's acceptable to have a well-thought-out mix of featured products (those given prominent coverage), minor mentions, adlike products in the margins, ministore-type displays, and full-blown stand-alone store environments.

You may discover that your most successful product displays are those accompanied by rich content you created yourself (you might find yourself in need of some writers!). Good examples abound at sites featuring in-depth reviews, product *shootouts* (comparisons), and featured products with lots of verbiage written (or licensed) by site owners. Not only do such presentations provide abundant information to assist consumers with making a purchase decision, but by offering a well-researched body of information, you come off as the credible source of that information. When that happens, incidental products that you place here and there—with no reviews or commentary—may benefit as well, the implication being that if they're on your site, they must be quality products. When unsure about what to do, it is this sort of subtle clue (along with brand name and price) that customers rely on to decide whether a product has value.

If there is a downside to hitting upon a magic formula for revenue generation, it is that you may feel pressured to do more of it. You may find yourself prioritizing your editorial calendar around new product releases that are sure to sell well. Or you may revisit a familiar topic—one that you've covered perhaps a bit too recently—because you know that this item category performs well. So the question is, will merchandising drive your editorial decisions or will your editorial goals drive your merchandising? The answer will probably depend on whether you (or your company) are revenue-focused or editorial integrity-focused. The short answer is, know your priorities. If you're unsure, fall back on the answer to the definitive question: What do our visitors really want to see?

## Will this boat float?

The answers you provide to the preceding questions lead to the following new questions:

How much will it cost?

How much will we make?

There are no quick and easy answers to these questions. Regarding costs, we can tell you not to bother making estimates until you've played around long enough to know how much time (and/or money) it takes to add or refresh a product link, multiplied by the number of links of that type you'd like to add or refresh during a given time interval. Once you have that information, you can project some cost estimates based on different scenarios, such as how much it would cost to create three new featured product articles per week, for example, or how much it would cost to add a new catalog-style page with 50 products, each week. And so on.

As far as revenue is concerned, be wary of broad-stroke estimates, such as "assume a 5 percent click-through and a 10 percent conversion rate." Sure, we (and everybody else) use guesstimates all the time in business, but that's all they are—guesstimates, which will vary based on the source and the situation. For instance, if you've got a high-traffic site related to a specific product like Palm Pilots, then click-through and conversion rates are going to be a lot higher than if you're running a free Web-based e-mail service and you suddenly start adding links to Barbie products. And the links themselves make a difference, just as one good banner ad can deliver 10 times as many clicks as a poor ad, all else being equal.

We repeat, as soon as possible, stop planning and start experimenting. Any test data you collect will help you to move forward and plan with confidence. Where possible, base your assumptions on data that is generated from your site. Data from other sites can give hints, but unless these sites are very similar to yours, and are visited by a similar audience, then the data may be misleading.

How will you measure the effectiveness of your plan and modify it accordingly? This process is easier if you are using only one merchant's affiliate program or a third-party service like CrossCommerce.com, which aggregates products from hundreds of merchants and presents cross-merchant reports revealing which products and merchants are performing best. You'll learn, for example, that the same product, displayed the same way, might sell better when it links to one merchant rather than another. Don't forget, once the customer clicks through to the merchant's site, what he or she sees there goes a long way to determining whether he or she will buy. Some merchant sites look better and are more organized, and thus make shopping simpler and more pleasurable. Others are up-front about their security and privacy policies. Still others aggressively cross-sell related products. Some perform well simply because they represent a well-known and respected brand.

Regardless, unless you check your statistics, you can't know what's going on. You may decide to check your reports only every few months, or forget to do so until a check shows up in the mail. Or you may set your browser homepage to these reports and check several times a day with the fervor and passion of a day trader. (Look for third-party services that make reports downloadable in spreadsheet form.) From analyzing the data, you might discover, for instance, that one product is a popular item but that its placement does not allow many of your visitors to see it. Placing it more prominently, such as on a more heavily trafficked page, might lead to a dramatic increase in sales.

## Summary

The size and type of site you're building or managing will drive how many products you place and how frequently you change them. Before you commit to launching a full implementation, experiment to discover what works best and how much it will cost to deploy your affiliate links on a large scale. Affiliate programs are a dream come true for experimenters and tinkerers. The results of your decisions can be observed and acted upon almost immediately, enabling you to optimize your commission revenues on an ongoing basis.

In the next chapter, we look at the details related to selecting and displaying products on your site.

# 9

# Designing Shelf Space and Picking Products

Now comes the fun part: deciding how you want to integrate products into your site at the page level. In this chapter, we explore 10 different methods for presenting affiliate links to Web site visitors. Most sites wisely implement only one or two of these methods. We say wisely because it is easier to maintain consistent design across a site when you don't have to juggle display styles, though of course there are situations where it is appropriate to mix and match. After we explain how to design your "shelf space," we will take a look at the process of selecting which products to show on your site.

## Designing Shelf Space

Throughout the shelf design phase, it is important, at all times, to be aware of how product presentation will affect your site's overall feel. The key variable should be how much weight to give to products versus other content. Naturally, giving a lot of weight to a product or store increases the odds that it will be seen and that a sale will be made. On the other hand, too much emphasis on e-commerce can detract from a site that ostensibly exists for another purpose. You will determine weight—which we're using as a synonym for *importance* or *clout*—by a number of factors that include size, colors, page placement, placement within the site's architecture, and so on. How much weight you should assign to a product is often obvious, but if a lot is going on at your site, you might want to do some user testing to gain some additional insight (see Chapter 10, "Increasing Hits and Selling More on Your Web Site").

## Featured Product: Substantive Review

Other than devoting an entire site (or portion of a site) to a single product, one of the most powerful methods for displaying a product is to feature it in an article (see Figure 9.1). The single-product feature article is an excellent

**Figure 9.1** Content as part of commerce: At a glance, we know that Outside Online strives to inform visitors thoroughly about this book. Notice the understated link to Amazon .com at the bottom of the review.

method for solving the commerce-versus-content dilemma. By providing your own substantive content related to a product, your site will not be seen as purely commercial or editorially barren, particularly if you fairly present both the strengths and weaknesses of the featured product. We've all had our "which do you recommend" question dismissed (whether in person or on-line) by the reply: "They're all good, which do you want?" By being honest, which means giving a negative review or including some negative comments when warranted, you will earn credibility among your audience.

This credibility, combined with weight/prominence and genuinely useful information is a winning affiliate selling combination, because it helps customers find what they want and be able to make a purchase decision with confidence. The downside to this approach is twofold: generating these reviews takes time, and the model does not scale well for sites with many products, unless you have many content contributors—which leads to high production costs, perhaps so high that the business cannot turn a profit.

In the future, product reviews of all kinds will be syndicated, meaning you will be able to use content owned by other sources in exchange for a fee or perhaps a small percentage of your affiliate fee. See this book's companion Web site for late-breaking developments (www.affiliateselling.com).

## Featured Product: Brief Review

If your site is devoted to more than just one category of product, or if you'd like to highlight more products than you have room to review at length, multiple, brief reviews might be your answer. A short, concise review (of three to five sentences, for example) usually is sufficient to cover a product's basic attributes, and to identify its strengths and weaknesses relative to other products in its class. As with longer, more substantive reviews, being honest about a product will go a long way to establishing you as a credible critic and not just another salesperson concerned only with making a commission.

Figure 9.2 depicts a site that, despite being produced by an amateur, provides visitors with the no-nonsense low-down on what's good and what's not. Using feisty editorial to tell us which guns "rock," which ones are "GP" (suitable only for grandparents), and how to modify the guns with rubber bands so you can "dent a door," we know we've come to the right place. This is a perfect site for adding affiliate links.

## Product Category Article or Shootout

An alternative to lengthy single-product reviews or short mini-reviews of multiple products is to craft an article that addresses a category of products, such as laser printers or children's books. This format enables easy product

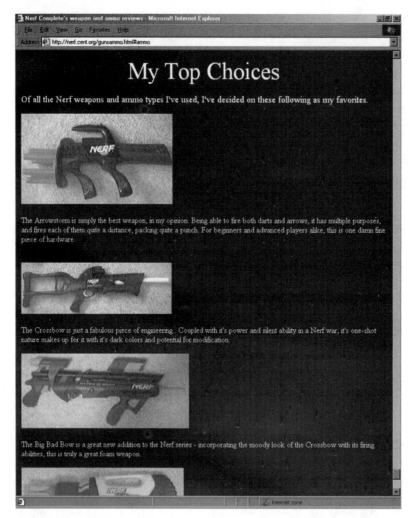

**Figure 9.2** This Nerf gun site doesn't need Hollywood production values to convince us that the writer is an expert.

comparison; you can point out differences between complementary or competing items, and include their respective strengths and weaknesses.

A product *shootout* is an extreme version of a category-comparison article, one in which you might establish a proprietary rating system (using one to five stars for example) for several product attributes, such as price, ease of use, quality, and so on. To the selection you deem as best overall you can give your own seal of approval, called, for example, Editor's Choice, Our Pick of the Week, and so on. These endorsements will carry a lot of weight with consumers who are in the process of sorting out the differences among multiple products, each claimed to be the best by its manufacturer.

Figure 9.3 shows one page of an excellent, thoroughly researched comparison between Nerf guns, complete with statistics based on tests performed by the site's authors. The only thing missing from this page is an affiliate link that would enable viewers to buy the toy after they've identified the one they want.

## Non-Product-Specific Content

Another good way to highlight multiple items in one piece of content is to reference tangentially related products in an article on a non-commercial topic.

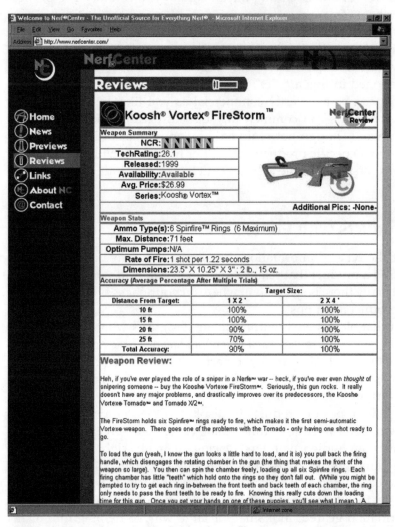

**Figure 9.3** Hardcore Nerf aficionados will appreciate NerfCenter's rigorous product comparisons.

For instance, let's say you decide to publish a narrative about your summer trek along the Appalachian Trail, and along the way, you mention that your trusty little MSR Whisperlite stove made you the envy of your traveling companions.

If you opt to go with this format, though, decide in advance whether the piece will be commercial-with-content focused or content with a commercial. There is a big difference, though the mechanisms for creating one versus the other may seem subtle. For instance, if you make an affiliate link out of every mention of every product, you won't fool anybody—you're producing a commercial. Alternately, you could add fewer links and even be intentionally casual about them, writing for example: "Gee, this is starting to sound like a commercial. Don't bother sending me an e-mail; you can buy one of these little lifesavers <u>here</u>."

Another way to avoid overt commercialism is to rave about a product within the editorial content, but *not* include any hyperlinks there, instead placing a highly visible link elsewhere on the page that reads: "<u>Information about products</u> mentioned in this article." This link would take visitors to a dedicated page that can be as overtly commercial as you like. In this way, your editorial never appears too commercially biased, because you have neatly separated the two. (Though not required, any additional insights or details you can give about specific products, no matter how brief, will go a long way toward helping persuade people to buy. Don't forget to include the bad as well as the good.)

## Margin Products with Photos

Regardless of the type of information that dominates a given page, chances are, you can find a product that relates to the material. And whether you plan for it or not, usually there is space somewhere on your pages where you can fit one or more product mentions.

One format that blends well with most site designs is what we call *margin products* (not to be misconstrued as *marginal products*). These are units of merchandising content stacked vertically in narrow columns that can be dropped into the columns of your Web site, usually on either the left- or right-hand side (see Figure 9.4, right-side column).

By choosing the types of products to display in the margins next to your primary content, you can subtly "tune" the level of commercialism, based on what you think your audience prefers. Placing golf clubs right next to an article about the same golf clubs is fairly blatantly commercial, but this is an acceptable choice, as long as it was made conscientiously. In such a case, you could almost say that the content supports the margin products; that is, it gives the user information geared, in a small or large way, to helping him or her make a purchase decision.

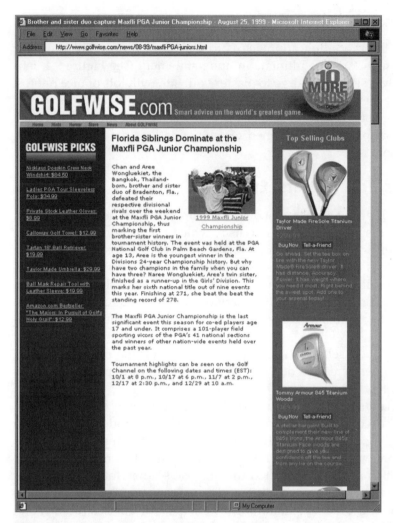

**Figure 9.4**  Margin products: Golf clubs with photos and descriptions (right) are displayed next to a general article about golf. This is a softer sell than showing them next to a review of clubs. Text-only links (left) are an even softer sell.

In contrast, you could relate the products less obviously to the topics explored on the page, for example, promoting a golf vacation package next to the article about golf clubs. Notice how it becomes a much softer sell? The margin products move farther into the background; and this can be extended by muting the brightness of the colors used in the display. In these ways, products take a back seat to your editorial, playing a role similar to (though much more effective than) banner ads, which more or less become part of the background to the reader.

## Margin Products without Photos

A variation of the preceding approach is to include text-only links in your margins. This method is the ultimate in understatement (see Figure 9.4, left-side column). By resisting the urge to plaster your site with lots of nice photos, you achieve subtle product endorsement, which takes on a flavor of recommended reading lists. This form is not a big commercial, not the solution to all problems, but simply useful, screened recommendations for those who seek more information.

## Best-Sellers, Top 10 Lists, Etc.

Text-only margin product links, just described, are perhaps the most common mechanism for displaying top 10-like lists, which range from the *New York Times'* best-sellers to the top-grossing films of the previous weekend to countless top-seller lists on e-merchants' and affiliate sites across the Web. Best-seller lists naturally require frequent or automated refresh, so look into CrossCommerce.com's free syndication services if you're interested in displaying this sort of merchandising content without having to do the ongoing maintenance yourself.

Other types of best-seller lists require more space on the page and, often, more custom content creation on your part, such as adding product reviews (see MysteryNet's Hit List, Figure 9.5).

Despite the labor-intensive nature of building your own best-seller lists, they are widely used because they are extremely effective. Indeed, you'd have a hard time finding a major e-merchant that doesn't post its top-sellers prominently on its home page. The short take on best-sellers is that most consumers don't know which products are rated the highest, so they look to others for this input. Social psychologists call this phenomenon *social proof*. Does this mean that some consumers are lemmings? Perhaps, but this is a rational and efficient (though not always correct) way for consumers to make, on average, good purchase decisions without spending precious time doing research themselves.

Enough on why people like these lists. The point is, they work, and you will find that the products you highlight as best-sellers will become—lo and behold—*your* best-sellers.

## Catalog Style

Catalog style is the straightforward, no-nonsense approach: You display a bunch of products and encourage people to buy them. No subtle this, no understated that; no trying to weave things in and out of "legitimate" content. Think about it: Catalogs don't pretend to be editorially based magazines.

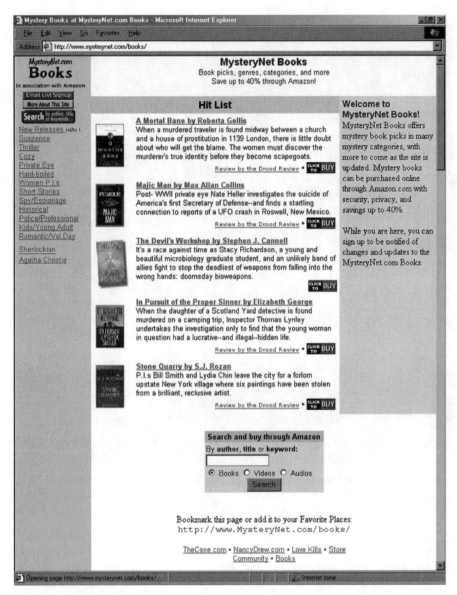

**Figure 9.5** Top sellers and top 10 lists require frequent updates but are a proven way to help people to buy with confidence.

Likewise, on sites that present products in a catalog format, the product information *is* the content (see Figure 9.6).

At catalog-style sites, no excuses are made about being overtly commercial, and none are necessary—the sites exist solely to sell products and they don't pretend to do anything else.

**Figure 9.6** Catalog-style sites like Tattoos.com display products using the most straight-forward approach.

**NOTE** The catalog layout style can be used in an "Our Store" portion of a larger site devoted to nonmerchandising content.

If you use this approach, you are, in effect, identifying your site as a surrogate, or virtual, e-merchant. You may therefore be excited by the hyper-enabled vision of the future we painted at the end of Chapter 1, "Affiliate Selling: The Next Big Thing." Until that future becomes the present, regrettably, we must hand over our visitors to the real merchants, except with third-party providers like Nexchange (www.nexchange.com) that provide affiliate-side shopping carts and other similar capabilities. Ostensibly, your primary reason for existing is to help customers to find what they want and to buy it. That means your site's entire architecture (or store architecture, if yours is part of a larger site) should be crafted to that end. To quote from *Increasing Hits and Selling More on Your Web Site*, good site navigation will fundamentally enable two things:

- Help visitors who know what they want to find it quickly, using as few clicks as possible.

- Help visitors who don't know what they want by taking them by the hand, leading them, and offering suggestions.

By 1999, most of the mechanisms for achieving these two capabilities have become commonly used, though unfortunately, not ubiquitously. On the other hand, perhaps it is fortunate that these mechanisms have not become ubiquitous, because that means there is room for you to one-up the actual e-merchants by making products easier to find. This is covered in greater depth in Chapter 10.

## Random Blurbs and Space Fillers

While perhaps not the most sophisticated or holistic approach to business or site design, numerous sites pay their bills by putting links pretty much anywhere they feel like it. To be fair, there are many loosely structured sites known for being a mishmash of whatever strikes the fancy of the developers on any given day. And who are we to criticize? If it works, it works.

Interestingly, only a few years ago, adding anything commercial to these "I am, therefore I code" sites would have been bluntly rejected by their loyal followers. Today, however, even the staunchest of the Internet old guard (some of whom are proud of their still-functioning 2400 baud modems) are known to issue statements to the effect: "My ISP started charging me more because I've got lots of traffic, so these products/ads are just here to pay the bills." It's a reasonable position to take, though undoubtedly, some of these sites that initially added product promotions "just to pay the ISP bill" have come to discover that real revenue can be generated with the model, enough to put a dent in the armor of the old guard.

## Bizarre, Funky, and Extreme

If your site ethos permits, and you're sure your audience would accept it, you might consider piquing their curiosity by using shock value to shamelessly draw attention. Imagine, for example, publishing a gratuitously gross, but funny, vomit story called "Prophets of Hurl," which could be fiction or nonfiction, and surrounding it with humorous animated GIFs depicting stickmen who are projectile-vomiting. Visitors who clicked on the linked iconic vomit chunks that randomly adorned the page might find themselves at a page at drugstore.com where they could buy, say, the behind-the-ear, anti-nausea patch.

And if you wanted to go really out there, you could link the vomit chunk icons to $40 baskets of potpourri from marthastewart.com—sweet irony. Such distinctiveness might not sell something every time, but it might encourage visitors to explore the links just to see where they end up. Some of your links could point to legitimately related products such as the book, *Man Eating Bugs: The Art and Science of Eating Insects,* by Peter Menzel and Faith D'Aluisio, which is about cooking and eating bugs. If you do this kind of "scavenger hunt" linking well, your visitors will have a good time, and probably tell their friends.

## Selecting Products

At this point in the book, we hope you've given some thought to which affiliate programs you'll join, how many products you want to place, and how to integrate them into your site. Now it's time to get down to the actual task of determining which products to select.

In many cases, the answer is self-evident. Sites or pages devoted to a particular product will, of course, provide links to that product; the only open questions might be which make or model to select or perhaps which merchant, if the same product is offered by more than one merchant. Likewise, developers of sites about a category of product (like computer games) or a topic that's closely related to a category of products (like golf) will have little difficulty figuring out which products to promote.

For the rest of you, the best product to choose may not be immediately obvious. It may not become obvious even after some thinking and searching. You might have a only few spots on your site that require hard-to-fill commerce opportunities; your entire site may be devoted to a sensitive subject (such as treating clinical depression); or your site may be operated under the auspices of an organization that has to monitor carefully what it contains (like a church or a school) to prevent giving the impression of making endorsements offensive to members of its audience. Whatever your boundaries, rest assured, there is a solution for affiliate selling on your site. We'll even go out on a limb and proclaim that there is an appropriate product available for every site (excluding, of course, those prohibited from selling at all, by government regulation, for example).

### Have You Got the Gift?

Coming up with less apparent product matches for odd topics can be tricky, though some people seem to have a knack for it. They can pull a topic out of a hat and start rattling off a diverse list of products that might appeal to somebody reading about that topic. If you don't have the gift, don't get discouraged, because this is also a learnable skill.

### First, Some Examples

Let's say you've got a golf site. "No problem," you think; I'll post links to merchants that sell golf clubs, balls, and maybe some shirts. Well, you might want to rethink that. For starters, to game aficionados, golf clubs are an extremely personal item, with a high dollar value. So unless you build a store with a wide variety of clubs, you're unlikely to pick the one that's going to trigger a typical visitor to buy, with the exception of a particularly hot seller (which will have to be refreshed regularly). What about golf balls? Probably not worth buying online, except in bulk at a great price, because of the shipping costs, or if you happen to need them before you can get to a store (not likely since golf courses sell game equipment), in which case golfers would probably go direct to a golf e-merchant anyway.

The point: Unless you're carrying enough products to be considered a virtual e-merchant (which you could do, of course), you'll probably do better by offering the hard-to-find, little-known but gotta-have-it items. Therefore, we recommend that you either make your site the whole store, target a particular niche (there is a site called golfballs.com, for example), or snag people serendipitously, resulting in the impulse buy. A golf game on CD-ROM, for example, is the kind of thing an avid golfer is less likely to hunt for, but likely to buy if he or she happens across it; and certainly it is a likely gift item. (Spouses and kids of golfers feel safe buying them books, CD-ROMs, and golfball shaped tie-tacks for fear of screwing up and getting something wrong that's actually related to playing the game.)

Want to add a high-dollar item that qualifies as a potential serendipitous purchase? No such thing, you ask? How about the latest gotta-have-it Palm Pilot? What's it got to do with golf you ask? Well, many—most?—golfers have discretionary income, they often like gadgets, and some even conduct business while on the fairway. What could therefore be more perfect for a golfer than a Palm Pilot?

And by merely placing a Palm Pilot on your golf site, it becomes a golf-related item, in the same way that Purell (a brand-name hand sanitizer) became an office-supply product once it was placed into office supply stores. The connection between hand sanitizer and office supplies may not have been initially obvious, but colds (hence, germs) spread like crazy in large offices. As an affiliate, you have much more freedom to experiment than does the typical e-merchant. Use it to your advantage by experimenting wildly to find what types of products will be of interest to your visitors.

## Coming Up with Ideas

If you don't know which products to place on your site, don't just start picking things randomly. Start by making a list, perhaps twice as long as the number of products you actually need, and then begin paring it down to the most appropriate among them. How do you generate the initial list?

### Ask Yourself What You Like

Perhaps you are an expert in the subject matter of your site. If so, the first source of items on your list should be your instincts—and don't be afraid to experiment. If you are a member of your target audience, think about what you like, even if it's only tangentially related to your site's primary focus. If you've got a lot in common with your site's visitors, chances are pretty good they share a lot of your other interests as well. If you need to make your case to somebody else, try calling it *"collaborative filtering"*—the emerging Web practice of tracking people with similar tastes to predict what other things they'll be interested in. If unique person 1 likes items A and B, then he or she is likely to be interested in item C if unique person 2 likes items A, B, and C.

### Look for Answers Elsewhere

Perhaps you're tasked with the difficult job of selecting products for your company's site, and you have little or no expertise on the topic. We've had the pleasure of working with some of the industry's best Web merchandising specialists, a couple of guys who know what virtually every major merchant carries, which merchants have the best photographs, which have good descriptions, customer reviews, and so on, in hundreds and hundreds of product categories. (They surf a lot.) Furthermore, they can access trusted Web resources to determine, sometimes in seconds, which products the power users prefer in any given category, even those categories about which these guys have no prior knowledge. We picked their brains about how to approach this problem, and the conversation resulted in the following recommendations.

#### Find Out What the Merchants Are Promoting

First and foremost, you should regard the merchants as experts in what's going on with respect to their product category, specifically as it relates to e-commerce. A quick visit to a relevant merchant's site will show you what the top-selling items are—usually those given the most prominence on their home pages. Others sites will tell visitors outright in the form of top 10 lists and the like. If you're looking for topics of interest to develop editorially, you might start with these top 10 lists and write about the items that are selling like the proverbial hotcakes. Not only is there a high likelihood that you'll make some commissions by offering products related to your content, but you're also guaranteed to be offering content that is currently of interest and value to consumers.

#### Learn What the Niche Experts Are Doing

Don't rely on merchants entirely, however. Unless you carry thousands of products, your value-add is to offer information that merchants *don't* offer. For example, at Reel.com (the online movie superstore) obscure, small, affiliate fan sites will literally sell out Reel's entire stock of an obscure release of a classic that has just been released on DVD. The point is, though the Reel staff certainly prides itself on their knowledge of movies, they are frequently surprised—pleasantly—when their fans tell them what's hot. Your job is to find that fan and get the latest scoop. There's nothing wrong with referencing the wisdom of others, and give credit where credit is due—hey, they might even provide a link back to you out of courtesy.

### Force the Question

This device almost always works, and yields great, unanticipated results. Ask yourself, "What has my topic got to do with product category X?" For X, start at the top of a long list of product categories or merchants in those categories. (Such lists can be found at CrossCommerce.com, BeFree, LinkShare, or ReferIt.) Force yourself to answer the question for every product category or merchant, especially the ones that seen *unrelated*. Trust us, what you'll learn may surprise you.

For example, suppose you have a site related to fitness. Applying this device, force the question, "What does fitness have to do with the product category of babies?" At first blush, it might seem like fitness and babies have nothing in common. But after some thought or by searching a site like Baby-Center, you'll find that there are fitness products aimed directly at new or expectant parents, such as jogging strollers and near-expedition-quality backpacks that comfortably seat babies. These two discoveries alone could lead you to create a new section at your fitness site, for new parents. Imagine the content that could come of such an intersection. And that's just one product category—babies. Imagine what you'd come up with by forcing the question for another 99 broad or narrow product categories. The results can be truly astounding, and will give you more exciting directions to follow than you could even hope to pursue.

### Focus on the User, Not on the Topic

For topics that are exceedingly difficult to align with products, and that prove resistant to the "force the question" technique, try focusing on the typical visitor to your site, instead of the site's subject matter. This approach was utilized successfully to come up with the notion of testing how well Palm Pilots would sell on golf-related sites. When you think not of golf, but of *golfers*, you quickly conjure up other assumptions about what the typical golfer does for a living, what kind of car he or she drives, his or her age, and so on. This technique is not a silver bullet, but it can yield some surprising and interesting results. Remember, not all sites have obvious matching products, but *all* visitors to *all* sites buy things daily to stay alive and comfortable. Identifying distinguishing characteristics of your visitors will help you not only to select appropriate products for them, but it will help you to understand them better as well, which can only serve to improve other aspects of your site.

### When All Else Fails, Book 'Em

Let's say you've tried all of the above techniques and have come up with nothing. Well, actually, we think it would be virtually impossible using these recommendations not to come up with something for a site, but if you're stumped on a particular section or page of your site, our first all-else-fails recommendation is to go with a book. We can't think of a single product category for which there is no book (probably a lot of books) related to it. Sound boring or like a copout? Who cares—books sell very well online. Need we say more?

But if you really don't want to use a book, our second all-else-fails recommendation is to select a magazine. It turns out that periodicals are almost as diverse as books (we bet you didn't know there's a magazine devoted to people with chronic gallstones). Furthermore, there's a good chance that the magazine you choose will have its own affiliate program or will be covered by Magazine.com's affiliate program, which, as of this writing offers a healthy 25 percent commission on any subscription you refer. Magazine.com also guarantees that its prices are the lowest available online, a nice value-add to be able to offer your visitors. (Magazine.com is featured in this book's appendix.)

And if you don't want to list a book and can't find an appropriate magazine, we say punt: Ask your customers what they'd like to have access to at your site. There are numerous ways of eliciting such feedback from your visitors, a few of which we outline in Chapter 10.

### Cross-Selling

Let's say you have identified a single product to place on a given page, but you are having difficulty coming up with additional products. Our advice is to find products related to the first product, rather than those that relate to the page content. Ask yourself: "If my customers buy this, what other things are they likely to want?" We'll assume you've racked your brain to come up with the ideal $10 item for a page for night watchmen, and the result is a wind-proof lighter. Rather than killing yourself trying to think of completely different items, consider adding links to lighter fluid and replacement flints.

This method is admittedly a bit problematic if the cross-sell items are accessories (useless on their own) and the links point to different merchants. So until cross-merchant or affiliate-side shopping cart technology becomes widely available, we recommend that you select accessories that are offered by the same merchant that sells the primary item. Even though the customer may have to do a little work to get all of the products in one shopping basket at the merchant site, at least your presentation has suggested a complete package, and increased the likelihood that the visitor will click through to the merchant in the first place.

# Refreshing Products

Once you've populated your site with a handful—or hundreds—of products, take the night off. Tomorrow, you start the exciting part of the affiliation process: figuring out what's working, what's not, and start making changes.

We address this topic in greater depth in Chapter 10, but for the purpose of the discussion here, we want to emphasize the following concept:

*When possible, select more products than you will initially need.*

Why? Because, typically, especially while you're still learning this process, product selection will be time-consuming, like doing in-depth research, and you'll often wind up with more than you need. Having a pool of extra products will give you ready-made substitutes when it comes time to experiment or to refresh your site's product content, with no extra work at that time. One caveat: Don't spend an inordinate amount of time finding a huge number of products that you don't need, because you might learn from your product testing that your overall strategy requires major adjustment, meaning you might not be able to use your surplus products at all. Rather, save *references* to additional potential products that result from your initial inquiries, and include them when it doesn't require much additional time or effort.

Having extra products "in inventory" will also make product rotations easier, an essential advantage for sites that depend on repeat visitors and can't afford to present stale content (more on this, too, in Chapter 10).

# Summary

There are many different methods to consider for presenting affiliate links to your visitors. You must decide how to integrate the products onto your page, choosing from formats such as product reviews, product category articles, non-product articles, margin products, best-seller lists, catalog-style pages, random space fillers, and creative/bizarre implementations. You must also choose which products to display, using methods such as tapping the knowledge of yourself and experts, "forcing the question" (what does A have to do with B?), focusing on the user, and cross-selling.

So far we've covered the different types of affiliate programs, how to choose one or two to join, how to add your affiliate links, and finally, how to place and feature the products. It's time for you, the affiliate, to get started, whether you're a business developing a new profit-and-loss center, a techie covering the costs of your expensive hobby, or a student hoping to earn enough cash on the side to keep you from penning "send money" letters from your dorm room.

A great affiliate site won't do well if nobody shows up. Once you build your site, you'll have to promote it. After people start to come, you'll want to refine the site to continue to improve and to increase your commissions. Chapter 10 covers how to build traffic and encourage people to buy.

# Increasing Hits and Selling More on Your Web Site

A great site with fascinating content might as well be a blank page if no one knows it exists. No matter how clever and useful they are, affiliate product links won't do you (or their merchants) any good if they have no audience. Clearly, you must create something worth visiting before attempting to attract visitors. But once built, your focus must shift somewhat to getting the word out and driving visitors to your site. This is not to say that building will not continue; indeed, as we've said before, many sites are never complete, but are forever being enlarged, enhanced, or simply updated. Remarkably, other sites continue to draw traffic after their owners have forgotten about them and have gone on to create their next site. Naturally, how you manage and monitor your site will depend on your reasons for putting it up in the first place. If your purpose is to create a modest fan site, then once you're done with the initial build, you may only update the site a few times a year. But if your purpose is to build a business from affiliate revenues, then more stewardship is required. This chapter provides some basic guidelines for:

- Building a site that people will want to visit.

- Getting the word out about the site.

- Making ongoing changes to the site to maximize your revenues.

**NOTE** If the title of this chapter sounds familiar, it's because it's the name of a book, by Greg Helmstetter, one of the authors of this book. Many of the ideas presented in this chapter, in abbreviated form, can be explored in greater detail in that book. For excerpt chapters and more information, visit this book's companion site at www.affiliateselling.com.

# Driving Traffic to Your Site

Want millions of visitors to start pouring into your site? Of course you do. We all do. But wanting them to come won't make them appear, best stated as a parody of the famous line from the movie, *Field of Dreams*: "If you build it, nobody will notice." We don't mean to sound pessimistic, just realistic. Though lots of sites are drawing lots of visitors, that's actually part of the problem—there are so many sites out there that it's become more difficult to get new ones noticed, no matter how great a site it is.

To restate, how you decide to promote your site depends on what kind of site you've built, coupled with what your resources and goals are. You may have noticed a recurring theme in this book, that one size does not fit all when it comes to creating Web marketing plans. If you're lucky enough to already be drawing heavy traffic to your site, then our advice is simple: continue doing what you have been doing, and skip to the later section of this chapter, *Selling More: Encouraging Visitors to Buy*. If, on the other hand, your site is new, or if you are new to promoting on the Web, read on. There are numerous approaches to spreading the word about your new site. Some are easy; others require extra work, special skills, or finesse.

## Search Engines

Eighty-five percent of Web surfers find Web sites using directories and search engines. So if you do only one thing to promote your site, submit your home page URL to all of the following: Yahoo!, Alta Vista, Lycos, Hotbot, Excite, Infoseek, MSN, Northern Light, LookSmart, Snap.com, and WebCrawler. (For links to submission instructions for these companies, visit this book's companion Web site at www.affiliateselling.com.)

## Posting to Usenet

Usenet is the mother of all Internet discussion boards, with tens of thousands of newsgroups devoted to literally every topic you can imagine. You can find out which groups address your site's topic at Deja.com (select "Discussions" and search using keywords related to your site).

## THE ART OF SUBMITTING

There are more than a thousand directory and search engine sites to which you can submit your URL, but doing so would be very time-consuming. A better way to go is to use a service like WorldSubmit (www.worldsubmit.com), which will submit your site for you, with packages ranging from $9.00 (for submission to 100 directories) to $89.00 (1,550 directories with repeated postings for six months).

If you are inclined to do the spadework yourself, be aware that submitting to search engines has become a specialized skill, particularly if you intend to modify your site so that it turns up closer to the top of the results list. There is even now a professional conference devoted to the topic. If you're interested in learning more, Danny Sullivan's famous newsletter, *Search Engine Watch*, is the place to start (www.searchenginewatch.com). And check out WebPosition Gold (www.webposition.com), which offers software to help automate the task of optimizing your placement within search engine results. It currently costs $149 for the standard edition (there's a professional edition as well), and a free trial version is available.

A word of caution: Some search engines have policies against "tricking" their technology into miscategorizing sites or attempting to elevate your site's ranking in the results. In the future, the FTC may even take steps to regulate the process, as abuses have become widespread (of particular concern are adult sites misrepresenting themselves as being suitable for minors).

Usenet has a culture all its own, further delineated by individual newsgroups that typically have their own vernacular, as well as rules for appropriate behavior. So though it may be tempting to blast an announcement about your site to the entire Usenet community (called *spamming*), doing so would be a serious mistake. First and foremost, it's simply rude, and completely inappropriate. Moreover, you will draw attacks ranging from, at best, harsh verbal criticism to, at worst, a focused onslaught of vengeful tactics designed to shut you down.

If your site has genuine noncommercial content and is highly relevant to a particular newsgroup's topic, then—*sometimes*—it is okay to make an announcement to that group. We say sometimes because there are groups that *never* welcome such announcements. The best way to find out which groups permit site promotions and which don't is to follow the group(s) you're targeting for a couple of weeks and read what gets posted before posting anything yourself. Not only will you get a feel for the culture of the group(s), but you will inevitably come across a FAQ (Frequently Asked Questions) document that specifies the group's rules in black and white. Read it and abide by it.

Again, rules vary from group to group, but in most cases, you will be welcomed if you legitimately participate in the discussions and mention your URL in your e-mail signature (no more than four lines), rather than merely dropping in once to post a purely commercial message.

**TIP** For additional online references to proper Usenet netiquette, go to this book's companion Web site at www.affiliateselling.com.

## Mailing Lists

Similar in scope to newsgroups are the tens of thousands of e-mail mailing lists devoted to individual topics of discussion. To find those related to your site, visit Liszt.com, eGroups.com, and Topica.com. Mailing lists operate much like newsgroups, except that the discussions take place over multiple e-mails (or one concatenated e-mailed "digest," usually sent out daily).

If posting anything remotely commercial to newsgroups is tricky, then doing so to mailing lists is downright treacherous. Mailing lists tend to be smaller, composed of more tightly knit groups of people who stay active on the list longer (for years, in some cases), and often get to know each other well. There are exceptions: small, cozy newsgroups and big, impersonal mailing lists. But in general, think of most newsgroups as a neighborhood bar and most mailing lists as a party in someone's home. As with newsgroups, legitimate participation within a list discussion is welcome, and it's usually acceptable to show your URL in your e-mail signature.

Also be aware that mailing list administrators often take a more active role in moderating what goes on, including banning offensive people from the list. But this can work in your favor. If you genuinely feel that your site would be of interest to a given mailing list, you can send a personal e-mail to the list administrator and ask if it would be okay to make your announcement. Asking permission will also serve to demonstrate your conscientiousness and anti-spam awareness, which will, in many cases, be appreciated. If given the green light, you know you're on solid ground.

## E-Mail

We know how tempting it is to send an e-mail announcement to every Web address you can get your hands on. Resist! Think how annoyed you get when you receive umpteen unsolicited e-mails (spam) in your in-box. Simply put, don't contribute to this widespread problem. Sending unsolicited bulk e-mail is almost universally regarded as inappropriate behavior, to the extent that Congress has been attempting to outlaw the practice.

Of course, the exception to this rule is that it's usually fine to send announcements to anybody who you're confident wouldn't mind receiving e-mail from you—friends, family, colleagues, and anyone else who has *"opted in"* (given consent) to receive e-mail from you. It's also permissible in some cases to send an *individual* (as opposed to bulk) e-mail to a complete stranger, announcing your site. An example would be contacting the Webmaster of a related site and asking if he or she would like to swap links to each other's sites (see the following section). Use your best judgment in cases like these. In general, if you believe that the other person may be interested in hearing from you, and if you are not indiscriminately sending e-mail to numerous others, then you are probably not going to annoy anybody.

## Web Rings and Trading Links

There was a time when Web sites were so few and far between that a sort of bond existed among Webmasters, even if they had never met. Just *having* a site indicated that you were part of the online family, and was reason enough to start an ongoing dialogue. Alas, the proliferation of Web sites has changed all that; the only thing most have in common now is that they are competing for a finite number of unique visitors.

Fortunately, though the window of opportunity has closed somewhat, it is still possible to find kindred spirits out there, particularly among Webmasters of noncommercial sites related to your site's topic. It is among these people with whom you might agree to trade links. The process is simple: just find an e-mail address on the site that seems a likely candidate, write, and ask. (Note: Commercial sites—other than amateur sites with affiliate links—are often resistant to providing reciprocal links, particularly if they have more traffic than you, because they feel that the deal will work against them on average.)

Fortunately, there are also sites that are really interested in swapping links, and a great service has emerged to facilitate getting likeminded Webmasters together. WebRing (www.webring.com) provides an infrastructure that enables sites with related content to link together in what are called, not surprisingly, *Web rings*. You can either join an existing ring or start your own. When you join, you place links pointing to some or all of the other members of the ring or to a link that randomly selects another ring member. The other members do the same in turn. In this way, you gain potential access to the traffic of all of the ring's sites combined.

## Partnerships

Another way of promoting your site and drawing traffic to it is to establish strategic partnerships with other sites or companies. Though partnership agreements might include placing reciprocal links (as mentioned previously), they typically involve more complex structures, usually requiring a legal agreement; and often technical integration is necessary and/or one site agrees to pay the other site. For instance, you might ask another site to provide a link to your site in return for a portion of the affiliate commissions you receive as a result of the traffic the partner site delivers to you.

Entering into such agreements are beyond the capabilities of many small sites because they require the technical resources to track the activities of your partner's visitors once they access your site (specifically, which of them made a purchase as a result of the affiliate links). For help on this front, look for affiliate programs that permit subaffiliation, particularly if the technical implementation involves something simple like appending your affiliate ID (in an HTML link) with your subaffiliate's ID (such as www.merchant.com/ yourID/subaffiliateID/productpage.html). Using one of these programs, you could form such a relationship without having to pay the partner, because the merchant or service running the affiliate program would pay your partner directly.

You might also consider partnering with Webmasters of numerous sites out there who don't even know about affiliate programs (or don't have the time to research them) and who might be happy to provide a link to your site if it meant they could automatically start receiving money. We know of one company whose sole purpose is to build out affiliate links onto K–12 schools' Web sites. The company receives all of the money from the e-merchants and then sends the schools a check for whatever percentage it has negotiated with them. The schools provide the traffic, and the company provides the schools with another source of funding, which they probably would not have developed on their own.

## Advertising

Perhaps the most obvious method of building traffic to a Web site is to pay to slap a few banner ads onto a portal like Yahoo! or Excite. If you think these companies aren't appropriate avenues for you to pursue because they're too expensive, think again. Excite, for instance, offers targeted banner campaigns for as little as $100, which, at the time of this writing, buys you 8,350 ad views (*impressions*). That's not going to turn you into an overnight media juggernaut, but it's an excellent way to test the waters and determine if advertising of this sort will pay for itself in affiliate commissions.

A potentially even more attractive option is to join the LinkExchange free banner network. Here's how it works: LinkExchange (now owned by Microsoft), gathers sites that want exposure and that have banner space of their own, and arranges banner swaps among its member sites. To participate, therefore, you must also be willing to show other sites' banners on your site. For every two banner impressions you provide, LinkExchange shows your banner once. This 2:1 ratio gives LinkExchange a surplus banner inventory, which they sell to paying advertisers—and is how LinkExchange makes its money and is able to provide the service to you for free. The system is automated, meaning that all you have to do is allocate banner space on your site; LinkExchange takes care of the rest. The service also provides reports so you can gauge your results, and offers features that enable you to specify the types of sites that you want displaying banners that direct surfers to your site.

Excite and LinkExchange are just two ways to spend your advertising dollars. Indeed, almost any site will take your money if you offer it, as will traditional media: radio, television, magazines, newspapers, and outdoor media (billboards and so forth). An in-depth discussion of serious advertising is beyond the scope of this book, so our purpose here is to highlight the low-risk alternatives worth checking into.

## Publicity

One of the most overlooked but potentially high-return methods of promoting your site is to be interesting enough to earn general media attention. But to get that attention, you'll probably have to hire a publicity or public relations (PR) firm whose job it is to send out press releases alerting journalists and editors to the goings-on at your company that might be of interest to their audiences.

In the early days of Web growth, just having a Web site was enough to get you mentioned in the media. Now, of course, it's so crowded online that Web companies and businesspeople are vying for attention in the same way as their brick-and-mortar predecessors. Nonetheless, media professionals are always on the lookout for items of interest. And that's worth remembering—newspapers and magazines *need* a steady supply of content. You never know what might be considered newsworthy; you might release some interesting statistic, for example, and the media reporting that information will site you as the source. It's entirely possible to go from zero to thousands of visitors a day from a single mention in a widely distributed newspaper article.

PR tends to be underutilized as a marketing tool, particularly by many small business owners, because they don't understand how the process works, or they believe that it is prohibitively expensive.

While it's true that good PR firms are budget-breakers for many small businesses, there are a number of guerrilla-type avenues for getting publicity on little or no budget. For links to such resources, visit this book's companion Web site at www.affiliateselling.com.

## The Only Sustainable Traffic Driver: Build a Good Site

If a good site is worthless without traffic, then the converse is also true—lots of traffic won't mean much if your site isn't interesting enough to induce visitors to stay a while. In fact, "staying a while" probably won't even cut it. You want people to dig deep, explore, bookmark your site, come back, and—most of all—tell all their friends about it. True, anybody who made millions of dollars from a recent IPO can buy television ads and build traffic that way, but it's a waste if there's no "there" there. Good sites are creative, interesting, and well executed. They are different from other sites, different enough to get noticed, recommended to others, and given mention in magazines and newspapers.

Large commercial sites whose purpose is clear and whose audience is clearly targeted already have this figured out. And those that don't know what value they plan on offering to their visitors have got bigger problems than where they should place a few affiliate links. We're more concerned here with the small and/or new sites that have not formulated a formal business plan. If you are serious—even just a little—about making real money with affiliate links, then you must, if you haven't already, give some hard thought to 1) why your site exists, 2) what value it adds, and 3) to whom it will be valuable.

Building your site without first answering these basic questions is a mistake, and we recommend that you stop what you're doing and go through the process. The good news is that, on the Web, you need to appeal only to a tiny sliver of a fraction of online users and you'll still have something interesting on your hands. That's because there are *a lot* of Web users. With hundreds of millions of surfers online (and more joining every day), you can make something that appeals to only .01 percent and still have tens of thousands in your target audience. So-called "sliver marketing" has always been appealing to Webpreneurs, and affiliate selling has made it even more so. If your low-traffic site is successful at selling just *one product* or at getting *one person* to recommend it to another, then there is a good chance that it will sell lots of merchandise and generate significant traffic once you've got some initial visitors to start building word-of-mouth.

## What's Your Hook?

This question is a bit of a chicken-and-egg problem, because significant traffic (without spending millions in advertising) comes from word-of-mouth. But people mention a site only if it's worth mentioning, so that is where you must begin. Build a site that 1) *you* would be interested in visiting, and 2) *you* would want to tell your friends about if you were to find it while surfing. Ideally, you want other Web site owners to add links to your site, and they're only going to do that if you've got something pretty interesting. We call it your *hook*.

Your hook might be a huge application such as free Web-based e-mail (although that one's been taken), or it could be something less ambitious like a program that converts numeric phone numbers into the words that the numbers spell on a touchtone keypad. This, too, has been done already, but there is no category-killer devoted to the topic, and there are plenty of sites that offer the same thing as other sites. Neat little gimmicky features can go a long way toward building word-of-mouth traffic. For instance, there are many Spanish/English translation sites, but the one at www.spanishdict.com also offers downloadable .wav files that enable users to hear pronunciation. Whether this sounds like a simple gimmick or a very valuable feature depends on whom you ask, and how likely he or she is to use the feature. Clearly, offering the feature is better than not offering the feature; and in this case, people building lists of their favorite links to, say, Spanish language resources, are far more likely to choose to link to the site that offers the audio files.

Too difficult? If building a technology-intensive, application-based site is beyond your capabilities, then take comfort in knowing that many sites draw heavy traffic simply by being the single best directory resource (in terms of links they provide) for a given specialized category. Others get noticed because they are the funniest. If your strength is a capacity for tirelessly conducting hours and hours of research, then put that to good use. If you are always the funniest person at the party, and you like to write, then put those skills to work. If you are an expert on something (we like the example of a Nerf gun expert because it demonstrates that if kids can do this, so can you), then take advantage of it. Identify your hook, your key *differentiator* that people like to talk about, and go from there. Any valuable differentiator will act as a traffic multiplier, converting whatever visitors you can coax to your site to become your promoters, who'll tell two friends, who'll tell two friends, and so on.

# Credibility

Building credibility among your visitors is *the* most important thing to do if you are an online merchant, that is, if you are selling something directly from your site. While most affiliate sites don't sell anything directly, establishing credibility is nonetheless important. Having credibility means that anybody who visits your site will believe who you are and what you say. If you are credible, then when you say a product is good, your visitors will believe you. As long as you are credible, even if you don't directly mention a product but it appears next to your content, your visitors will assume you have screened out bad products and merchants. This is all good, and will enhance your revenues. But how do you go about establishing credibility?

## *Tell, Don't Sell*

Every story has at least two sides, probably more, and you should tell the different sides of the story, just like any good journalist. Whether you are discussing your favorite/least-favorite movie, describing an incident from your childhood, or telling people which kind of car stereo to buy, present all of the facts and be fair. Do this even when, ostensibly, you're not promoting a product; convey that you are even-handed in your appraisal of *everything*. This will establish your editorial credibility, which will carry over into your merchandising efforts, particularly if you remain neutral when discussing products. It's okay to be excited about a given product and say great things about it, but by presenting both sides—pointing out any downsides you can think of—your readers will believe that you are not just trying to sell them something. Going one step farther and discussing less favorable products will help establish your credibility as a resource for comparative information, rather than as a mere front-end to a merchant.

## Invest Heavily

Is yours a serious site? Or is it an HTML diversion from studying for midterms? This is not to say that your affiliate site can't be just for fun, as long as you realize that just for fun is just that, and you aren't likely to make much money from it. But if you are interested in operating your site as a business, then you not only must operate it as one, but you must signal to your visitors that you are serious if you expect them to take you seriously. We encourage you to "invest heavily." For companies, that means spending money; and if you are part of such a company, no doubt you are already planning to do so. But if you are one of the many do-it-yourselfers out there, investing heavily does not necessarily refer to money. More likely, it refers to spending *time*, to continuously add to and improve your site. Even if you're just having fun, we recommend that you take your fun seriously, too.

### More, More, More

One way to send the message to your visitors that you are for real is to take whatever you're doing on your site and do *more* of it. Even with the automation offered by computers, little gets put onto a site without some effort. When you put forth more effort, two things happen. First, you have more value to add, which means there is a greater chance that something on your site will be useful to visitors. Second, whether the average visitor consciously recognizes it as such, you are demonstrating a high level of investment. This will automatically translate into greater credibility.

The following are ways to offer more:

**More info.** Have you reviewed 10 products? Try reviewing 100. Have you posted a few articles? Post several. Don't have the resources? Encourage your visitors to contribute.

**More details.** Have you written a paragraph on each product? Try writing five paragraphs on each. Just keep in mind that substantive content matters more than fluff. Take a look at NerfCenter's product evaluations

(Chapter 9, "Designing Shelf Space and Picking Products"), and strive for such admirable levels of quality *and* quantity.

**More pages.** Got lots of content? Break it out into a larger number of shorter pages. (But don't make pages annoyingly short; the point is to avoid extremely long pages, the bottom two-thirds of which aren't likely to get read.) By having more pages, you can have longer lists in your navigational cues and site maps, demonstrating that yours is a content-rich site.

**More pictures.** Got the gift of gab but no pretty pictures to go along with your wonderful words? Then add pictures. If you're an amateur on a budget, it doesn't have to cost you much money. Digital cameras are affordable these days, and lots of fun. Need better quality? Put slide film into your point-and-shoot 35mm and have the slides digitized at any local Photo-CD place. The results will amaze you. Finally, there's always the option of using others' photography. Don't steal, ask. You'll be surprised how many amateur and professional photographers will let you post their photographs as long as you give them credit—and perhaps a link to their sites. Most manufacturers are interested in getting their products in front of people, and they won't object if you use their images to sell their products. When in doubt, fire off an e-mail to check with either the manufacturer or the merchant at the other end of your affiliate link.

**More functionality.** This should go without saying: Any site that is built around a Web application will become more useful as pieces of functionality are added to that application. But resources are scarce, and development must follow a prioritized product road map. If your site does not have dynamic features of its own, you might want to add somebody else's dynamic features. For instance, Merriam Webster (www.m-w.com) allows you to place a dictionary lookup search box onto your site for free. Hundreds of other sites will let you add such functionality (stock quote lookup, sports, weather, and so forth) because it helps draw traffic to their sites. Of course, you want to be careful about sending your visitors elsewhere, but keep in mind that offering more features demonstrates that you're serious about making your site a useful place to visit.

**More frequent updates.** There is perhaps nothing more compelling in terms of establishing credibility at an amateur site (it's a given on large-scale professional sites) than updating your content frequently, even daily or multiple times per day. Fortunately, you need to update only one page, such as your home page, to be able to say that the site has been updated. When visitors see that "Last Updated" spot at the top of your page filled in with today's date, they'll immediately know they've come to a serious site. But note, you won't be able to get away with updating only your home page for long. To remain credible, you'll have to continue adding content to the heart of your site. Small fan sites don't need to be updated daily, though doing so certainly will encourage a visitor to return in the near future. Site updates naturally require extra work, but this is your passion and/or your business, right? If it's too much work, again we say, enlist the help of others. Solicit input from your visitors and tell them you'll post their work if it's appropriate. You'll be surprised at how many people will contribute, just for the byline and to feel part of an online community. (We know of more than a few aspiring writers who are still too afraid of technology to attempt publishing their own sites, so sites like yours for which they only need to learn how to hit Send in their e-mail client are a godsend.) In short, we say: Beware of the stale page; anything that talks about Leonardo's *upcoming* movie about a sinking ocean liner is going to sink with your audience. Scan your site periodically and keep it fresh, even if it means deleting old content or relabeling it as "archive material."

## TIPS FOR DO-IT-YOURSELFERS

Prior to the invention of Web affiliate programs, it was difficult for individuals (particularly those lacking technical skills) to use their Web sites to generate income. Aside from participating in banner ad exchanges, developers of small sites who wanted to make money had to be able to take transactions online and sell something directly to users.

Affiliation has changed all that, turning the economics of developing Web content upside down. There are now literally hundreds of thousands (perhaps millions) of small, do-it-yourselfer sites out there taking advantage of the great opportunities created by affiliate programs. The lure of relatively hassle-free income has drawn a lot of entrants, large and small, making it more important than ever for amateur Web developers to make their sites look their best in order to stand out from the crowd.

We've included a number of resources in this book to help nontechnical people get into affiliation in almost no time. With that said, we urge everyone interested in more than just experimentation to become as technically skilled as possible (or hook up with people who are). At a minimum, that means learning HTML well enough to manually edit and tweak the code spit out by visual HTML editors, many of which are the laughingstock of "real" Web developers. To be fair, the tools are improving all the time. For an up-to-date list of site-building resources, visit this book's companion Web site, www.affiliateselling.com.

One tool is essential for every Web developer to own, if not master—Adobe Photoshop. We know of no serious Web professional who does not reach for Photoshop to do graphics work; in fact, most of them have it open constantly during their production hours. Indeed, the computer world would be a much

## Production Values

To ensure that your credibility enhances your product recommendations and makes your site more likely to be revisited and recommended to others, you should give some thought to how your site's production values measure up against those of other sites. For purely commercial sites (particularly those that sell their own products direct), top-notch production quality is a must. This means hiring expert employees (or a design firm) or getting serious about refining/expanding your existing team's (or your own) skill set. While a certain honesty comes across in sites that are clearly of amateur origin, the charm will only carry a site so far. Moving beyond the college student-level site to, say, a large-scale site with lots of products will be seen as a hack job if your production values still look like those of a typical do-it-yourself site. Fear not, however; with a little effort, ratcheting the quality up to the next level is very doable. See the sidebar, "Tips for Do-It-Yourselfers."

simpler environment if only there were such unanimity with respect to other tools. Simply put, everybody loves Photoshop, and you will, too.

At the time of this writing, Adobe had just released Photoshop 5.5 (for Mac and Windows), thereby making the longtime international standard of image-editing software into a truly Web-oriented tool. Those of you familiar with optimizing Web graphics by hand (which makes for smaller file sizes that download faster) will appreciate the Save for Web option, which shows you the effects of your tweaks in side-by-side windows, before you commit to indexing an image's color palette. To those of you not familiar with such things, don't worry: This formerly complex process has been made simple enough for anyone to do. You will be able to build your pages as lean and clean as the best of them.

Photoshop now also includes other Web-related niceties (well, necessities) such as transparent backgrounds, *rollovers* (images that change when the user's mouse passes over them), animated GIFs, image maps (images in which parts of the graphic link to other Web pages), and *slicing*, (chopping up large graphics into smaller pieces that can be independently optimized).

These are all exciting additions to the experienced digital artist; and beginners will be amazed by their newfound ability to make professional-looking graphics. But let's be realistic: The quality of the graphics will always be highest when such tools are used by people with innate or learned design sense. But much of Web graphics production is mechanical, as opposed to artistic, such as creating links that look like buttons with text on them. Whether you're the next Monet or can't draw a stickman, Adobe Photoshop will help you look like you know what you're doing.

Go to www.affiliateselling.com for the best price we've found on this must-have tool.

### *Attention to Detail*

We close this section with a discussion of one of the best ways to establish credibility with your audience—whether yours is a glitzy expensive site or a homemade, just-for-fun, creative hobbyist place: Pay attention to the small stuff. Anything worth doing, big or small, is worth doing well. An amateur site whose editorial content contains accurate spelling, grammar, and punctuation will, all other things being equal, beat out another amateur site whose content is peppered with typos. Sure, some mistakes are bound to go unnoticed by viewers, but others are so blatant that even a cursory review will catch them. We see sites with blatant, egregious errors all the time. If you're doing the work yourself, be sure to give it a thorough once-over; better, however, to have a couple of trusted friends or colleagues look it over for you. If you work at a company or in a more formalized production environment, be sure that one person is ultimately responsible and accountable for accuracy, for finding and fixing errors quickly. If nobody on your team is obsessive and completely anal about attention to detail, we suggest you enlist the help of somebody who is.

Most folks in the Web industry have worked in environments led more or less by engineering teams whose first priority is not the user interface and verbiage, but rather the technical aspects, such as how quickly and reliably pages download. Their logic is that "it doesn't matter what's on the page if the user never sees it." Obviously, this is true, but so is the converse: "It doesn't matter how quickly it loads if they're disappointed once they see it." In practice, both are correct, so attention to detail should apply equally to all aspects of your operation. Encourage everybody (including your users) to report bugs and to offer suggestions of all kinds; then be committed to addressing them as quickly as possible.

# Selling More: Encouraging Visitors to Buy

Okay, now you've built a site, implemented a thousand minor tweaks, buffed it to a high sheen, and announced it to the world. Now what?

## Watch Your Traffic

Before making any plans to modify or improve your site, you must first find out what's already working and what's not. To find out, study your site's traffic patterns. Depending on who hosts your site, you may have direct access to your traffic logs, high-quality reports, or be given little or no information at all (in which case, you might consider switching Web service providers). It's possible to learn a lot about individual user habits over time by using cookies, the mechanism we described in an earlier chapter, which essentially mark a user's browser so that your Web server can recognize each user from one pageview to the next or between visits that may be days apart.

If you have such capabilities, there are a lot of high-end (read: expensive) options, such as employing personalization engines to deliver customized content to each unique visitor in real time. An in-depth discussion of such technologies is beyond the scope of this book, but we do provide links to traffic analysis services and software at this book's companion site at www .affiliateselling.com. Here, we assume that you have reasonably good traffic analysis reports at your disposal.

## The Data You Need

In particular, you're interested in knowing the following:

- How many people are visiting? Is this number increasing over time?
- How are visitors finding you? (Which sites did they click from to get to you?)
- How many pages are they viewing?
- How frequently do they return?
- Which paths are they using to navigate through your site?
- From which page do they exit your site?
- Which products are they seeing?
- On which product links are they clicking?
- Which products are they buying?

The last two require looking at your affiliate program provider's reports.

## What to Do with the Data

Based on what the numbers tell you, here are some strategies to consider:

**If you have no traffic.** Don't worry about improving your site. Put all of your effort into building traffic.

**If you have traffic to your homepage but little or no traffic beyond that point.** You are losing your visitors, probably either due to poor-quality presentation or lack of interesting content. You could consider trying a new look or improved content. We know, it's scary to invest further without knowing exactly what's causing the problem, so encourage people to provide feedback wherever possible. If you desperately need such information, enlist the help of friends or other people who might be interested in visiting a site devoted to your topic (such as newsgroup members).

**If you are receiving a large percentage of your traffic from a particular site.**
Consider doing a deal of some sort with that site to make the effect last as long as possible. You could either agree to provide a link back or even to advertise on that site. Always try to get the most prominent placement possible, and remember that advertising rates are *always* negotiable.

**If people return frequently to your site.** You must refresh your content more often. And don't wait until you have evidence of repeat visitor traffic to begin implementing this approach. By then, it may be too late. It's best to have some form of content refresh (even if minor) working by the first time somebody returns. Then he or she will know that you refresh regularly and will be more likely to return again soon. Display your refresh dates (e.g., "Last Updated: 01/01/00") if you are refreshing content more often than monthly.

**If people are exploring your site in depth.** That's a strong sign that you are doing something right. If they go deep but never click on products (for example, less than 1 percent of those who see a product click through to it), then experiment with different products. Be sure to wait until you've had a couple of thousand pageviews on any given page before making changes, just to make sure that your conclusions are statistically valid.

**If people are exiting your site from the same page or same type of page.**
This indicates there's a good chance you're either not providing enough enticing content to keep their interest or they've become frustrated in some way. Review these common exit points and see if there is anything wrong, confusing, or unappealing on these pages. Perhaps they suffer from too much text, too many products, poorly written product descriptions, errors, or confusing navigation.

**If people are clicking through on a product but failing to make a purchase.**
There could be a problem with the product link on your site (maybe it's confusing—suggests a different product, for instance), or a problem with the merchant. Consider switching to a different merchant, or try to find the product elsewhere at a lower price.

**If people are clicking through and buying a particular product more than other products.** Make it easier to find that popular product on your site. For instance, display it prominently on your home page, if that makes sense given the nature of your site.

**For hot-selling items, attempt to cross-sell.** That is, find similar or complementary products, and display them next to the popular item.

**If your traffic does not comprise many repeat visitors.** It's okay to leave top-sellers in their prominent positions for a long time. However, you must weigh the potential downside of not actively encouraging repeat traffic—repeat visitors expect to see *different* content when they return. If your site is interesting and dynamic enough to draw repeat visitors, you probably want to rotate new products into the mix, even at the risk of displacing top-sellers and losing some short-term sales. In the long run, you'll be better off because you'll have earned a more loyal user base that has come to expect fresh content at your site. The suggestion to remove a product despite its strong performance is just that, a suggestion. The idea is to make sure your site looks—at first glance—as though it's new and different from the last time a regular customer visited. The best way to do this is by showing a new date and new graphics (including product photographs). Even if you created all new editorial content, you could still risk losing repeat visitors because, at first glance, the page looks the same due to one prominent product photo that has not been changed. A solution to this dilemma might be to find new ways of promoting the *same* hot-selling item. Perhaps locate a different photo of the product (images with different colors will be seen as new) or place it elsewhere on the page. If the item is doing extremely well, then maybe it's time to consider devoting an entirely new section of your site to that product or product category. In this way, you are creating new content devoted to a topic about which there is a known interest among your site's visitors.

## A Few Basics on Site Improvement

No matter how good you think your site is, it can always be better. No matter how simple it is, it will confuse someone. More often than not, sites are more confusing to viewers than their creators think they are. This is because Web site developers in general are more technically knowledgeable and have a lot of experience finding things online, in a variety of formats. Designers and engineers often take things for granted that are beyond the range of experience of the typical user, let alone the novice user.

A research report put out by Creative Good estimated that the "99/00 holiday season would confuse shoppers to the tune of $6 billion in unrealized revenue to e-merchants who failed to make their sites easy to navigate." Many sites spend millions of dollars on technical wizardry, when in fact, simplicity is what works best. In conducting Creative Good's research, testers tried to find things on 10 major sites and failed, due to the sites' unnecessary complexity; moreover, a whopping 39 percent of shoppers failed during usability tests.

"Simple links to simple categories" is what works, says Mark Hurst, president of Creative Good. As an affiliate, you'll probably have an easier job than that of the e-merchants, because you aren't taking the transaction—an inherently complex process because many variables must be taken into consideration. But you must still be sensitive to the fact that no user, no matter how experienced, will feel as comfortable as you are when you first enter your site.

You must take this into account; anticipate some confusion, or, at least, a bit of clicking around before users orient themselves.

## If They Can't Find It, They Won't Buy It

Traffic reports only tell so much of the story of your site. For example, the most commonly used paths through your site might not be the ones that lead to the highest percentages of sales. Recall that there are two types of site visitors: those who know what they're looking for and those who are just looking around. Good navigation tools at your site help both groups. For those who know what they're looking for, it should be clear that clicking on this will lead to that—again, "simple links to simple categories." Those who are looking around are more likely to appreciate a bit of handholding in the form of straightforward navigational cues, which imply or state outright how to get from here to there. By state outright, we mean links that literally say, "Start Here." Implied navigational cues are more subtle; they're design features that suggest one path over another, such as making certain links bigger or more prominent than others, or placing them at the top (of a vertical list) or to the left (of a horizontal list), where readers are most likely to start.

### Usability Testing

So how do you ensure you're doing the best you can for your site? Simple. Test. Sit people down in front of a computer and let them go at it. Use your friends or hire a dozen or more people from a pay-by-the-hour, human factors lab. But unless you're a company with a big budget and/or a shortage of time, implement one of the numerous do-it-yourself approaches that work almost as well. The trick is to make participants forget that they are being watched. Sure, you can use a two-way mirror, set up a little video camera to watch from another room, or just pretend to be reading a magazine while your tester goes at it; what you want to find out is what he or she does when left "unattended."

This process usually amazes whoever designed the site being tested. Users start clicking on things that don't even look clickable. Or they start clicking in what appear to be random monkey clicks. This behavior is related to the orientation issue and is more apparent when users are let loose with no instructions. But your aha! meter will really go off when you simulate the "directed" browsing experience, that is, when you ask your tester to find something in particular. You'll watch, your mouth agape, as he or she clicks on choices that, to your way of thinking, couldn't possibly lead to the right area. If only one person uses your site this way, it's probably no big deal, but if all or even most of your testers do the same thing, then it's *your* assumptions that are out of synch with the average user. If this happens, don't be discouraged. First, rest assured there's nothing wrong with your brain; it's the result of building a thing from the ground up as opposed to seeing it for the first time after it's built—it will *always* look different to its creator. Second, be grateful, for you will have discovered a potentially disastrous problem with your user interface, one that has, in all likelihood, a simple solution now that you are aware of it.

### User Feedback

We think all would agree that the Web could be a little easier to use, but for whatever reason, conducting usability studies, even the quick-and-dirty variety, does not seem to be a high priority to many site developers. Even the pros mess up on this front. More than a few merchant sites out there with otherwise good affiliate programs are risky to use because their shopping environment interfaces need some work. No one wants to send their visitors to a merchant site if they're going to get lost before they can buy something.

Usability testing is a great idea and, as just noted, need not be expensive. But whether you test or not, there is another method of figuring out what to do next that is an absolute must: generating some user feedback, such as the following:

**Passive feedback.** *Passive* methods, by definition, require little effort, therefore, this is what we see on most sites—a link somewhere that reads "Feedback," "Send us your comments," "We'd like to hear from you," and so on. On the more basic sites, the link is a "mail-to" link that activates the user's e-mail client with a preaddressed e-mail ready to be written and sent. On more advanced sites, the link goes to a page that contains a form, usually requiring the user to make a few selections, such as to indicate whether the feedback is related to the site, the company, a product, and so on. Such forms are most useful for helping either an automated process or a support person to accurately route the e-mail to the appropriate individual. An incidental benefit of such a form is that it gives a strong impression that quality and customer support are among the company's highest priorities, otherwise the company would not have implemented such a refined process for handling complaints and feedback.

If placed prominently, feedback links (pointing either to an e-mail address or to a form) can generate a lot of information. One Fortune 500 company we consulted for pulled down its feedback form because "all it did was generate complaints." Suffice to say that this business unit did not receive high marks for customer service. (The business unit has, in fact, since been dismantled.) Contrast this to the infinitely more intelligent attitude expressed to us by a seasoned executive at US West (one of the Baby Bell phone companies): "Think of your pile of complaints as a pile of gems—each one is extremely valuable in that it tells you exactly what you should be doing next."

While much, if not most, feedback will be courteous, you will sometimes receive nasty remarks, made either by nasty people or by normal people having a nasty day. You should regard a negative remark as an opportunity to turn a potential source of bad word-of-mouth for your company into a loyal visitor or customer. Respond to negative feedback promptly and courteously. By showing respect for the person and acknowledging and addressing the problem quickly and professionally, you send a strong message that your business is on top of things, even if you had made an error on your site. Research has shown that customers who receive prompt, courteous resolution to problems become *more loyal* than customers who experienced no problems at all.

**Active feedback.** In contrast to passive mechanisms that wait for users to act, active methods seek out and encourage user participation. For instance, let's say you have given your site a facelift and are eager to get some fast feedback; or you might want some data to help you prioritize your development road map. In either case, not only could you display your feedback link prominently on the home page, but you could also offer an incentive to users who submit comments and ideas. The incentive could be as minor as posting the user's comments (you'd be surprised what some people will do for an acknowledgment) or as major as sending the winner of a drawing on an all-expenses-paid trip to Hawaii. True, the former may not generate many responses, but the latter may do the opposite: encourage people to submit garbage comments because they want a chance to win and have nothing of value to contribute. A more appropriate offering might be to reward each participant with a free T-shirt emblazoned with your logo; or just offer T-shirts to the 10 best submissions.

Another, less common active feedback method that is quite effective is to personally contact one or a few individuals whose e-mail addresses you have on hand (perhaps from feedback they have previously submitted via passive means). Naturally, you want to avoid bothering any of your users, but if you write an obviously nonform/nonautomated e-mail to a person courteously asking for some feedback, many people will be happy to oblige. It will be obvious that you value their input, and this makes people feel important. Keep the initial e-mail short; later you can engage in a more substantive dialogue if the individual seems willing to participate in an ongoing discussion. Some people will be eager to do so. Having a few of these "friendlies" (users or customers who are eager to offer help occasionally) you can "run things by" can save you time and money, saving you from doing real research or building pilot pages to test your ideas. Just beware of the natural tendency to put too much weight on testimonial evidence in the absence of numerous data points. Still, a testimonial data point from an actual user can be worth more than all of your company's managers' best input combined. The user knows best what he or she wants, and any given user can be much more representative of your broad user base than you, your employees, or your consultants.

# Summary

Once your site has been built, you can attract traffic by utilizing traditional and nontraditional marketing techniques, such as advertising, publicity, submitting to search engines, posting to newsgroups and mailing lists, and by seeking partnerships or trading links with other sites.

But generating traffic to an uninteresting site is a waste of time and money. At the core of any successful site and Web-based business is content, a clear reason that entices people to visit. Sites must earn their repeat traffic and referrals by being useful and interesting. Any site that merits these advantages will get much more value out of any promotional resources, because users will like what they see and promote the site themselves via word-of-mouth. You must find a hook that makes your site important to a defined group of people.

In addition to identifying an interesting hook, you must execute site development so that it establishes your credibility among your users, to the degree that they will accept your affiliate product recommendations as honest and helpful. Credibility can be established by telling all sides of the story, investing heavily in your site's development, instituting professional-caliber production values, and paying attention to detail in every aspect of your operation, Web-based or otherwise.

Finally, to maximize your revenues, maintain quality, and intelligently prioritize future site development, you must study your users' habits and perceptions by analyzing traffic reports, conducting usability testing, and gathering feedback passively and actively.

The next chapter departs from the focus of the rest of the book, to discuss the strategies and options available to merchants that would like to create affiliate programs of their own.

# For Merchants: Building a Program

The body of this book has looked at affiliate programs from the point of view of the affiliate, or the potential affiliate; that is, companies and individuals who own Web sites and are interested in referring traffic to other sites—merchants—for a commission or other incentive. This chapter looks at this issue from the other side, from the point of view of the merchant interested in offering such a program to affiliates.

> **NOTE** Because most programs are offered by e-merchants, companies that sell physical products, we use the word *merchant* to refer to any site that offers an affiliate program. For our purposes, the word could also apply to sites that offer affiliate programs but that *don't* sell physical products, such as advertiser-sponsored sites that pay bounties for visitors, e-zine publishers that pay for user registrations, insurance brokerages that pay for lead generation, and the like.

Once the exclusive domain of large e-commerce sites, affiliate programs have been sprouting up on sites big and small, thanks largely to the array of third-party solutions providers that have emerged to help set up and administer such programs. Indeed, just about any site able to convert visitor traffic into revenue—by selling products, displaying ads, or any other means—is a candidate for paying other people to refer visitors to it.

# Why Start Your Own Affiliate Program?

Simply put, affiliate programs exist to generate traffic. But as we discussed in Chapter 10, "Increasing Hits and Selling More on Your Web Site," there are lots of ways to generate traffic. Why not just buy a banner ad placement on a major portal site? Isn't that easier? Why bother spending the time and expense of building an entire affiliate program?

> A merchant that can increase affiliate sales from 10 percent to 20 percent will be able to decrease sales and marketing expenses by 10 percent—savings that benefit the bottom line directly.
>
> —Jupiter Communications

## Low-Cost Customer Acquisition

The advertising and promotional budgets for many firms show that many Web sites are currently paying between $20 and $42 to acquire each new customer. Why, you might ask, would Barnes & Noble let you use a $10 coupon on a $12 book? Are its margins so steep that they still make almost $2? No, B&N is losing its shirt on such a transaction. But company managements sees this type of promotion as a long-term investment. If they can get you to buy from them once, there's a much better chance that you'll buy from them again, not just the next time you buy, but always, rather than going to Amazon.com or the Border's down the street. They think of each new customer in terms of that person's "lifetime value" to the company. (Lifetime value is notoriously difficult to estimate, given the newness of the Web.) As such, you will notice that many of the $10 coupons are good for "first-time customers" only.

**TIP** The first-time customer restriction is usually easy to foil. You can, for example, use a different e-mail address each time you buy; so, by opening a free, throwaway Hotmail account you can save 10 bucks.

While portal managers argue that they give merchants the opportunity to pay only from $.90 to $2.67 per customer, they have a much more difficult time proving that they contribute to customer retention—which is necessary if you want to generate repeat business, and hence, long-term profitability. And, portals, unlike affiliate sites, are notoriously broad in their reach and therefore cannot provide what affiliates can: the opportunity to address many different specialized markets (see the upcoming section *Extend Your Marketing Reach*). Furthermore, affiliates build your brand awareness on a more even playing field because you're not competing for attention with the portal's dominant brand. Affiliates also allow you to establish what amounts to a diverse (therefore robust) sales channel—in actuality, *multiple* sales channels—

each of which drives *new* customers to your site. Finally, the most important reason that affiliation tends to beat advertising hands down is that affiliate programs generally use the *pay-for-performance* model.

## Pay for Performance

Under the terms of affiliate programs, you pay only when a successful transaction takes place, whether that means a new visitor coming to your "front door," making a sale to a new or existing customer, or getting a sales lead. You designate the type of transaction for which you're willing to pay a commission or bounty. If you are not willing to pay for traffic only, you can establish a commission-based program, in which case, rather than paying per click-through on a banner ad placed on a high-traffic site, click-through is free. That means that your brand exposure is *absolutely free* unless it results in a sale on your site. This can be compared to placing a billboard along a busy highway and having to pay only if a driver pulls over and buys something from your corner store. And to extend this analogy, the billboard owners are responsible for placing the billboard and adding the marketing copy that will encourage the drivers to pull over.

The bottom line is that you don't have to spend a dime (except for setup costs) to acquire a new customer until that customer actually makes a purchase on your site. The pay-for-performance nature of commission-based affiliate programs makes them completely risk-free. In the pay-and-pray world of marketing, that's golden.

## Drive Traffic to Your Site

Let's say that you're *not* interested in acquiring more customers; rather, you're interested in acquiring more users for your free Web-based service. You're looking for a grassroots marketing strategy that can leverage the viral aspects of your new Web service and drive first-time users to your site. Many Web-based companies that offer free services have a difficult time reaching their core market segments through traditional on- and offline marketing methods because they can be prohibitively expensive (except to those firms with established brands). Additionally, it takes more than just an ad on a high-volume site to get the attention required to convince someone to register for yet another Web service.

Given the number of Web-based services floating around in cyberspace, you need something special to make your site rise above the noise, say something like having your site personally recommended by the Webmaster of a popular affinity site. (The fact that these Webmasters are receiving payments for making such recommendations is little known, or at least seems to be of little importance to many users.) In other words, effective grassroots marketing plans require active word-of-mouth promotion, and the best of it will come from respected, third-party sites with a broad reach of their own. Affiliate programs allow you to generate interest from third-party reviewers, essentially turning them into your own army of resellers and evangelists.

## Extend Your Marketing Reach

Affiliates act as the online equivalent of offline sales reps. Your affiliates, potentially hundreds or thousands of them, make up your reseller network, a network from which you can leverage the reach of topic experts, qualified content and commerce providers, and even over-the-top fanatics. In exchange for acting as members of your affiliate network, your affiliates receive a small percentage of the revenue that they generate—just as a salesperson would.

Affiliate programs also provide you, the merchant, with the opportunity to extend your reach to more niche-type segments that might be overlooked (by accident or by necessity) in your current market positioning strategy. In effect, it enables you to use in-context selling, which would be nearly impossible without providing the context portion—that is, the content—yourself. Here's an example: Let's say you're the Webmaster at an online bookseller, and one of the thousands of books that you sell is *A Guide to Zuni Fetishes*. Are you willing to dedicate a page of information about these small, stone totems carved by Native American artisans, which includes where to buy them, who the best carvers are, and what the fetishes represent to the Zuni people? How many marketing dollars would you want to spend advertising the newest *Guide to Zuni Fetishes* specifically to Zuni fetish collectors? Now, you could launch a marketing program aimed at driving Zuni fetish collectors to your site, but it would be a lot cheaper (and quicker) to determine where those collectors hang out on the Web (in newsgroups, mailing lists, etc.) and entice a few of them to become affiliates by offering to share your revenue with them. Those affiliates, in turn, would be tasked with driving the "right" people to your site. If it costs you $100 bucks in commissions to sell 100 copies through one affiliate, wouldn't you be delighted? You'd pay $100 for 100 customers—that's a dollar per customer. With the average cost of customer acquisition currently between $20 and $42, that's quite a bargain!

*Portal deals* are long-term, paid sponsorships by a merchant on a portal site (also called *portal tenancy deals)*. Refer back to Chapter 1, "Affiliate Selling: The Next Big Thing," for more on portals. These deals can be undertaken for years, but can also cost the sponsoring merchant more than $100 million dollars. Can you afford to cut a portal tenancy deal? If so, can you afford to maintain alternate deals so you're not dependent on one source for all of your sales leads?

## Competitive Necessity:
## The Next Land Grab

We're all familiar with the metaphor of the Web as a wide-open frontier, a nascent market where being the first to show up gave a merchant a good chance at becoming a market leader for the long term. That viewpoint spawned "land-grab" behavior, and spending money to acquire customers and market share became (and continues to be, for the time being) more important than demonstrating the ability to produce revenues, let alone profits.

Today, firms still spend a lot to acquire new customers, but affiliated selling has started a new land grab: the race to sign as many affiliates as possible before they sign with somebody else. Does your competitor offer an affiliate program? If not, there's a good chance that it will soon. If so, the features, terms, and service you offer should be at least as good as what your competitor offers to potential affiliates.

Recall from Chapter 8, "Planning Your Implementation," the concept of stickiness, the tendency for a service or feature to get users to stick with that service, not switch after they've visited or joined. (Web-based e-mail is the ultimate example of a sticky feature; who wants to switch to a different Web-based e-mail system after giving your e-mail address to everybody you know? It'd be like having to send change-of-address cards when you move.)

If there's anything potentially stickier than Web-based e-mail, it's affiliate programs, for a similar reason: the nature of their labor-intensive implementation. Once an affiliate searches for and finds an appropriate program, signs up with Merchant A, adds product links, and begins collecting commissions, it's difficult to entice that affiliate to abandon Merchant A's program in favor of a competitor's, Merchant B—even if Merchant B offers a slightly better commission rate or broader product selection. The advantages must outweigh the switching costs associated with transferring from one program to the next. These costs comprise not only the manual process of swapping out dozens, perhaps hundreds, of product links, but also breaking habits, such as an affiliate's pattern of checking his or her commission reports daily, perhaps from a reports page set to appear each time he or she logs on.

In the same way that e-merchants offer major incentives to encourage consumers to get into the habit of buying from them, you should consider offering enticing incentives aimed at signing as many affiliates as you can. As of this writing, there are more than 2 million affiliates out there, with more signing up each day. Though it is true that many join multiple programs, fewer join multiple programs within the same product category. Let's face it, there's not much reason to be a member of both Amazon's *and* Barnes & Noble's affiliate programs. So given the stickiness of affiliate programs in general, it behooves you to offer not only a competitive program, but to do it quickly.

Currently, there are more than 2,000 affiliate programs available. The Gartner Group predicts that the number of affiliate programs will grow to 100,000 by the year 2001! Will yours be one of them?

## How Affiliate Programs Work

Affiliate programs work by tracking affiliate referrals to and throughout your Web site. Tracking systems allow you to trace your customers' movements from the time they enter your site to the time they make a purchase, complete a form, or perform any other action. The more complex the affiliate program, the more complex the tracking tools must be. For instance, if you are offering a click-through affiliate program, you only need to be concerned with tracking the referring URL (which contains the affiliate's ID) and the page on which the URL was clicked (the referring site). In contrast, if you are offering a commission-based program, you need to track not only the initial visit, but subsequent activity as well, including any orders your visitors make. That means you need to follow the customer from the point where he or she clicks on the affiliate link to the point where they make a purchase; then you must record the details of the purchase (item quantity, prices, total sales, and so forth), and log the results in a database, from which later you will generate commissions reports that will be used by your affiliates, your company's managers, and any third-party you might use to cut checks to your affiliates.

Most commission-based or flat-fee programs require you to change your order confirmation page (also called a thank you, receipt, or fulfillment page) to include a unique order-tracking ID. This ID can be a transaction number or any other unique string of characters that indicate that a sale or lead has been made (i.e., that an exit page was reached). If you do not have the capabilities in-house to develop such tracking mechanisms, don't worry; you can purchase software or hire an affiliate solutions provider to make these types of changes.

## Starting an Affiliate Program

We'll assume that you've already registered your domain name and have designed and built your Web site (and added shopping/order-tracking functionality if you're selling products or services online). Now you're looking for an automated way to compensate other sites for referring traffic, leads, and/or buying customers to you. Before you begin building your own program from scratch, or searching for an affiliate solutions provider, or shopping for third-party affiliate software, answer these questions:

- What is your objective? Do you need more traffic to your Web site? More registered users? Do you need to increase sales?

- Who are the affiliates you're targeting? Are they members of your current user base?

- How much are you willing to pay to meet your objective? How many cents per click-through? How much per new registered user? What percentage of the sale?

- What's your development budget? How much can you spend to build the program's technical and business infrastructure? Can you afford to maintain it? To promote it?

- How quickly do you need to move? Did you need it yesterday? Do you have enough time to build your own?

- How will you promote the program? Will you need someone else to do it for you?

- What type of program and compensation terms are your competitors offering? Is there some way you can make your offering more appealing than theirs?

- What resources do you already have to work with? Will you need additional resources? Engineers to build it? Customer service reps to support it? Marketing personnel to design and promote it?

- Are there other technical constraints that you must consider? Do you have legacy back-end systems to reckon with?

- Is there potential for channel conflict or problems with your other business partners? Do you have existing contracts or business relationships that might conflict with aspects of your affiliate strategy? Do you have an existing reseller network whose members will be upset if you create an affiliate program that competes with their efforts?

Let's take a look at each of these questions in greater detail.

## What Are Your Objectives?

What is your primary objective for starting your own affiliate program? What is your secondary objective? As we've discussed throughout this book, there are many reasons for launching your own affiliate program. Are you looking to drive traffic to your site? Do you need more registered users to add to the value of your online community? Do you want to leverage the expertise and reach of Webmasters and convert them into a sales channel? Are you looking for a way to create a buzz around your site?

If you use a click-through program to drive traffic to your site, make sure it's relevant traffic you're driving and that valuable content is available when your visitors get there. The affiliate program should act only as a door to your site; it isn't intended to replace the need for a solid foundation, attractive décor, and purpose. Again, your affiliate program is an invitation to the party, not the party itself. If there is nothing worthwhile once they arrive, your money will be poorly spent.

Do you seek to add members to your online service or community? If so, offer an incentive to join and additional incentives to encourage others to join, and make sure to dangle the carrot in a valuable spot. For example, you probably want more than just another username showing up in your database; what you'd really like are visitors who actually use the service or participate in the community you've so painstakingly created for them. So why not offer affiliate fees for referring new users who complete specific actions, say for creating and moderating a message board. Then encourage those new users to act as affiliates by offering them a few cents for every new user they sign up who participates on their new message board. Don't get us wrong; we're not suggesting you pay everyone for every action they make within your service or community—especially if you're a free service—but this is a great way to get the user acquisition ball rolling in a good direction.

Are you trying to increase sales? Commission-based incentives are probably your best bet, unless your product involves complex or customized pricing, as with build-to-order computers, travel packages, and insurance products. For these, a flat rate (such as $25 for each insurance policy sold) can be much simpler, as well as dramatically appealing to affiliates.

## Whom Are You Targeting?

Before you start defining, building, and promoting your program, you need to perform an affiliate analysis to determine exactly the makeup of your target audience. You can cast your net to catch as narrow or broad an affiliate audience as you need, as long as you know at whom you're aiming before you cast it.

Are you looking to convert your existing user base into affiliates? If so, how Web-savvy are they? Will you need to educate them about the benefits of affiliate sales, or will they already have some familiarity with the concept and its reward system? Or do you want to leverage the existing affiliate channel (built by other online merchants) made up of Web-savvy individuals with experience and clear goals for earning good commissions from the products and service they promote? In this case, you'll spend less time on educating and more on describing your key differentiators relative to other affiliate programs.

Finally, consider the type of affiliate you need to drive the *right* users, traffic, or sales leads to your site. Do you really want to attract Webmasters from gaming sites to join your affiliate program for your Conservative Silk Ties Galore site? We think not. Do you want to attract the Webmaster from a popular online high-tech community to join the program for your software developer online recruiting service? Definitely.

## How Much Are You Willing to Pay?

Now that you know whom you're targeting and why, you need to figure out how to entice them. How much can you afford to invest to acquire one new user/visitor? One new customer? To make one more sale? This is a tricky game: Aim too high and you give away the farm. Aim too low, and no new chickens will roost there. Be aware that most affiliate program terms allow merchants to change the incentive structure as needed. But this option is best used carefully or you risk upsetting or confusing your hard-won affiliate base.

If your margins are steep, don't be stingy. Better to share the spoils with your affiliate partners than to miss out on the land-grab for potential affiliates to your competitors who offered more. If you're selling a low-margin or high-ticket item, then either offer a flat-rate lead amount or a small percentage of the sale (for example, at the time of this writing, Dell gives 1 percent commission for sales).

Haven't got a product to sell? Offer $.02 per click-through to your site. Just interested in boosting brand awareness? Try using a pay-per-impression compensation model (of which banner ads are just one example). You get the picture. Structure the incentive to deliver exactly what you need. This could be the most strategic decision you make about your new affiliate program.

## What's Your Development Budget?

We'll assume you've decided you need a program and that you want to move fast. How many development dollars do you have to spend on building your affiliate program? Can you afford to outsource the whole enchilada if you have to? Have you earmarked the marketing dollars required to define, design, and promote the program?

Building an affiliate program can cost anywhere from a couple of hundred dollars to $6,000 or more, depending on the complexity of your offering and your degree of participation. If you have no money to spend, but you do have time on your side, your best bet is to either invest in a low cost third-party tool or build the software you need yourself. If you have some money but no time, consider hiring an affiliate solutions provider (see the upcoming section, *Third-Party Tools*, and this book's companion Web site at www.affilateselling .com for a list). If you have no money and no time, you may be in over your head if you launch a program. Although affiliate programs can be launched for less than two hundred dollars, it takes time and money to maintain and support them. Don't build a program unless you intend to keep it running for the life of your business.

In addition to development costs, you'll have to allocate resources to promotion, maintenance, support, and affiliate reporting. Even if you're targeting only 100 affiliates, producing quarterly commission reports and writing checks takes time (and costs your company additional processing fees). Be prepared, but don't panic. If you find your affiliate base is growing out of your control and you secure the capital required to outsource it, it's fairly easy to upgrade your a homegrown program to either a more robust version or to another program provided by a third-party.

## How Quickly Do You Need to Move?

Do you have a few months to define and build your affiliate program, including time for testing, tweaking, adjusting, and troubleshooting? Or did your VP of sales and marketing just tell you that you're responsible for showing affiliate revenue on your next quarterly earnings report?

Typically, it takes anywhere from a few hours to six weeks to build a program. Note we didn't say to *define* a program. Defining a program—deciding whom you're targeting, what you're offering them, and how it will all work with your existing architecture—can takes weeks or months, depending on who's involved in the process. Can your team move as quickly as they need to? Do they have the know-how to make these decisions in a timely manner? If you need a program yesterday and you think you'll need a lot of assistance getting it off the ground, consider hiring a consultant, not only to lend expertise, but to cut through interdepartmental conflict and politics with objectivity, and offer take-it-or-leave-it advice. If you want to and can afford to outsource it all, use an affiliate solutions provider.

## How Will You Promote the Program?

Do you have anyone on your staff with the time and know-how to promote your new program? Promoting your program is similar to, but not the same as, promoting your Web site. You'll need someone who knows the difference and who has up-to-date knowledge of what's going on in the world of Web affiliation.

There are a few exceptional affiliate directories online where you can promote your affiliate program for free, including AssociatePrograms.com, Associate-It, CashPile, ClickQuick, and Refer-It (go to www.affiliateselling.com for others). But how do you reach individuals who know nothing about affiliate programs? Where do you go to nab *them*? Certainly you can advertise on your own site, but if you're a new Web-based service with 300 registered users, you might need some external influence as well.

The bottom line is, you need to develop a plan of attack for promoting your program and have the attackers on hand to execute. The directories can get you on the typical affiliate's radar screen, but unless you have a marketing communications person or a department with free capacity, you might need assistance from an affiliate solution provider to really spread the word (for a fee, of course).

## What's the Competition Offering?

Affiliate programs can increase traffic, sales, and brand awareness, the three crucial reasons for starting an affiliate program. Though sometimes it's okay to share a user with a competitor, if your competitor snags that user as an affiliate, guess whose site that user is going to promote to his or her friends, family, and colleagues? Most Web-based companies still depend on "word-of-mouse" to drive traffic, make sales, and build their brand, but money is talking louder than ever before on the Web. Though some will refer for free, others charge a fee—and refer far more.

The key is: Make the best offer you can afford to secure that initial relationship—that sticky relationship in which your loyal user invests in your site by committing as an affiliate. As stated earlier, once someone signs up with a given affiliate program, adds links to his or her site, and starts promoting heavily, the costs of switching programs are too high, and even if you're offering a better deal, it might be too late.

So spend the time it takes to find out what your competitors are offering; then offer something better. It doesn't necessarily have to be a higher commission percentage or higher flat fee. Offer more powerful features and more affiliate-friendly terms; for example, more flexible linking options (like e-mail-based links or co-branded store fronts), better online reporting tools, a cooler interface, fewer restrictions, or a lower minimum threshold. Be creative.

## Do You Need Additional Resources?

If your site is up and running with full e-commerce functionality, you have a team of engineers chomping at the bit to take on a new challenge and a marketing department that wants to be 100 percent hands on when it comes to defining and building your affiliate program, and you are all aware that cutting checks, generating affiliate commission reports, and handling support issues are significant challenges, you're probably a good candidate for building an affiliate program from scratch. If you're up for it, and you have the support, a primary advantage is that you won't have to share a dime of affiliate revenue with an affiliate solutions provider. And if you need help getting started, try one of the third-party software tools described later in this chapter.

More likely, you are part of a typical Web-based company that just plain doesn't have the time or the people required to build a full-fledged affiliate program in the time frame set to meet your company's goals. Or, perhaps, you're looking for the opportunity to partner with one of the better-known affiliate solutions providers. In these cases, it's probably worth the dollars (about $5,000) to get a jump-start on your program development (programs can be custom-built in one to six weeks), and not disrupt or, heaven forbid, slip the deliverable dates on your other development projects. Affiliate solutions providers can help you define, build, launch, promote, and maintain your affiliate program. You simply decide how much you're willing to contribute to the cause (either resources or dollars).

## Are There Other Technical Constraints?

Will an affiliate program work with your current system architecture? Will a third-party integration require more than a few hours to implement? Are you aiming for a commission-based program but haven't added e-commerce functionality to your site yet?

Depending on the amount of money and time you have, this aspect of starting an affiliate program could be very scary or a walk in the park. Do you have time to reconstruct pieces of your architecture or to build the necessary pieces to implement the type of program you want? You have a few choices when you encounter technology constraints:

- You can build or rebuild.

- You can pay someone else to build or rebuild (there are many companies that offer e-commerce software, such as shopping carts, personalization engines, gift registries, credit card services to merchants, and so forth).

- You can choose a different type of program. For example, if you have no e-commerce functionality but offer a catalog and an 800-number for ordering, you could offer a flat fee for referrals to your Call to Order page. Then all you'll have to do is to track the referral ID through your service and request the affiliate's ID when the user clicks the Order button.

It's the combination of the answers to all of these questions that will help you determine whether you should tackle your affiliate program using the internal resources at your disposal to build your own affiliate program from scratch, buy affiliate sales software to integrate to your existing site, or outsource it all (or most of it all) to an affiliate solutions provider.

# Is There Potential for Channel Conflict?

Finally, you must consider how an affiliate program will mesh with your other business relationships. Do you have any exclusive relationships that would prevent or complicate your implementing an affiliate program? In particular, are there any online or offline resellers who would have concerns—legitimate or not—or outright rage if you began signing up "just anybody" to act, in effect, as a reseller? Keep in mind the frequently voiced trade-offs: Traditional resellers usually offer additional service or domain expertise about your products, whereas dime-a-dozen affiliates might not know anything about your products. At first blush, this is a simple quality versus quantity debate. A closer look reveals that quality traditional resellers almost always offer your competitors' products as well, and so-called dime-a-dozen resellers are often extremely knowledgeable about their subject matter and, possibly, your products. In fact, a devoted affiliate may know more than a lot of not-so-devoted resellers.

To solve this conundrum, take a good look at your existing distribution network to see how it might successively coexist with an affiliate network. Can you offer better commissions to those—whether affiliates or traditional reseller—that surpass a predetermined sales volume threshold? Traditional resellers are all too familiar with such tier structures (silver/gold/platinum levels, and so forth).

You might even present your affiliate network as an easy way for your resellers to make money directly from their Web sites, without ever having to deal directly with customers. For traditional resellers too small or slow to offer e-commerce directly from their own sites, your affiliate program might provide the low-cost way to create a Web-based revenue model for themselves. Some resellers are notoriously lax about following up on what they regard as minor leads, because they must spend their limited time beating bigger bushes. Therefore, providing a zero-labor, secondary revenue stream can result in a win-win-win for them, you, and the customer who might otherwise go underserved.

In this light, you might suggest to your resellers that they use your affiliate program to provide their customers with Web-based, self-serve access to items that the resellers do not have the desire or resources to sell directly. Low-ticket, low-margin items (such as power cords and other electronics accessories) are the sort of thing that resellers tend not to stock; or sadly, some seem to regard it as an imposition to have to make such items available to their "smaller" customers. Under the terms of your affiliate program, however, resellers could, at their discretion, direct their visitors to you for such low-margin items, meanwhile directing users to themselves for higher-ticket items or those requiring the value-added by resellers (consults, installation, integration, service contracts, and so on). As long as your pricing does not undercut your channel partners, you should be able to come up with a solution that's good for both you and your resellers. (If your direct-sale prices *do* compete directly with your resellers, then an affiliate program probably is not the source of channel conflict, but it may act as a catalyst that forces your company to decide whether it wants to be a wholesale or direct sales firm.)

## Affiliate Solutions Providers/ Affiliate Networks

If you choose to use an affiliate solutions provider, probably it's because you 1) require a robust affiliate program, 2) don't have the bandwidth to build and maintain your own program within the required time frame, 3) believe the partnership with the affiliate solutions provider will help drive traffic to your site. These are all good reasons. Affiliate solutions providers (ASPs) are companies that provide a number of services (usually packaged based on different types of requirements) to merchants that want to offer an affiliate program to generate traffic and/or increase sales. If you decide you use an ASP to help you develop your program, in addition to providing the technical infrastructure, the ASP will promote the affiliate program, pay commissions to affiliates, police affiliate sites (to ensure they aren't promoting offensive material), provide customer support/service, and supply reporting tools so affiliates can track their earnings, and merchants can track their affiliates' activity.

All that said, it's important that you recognize that you'll still have to spend the time it takes to add the affiliate program to your Web site. Initially, on partnering with an affiliate solutions provider, you'll describe your program requirements and the ASP will offer a somewhat customized solution. Once you agree on the solution and the price for that solution, you're ready to begin. Your responsibilities at this point will depend on the solution you've chosen. Typically, you pay the affiliate solutions provider a set fee to launch, then a percentage of the payout you make to affiliates on an ongoing basis.

In the subsections that follow, we describe the services and benefits offered by some of today's most prominent affiliate solutions providers: BeFree, Commission Junction, and LinkShare. Also be sure to read the sidebar *PeopleScape: A Case Study* for an example of a company that shopped around to determine which of these affiliate solutions providers' services were most appropriate. (This book's companion Web site contains updated lists and reviews of major solutions providers.)

# BeFree

BeFree (www.befree.com) is a leading provider of performance marketing technology and services. BeFree helps top-tier merchants build and manage affiliate programs (in other words, online sales channels) that carry the merchants' brand, which enables revenue generation by selling products in context on affiliated sites throughout the Web. Each BeFree implementation is customized to fit the individual needs of their merchants. Its offerings are extensive, and include powerful tools that enable merchants to build their programs, generate popular revenue tracking/usage reports, and communicate with affiliates on a one-to-one or one-to-many basis.

> **NOTE** BeFree is one of the most costly and time-intensive solutions, so it isn't for mid- or low-budget companies seeking to "test" an affiliate program for their site.

With BeFree, your affiliates' personal information is kept confidential when they join your program; you don't have to share their contact info (e-mail address) with BeFree or other participating merchants. This type of partnership is especially important for sites with strict privacy policies that state restrictions regarding direct marketing.

BeFree's impressive list of merchants reads like a veritable Who's Who of Web category-killers, including BabyCenter, eToys, Barnes & Noble, Reel.com, Travelocity.com, CNet, Yahoo! GeoCities, and many more. If you consider your site to be a category-killer—or intend to position your site as one—you should consider BeFree.

## *What You Get*

When you join BeFree's list of category-killer merchants, you get a performance marketing tool that enables you to enroll, track, and manage affiliates. You can:

- Offer a branded affiliate program built, maintained, hosted, and audited by a dependable third party.
- Reach more than 1.75 million existing affiliates (and affiliate recruiting services).
- List your company alongside other category-killers.
- Offer your affiliate program to anyone with a Web site or just an e-mail address (your affiliates don't have to have a Web site to act as an e-marketer for you).

- Send targeted messages and e-mail to specific affiliates (or groups of affiliates) based on their number of impressions, click-throughs, and other performance criteria.

- Provide flexible compensation for affiliates; you can set up five different compensation tiers based on performance levels and/or incentives; pay accelerated commissions for a specified period of time, or after a specified performance level has been reached, and so forth.

- Measure your success by generating more than 75 different reports.

- Access key metrics (such as click-through rates, impressions, and net shipped sales) without running reports.

- Change your site's navigation/flow as often as you like without invalidating your existing links.

- Enable your affiliates to create links to different areas of your site by offering product links, product category links, a search box, a link to online promotions, a link to your home page—even a prefabricated storefront that contains many different types if links.

- Offer your affiliates a co-branded sign-up and account management site (www.reporting.net) that lets them create a variety of affiliate links (text, banners, images, and prefabricated storefronts); give them access to more than 15 online reports; send them targeted messages, give them marketing tips; provide account maintenance (in other words, enable them to change their password, and so forth). Figure 11.1 shows an example of the Lycos Reporting.net site.

## Outsource Everything

BeFree offers additional services for merchants that don't have the bandwidth to run a full-scale affiliate program and don't want to hire additional help to do so. You can use BeFree to provide e-mail-based support to your affiliates, implement promotional campaigns, review applicants, and even cut checks. You name it, BeFree offers it.

## Getting Started

Because BeFree customizes each affiliate program implementation to meet the needs of its merchants, no online sign-up process is available. Rather, you must complete the BeFree online form to request additional information. This will be followed by a discussion about your needs/requirements, which will be followed by a proposed solution.

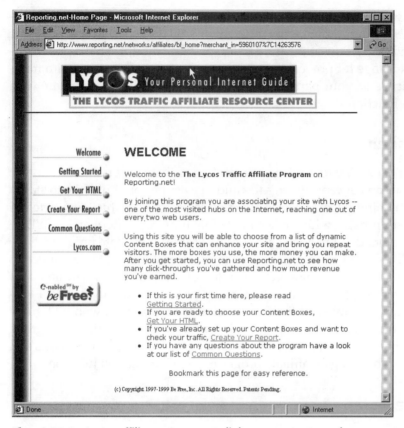

**Figure 11.1** Lycos affiliates can create links, run reports, and get answers to questions from Reporting.net.

Read the sidebar *PeopleScape: A Case Study* for an example of the costs and requirements of building an affiliate program with BeFree. Again, each implementation is customized, so this is just an example.

# Commission Junction

Commission Junction (www.cj.com) enables you, the merchant, to quickly establish a pay-per-click, pay-per-lead, or pay-per-sale program (or any combination of these programs) and connect to a network of prescreened affiliates. (See Chapter 2, "Types of Programs," for an explanation of these types of affiliate programs.) Commission Junction manages your entire affiliate program, including affiliate recruiting, affiliate approval, online tracking and reporting, and commission payments. You can even earn affiliate revenue yourself by recruiting your own affiliates via Commission Junction's Web site.

As of this writing, Commission Junction offers affiliate solutions for a one-time fee of $795, a minimum escrow amount of $250 (which is used to pay your affiliates), and 20 percent of the transaction payout amount. That's pretty reasonable in exchange for powerful reporting tools at your fingertips with minimal maintenance on your part. Currently, 230 merchants have signed up with Commission Junction.

### Getting Started

Whether you're looking to offload your existing affiliate program onto another vendor so you can concentrate on sales and marketing, or you'd like to start a new program, joining Commission Junction is pretty easy. Just complete the four-step sign-up page, which takes just a few minutes. Afterward, you'll be prompted to upload the banners and/or links for your affiliate program.

Next you'll configure the exit page of your site to enable Commission Junction to calculate the credit commissions generated by your affiliates. Within about 48 hours of reaching this point in the sign-up process, you will receive a telephone call from a member of the Commission Junction team, who will guide you through the remaining setup procedures for your new affiliate program. Read the sidebar titled *PeopleScape: A Case Study* for an example of the costs and requirements of building an affiliate program with Commission Junction.

## LinkShare

LinkShare (www.linkshare.com) was the first affiliate solutions provider on the scene, and it currently boasts partnerships with more than 400 merchants representing a broad range of products and services. LinkShare offers merchants the ability to create affiliate programs using the LinkShare Network (a marketplace where merchants and affiliates come together to form partnerships), a Private Label Network, or a combination of the two.

LinkShare lets you:

- Offer a branded affiliate program that is built, maintained, hosted, and audited by a dependable third party.
- Control your brand by blocking competitive programs.
- Reach more than 2 million affiliates.
- Highlight your affiliate program on the affiliate login page.
- Send targeted, customized e-mails to affiliates based on site category, join date, demographics, and so forth.
- Provide one location from which your affiliates can join your program, access reports, create links, update their account information, and receive targeted messages from you.

- Compensate different affiliates using different methods or combinations of methods, based on numbers of impressions, click-through rate, commission percentages, return days, monthly minimums, or any combination of these.

- Group affiliates in order to create and track offers targeted toward specific market segments.

- Dynamically update your links, images, and promotional copy easily from any computer connected to the Internet.

- Provide your affiliate with a variety of linking options: text, banners, images, search boxes, or virtual storefronts (containing products you can change as often as you'd like).

### Getting Started

You must install LinkShare's Synergy software on your server in order to accurately track, manage, and evaluate your affiliate transactions. (Upgrades are installed automatically through the LinkShare Network.) Synergy enables LinkShare to track visitors from when they click on a link on an affiliate's referring Web site to the point at which they complete a transaction on your (the merchant's) site. It usually takes about two to three days to install Synergy. Check LinkShare's Web site for a list of compatible e-commerce engines.

LinkShare does not have an online sign-up process. Rather, you must complete its online form to request additional information. You'll receive a call from a sales representative, with whom you can discuss your needs/requirements in order to estimate an implementation fee. See the sidebar titled *PeopleScape: A Case Study* for an example of the costs and requirements of building an affiliate program with LinkShare. As for the other services, the specifics will vary based on your individual criteria and parameters.

## Third-Party Tools

If you'd rather build and maintain your own affiliate program, you have a few options. One is to buy and integrate a third-party script that enables you to automate the affiliate sign-up process, track revenue, and perform some

**NOTE** The market for third-party tools changes rapidly. Check out this book's companion Web site at www.affiliateselling.com for a current list (including where to find them), plus reviews of the most popular tools available.

## PEOPLESCAPE: A CASE STUDY

PeopleScape (www.peoplescape.com) is a next-generation services company, offering a new model for hiring great people. It delivers powerful staffing solutions and human resource information tools for high-growth, high-technology companies nationwide. As your strategic staffing partner, PeopleScape helps you find and retain the industry's best talent.

### The Initial Program
PeopleScape pays affiliates $2 for each referral who: 1) completes the registration form on www.peoplescape.com and 2) is in sales, marketing or a technical field involved with the Internet, new media or hi-tech industry.

### Valid Registration
- A registration will include at a minimum: name, company, title, e-mail, phone number and/or zip code.
- The individual must be in sales, marketing, or a technical field, and have experience in the Internet, new media, or hi-tech industry.

### Payment
Participants will be paid on a monthly or quarterly basis, and a $25 minimum must be accrued before a check is cut. The time frame will depend on the capabilities of the affiliate solution provider chosen. Due to PeopleScape's current size, the affiliate solutions provider will have to offer check payment services.

### Who Can Participate
All sites must be approved by PeopleScape in order to participate. It is important to PeopleScape to manage its brand by choosing appropriate affiliates.

### Affiliate Marketing Companies
Initially, PeopleScape will roll out the program on an individual basis, based on demand generated through one of these affiliate solution providers:
- BeFree
- Commission Junction
- LinkShare

### Target Web Sites
Target sites are those that attract the candidate community such as:
- Industry Insite
- MBAZone
- Infomediary
- Golden Parachute

### Cost
Cost considerations are important to PeopleScape, which is in a high-growth phase and needs to spend its dollars and resources wisely. PeopleScape's goal is to focus at this stage on guerrilla marketing techniques to build its database.

Once it reaches critical mass, the company will begin to spend more dollars on a branding campaign.

### Technical Considerations

It is important that the PeopleScape engineering team invest minimal time in the project, so as not to necessitate pushing back the delivery dates of their current engineering efforts.

### Comparison of Proposals

|  | *BeFree* | *Commission Junction* | *LinkShare* |
| --- | --- | --- | --- |
| **Startup cost** | $5,000 | $795; $250 in escrow account | $5,000 first-year software licensing fee; $1,000 license renewal fee |
| **Per lead cost** | 25%, or $3,000 per month, which-ever is greater | 20% | 25%, or $2,000, whichever is greater |
| **Bill payment cost** | $1 per check, plus postage | $0 | $1.5 per check, plus postage |
| **Relationships with target** | N/A | N/A | N/A |
| **Advertise to affiliates** | Yes, strong program | Yes | Yes |
| **Access to account manager** | Yes | Yes | Need $2,500 in affiliate-generated sales to have an assigned account manager; help desk is available otherwise |
| **Work with IQ.com** | Yes | Yes | Yes |
| **Ability to track complete registrations** | Yes | Yes | Yes |
| **Well funded?** | Second-round $25M from VCs, 4/99 | $7M from CyberCash | Revenue supported; have not taken significant funding |

*Continues*

**PEOPLESCAPE: A CASE STUDY** *(Continued)*

**Comparison of Proposals**

| | BeFree | Commission Junction | LinkShare |
|---|---|---|---|
| Online reporting (for PeopleScape) | Need CD from BeFree | Yes | Yes |
| Will customize lead fee for target affiliates | N/A | Yes | Yes |
| Time for setup | Average 4 weeks once contract is signed | 2 days, after payment is received | 3–4 weeks |
| Ability to manually approve affiliates? | Yes | Yes | Yes |
| Difficulty of integrating system into PeopleScape technology | High; 20–25 hours of programming time from our engineers | Low; 30–60 minutes | 6–8 hours |

**The Winner**
PeopleScape chose Commission Junction because of its low startup fees, quick setup time, and ease of integrating the program technology into its own.

For an update on PeopleScape's affiliate program, go to this book's companion Web site at www.affiliateselling.com. To join PeopleScape's affiliate program, go to www.peoplescape.com.

report generation. If you have a few techies onboard who have a few hours to bring your affiliate program to life, try one of the following third-party tools. Some argue that these tools are as robust as those offered by affiliate solutions providers, just a lot less snazzy. Here we describe three of the most popular third-party tools (scripts, really) available, including the benefits of using them.

# AffiliateZone.com

AffiliateZone's Affiliate Link software offers an inexpensive, complete, easy-to-use affiliate program solution. The software is installed on your server by

AffiliateZone's programmers, which means you can spend more time promoting your site and less time maintaining your affiliate program. Affiliate Link supports one- and two-tier pay-per-sale (commission-based), pay-per-clicks, and pay-per-sign-up programs, and enables you to offer customized commission rates for different affiliates. Its automated affiliate sign-up procedure and affiliate management and e-mail notification tools will keep you in close contact with your affiliates, which is key to any successful business partnership.

Find out more about Affiliate Link by visiting www.affiliatezone.com. For a $75 setup fee and a monthly charge of $29.95, many agree that this powerful tool is quite a deal. We recommend you take advantage of AffiliateZone's online demo at www.affiliatezone.com/al16plusdemo to see if its solution is powerful enough to meet your needs.

## The Affiliate Program™

The Affiliate Program software comes completely customized, and is installed on your server, for anywhere from $499 to $1,245. Are you currently processing orders using shopping-cart software, or receiving faxed or phoned-in orders? It doesn't matter. The Affiliate Program can be customized to work with most existing order-processing technologies. With The Affiliate Program Software, you can customize commission rates for your affiliates and offer multiple banner support, multiple click-through page support, two-tier commissions, and more. The program also provides administrative pages for both you and your affiliates. You can track traffic, banner location (where your banner appears on your affiliates' Web sites), and all methods of sales (phone, e-mail, and Web). Your affiliates can track their revenue earnings and statistical data (click-through rates, and so forth).

Finally, using The Affiliate Program, your affiliates receive an e-mail notification when a sale is made, plus automatic monthly statements and customized thank-you pages seen by their referrers (if you want them to) when they complete a sale at your site. You also get a few "treats," like the ability to send out a broadcast e-mail to all of your affiliates and a nice little e-mail reminder that tells you when it's time to cut the checks.

To find out more about The Affiliate Program software, check out www .theaffiliateprogram.com/features.htm.

## Groundbreak.com

Groundbreak.com, one the hottest affiliate program toolmakers, offers a full-featured affiliate program CGI script that integrates with your existing payment system on your server. Groundbreak's Ultimate Affiliate software offers a low-budget solution ($100 for the script, $100 for customization, as of this writing) that enables you to recruit affiliates and give them access to a detailed statistics page that tracks their referrals and their commission earnings. You can edit the affiliate CGI script; add, view, or delete affiliates; view or add the commissions due to those affiliates; and track your traffic through a detailed administration page.

This is not a solution for a site that is looking only to drive more traffic to its content, but it's a good choice for a well-established e-commerce site with a spare programmer or two on hand to integrate the script to your Web site. Take a few minutes to review the program demo at www.groundbreak.com/demo.html.

# Building a Program from Scratch

If you're one of many who thinks it's wasteful to pay for a CGI script when you can write your own, you're probably a candidate for building your affiliate program from scratch. Certainly doing so isn't rocket science; it just takes a lot of time to develop, and more time and resources to support. The following sections provide an overview of the typical requirements for designing, developing, and supporting an affiliate program without the assistance of third-party affiliate solutions providers or toolmakers.

## Your Team

Before embarking on the task, make sure you've got the staff required to handle all of the program-building tasks (though it may be possible for some talented individuals to wear multiple hats):

**Affiliate program manager.** The affiliate program manager is tasked with designing and implementing the affiliate program. This person should have a clear understanding of your company's business model and how affiliate selling plays into your business and/or user acquisition goals. The program manager interfaces with your customers, your marketing/business development teams, and, of course, your engineering team, to define and deliver your homegrown affiliate program. This manager should either recruit or solicit the following assistance: affiliate administrator, customer service/support analyst, and accountant, all of which are defined here.

**Affiliate administrator.** The affiliate administrator is the equivalent of an account executive. This person will handle your premiere (or premium) affiliates, such as the owners of high-volume Web sites or Webmasters who send a significant number of new customers to your site on consistent basis.

**Accountant/bookkeeper.** The accountant or bookkeeper is responsible for generating revenue reports (or at least reading through them) and for using accounting software to produce affiliate earnings in the form of paper checks that are mailed to the right person at the right time. His or her job is to ensure that affiliates are paid on time, after, of course, they meet the required minimum earnings threshold. (The accountant is also responsible for generating the subthreshold checks, payable to those affiliates who fail to reach their threshold but must be paid in order to balance the books at the end of the fiscal year.)

**Customer service/support analyst.** The customer service/support analyst is responsible for fielding phone calls (or, preferably, e-mails) from affiliates who need, for example, assistance placing links or generating revenue reports, or who simply prefer to contact you directly rather than use the FAQ and help pages available via your Web site. If you don't provide online reporting tools (or used a third-party solution that does), consider hiring additional customer service analysts to handle the onslaught of customer inquiries. The bottom line is that you should expect questions and comments from your affiliates. After all, there's money involved.

## Costs

The costs of building your own affiliate program can range from a couple of hundred dollars to tens of thousands of dollars, depending on whether you need to add people to your development team, shuffle revenue-generating deliverables to make room in the development schedule, pay to promote your program, and so forth. This section provides some guidelines for preparing for the costs involved in designing and building a homegrown affiliate program.

### Development Time

Even if you use an affiliate solutions provider, you're going to end up spending time adding an affiliate program to your Web site. As previously mentioned, the most complicated pieces for which you'll need to allocate resources are the tracking system and the reporting tools.

It's imperative that you use dependable tracking software so that you can effectively and efficiently monitor the sales you make through your affiliate channels. (Affiliates should require it.) Tracking software costs anywhere between $250 dollars and $20,000. This book's companion Web site at www.affiliateselling.com contains a list of tracking software applications.

Your marketing department, executive team, and affiliates will want to be able to track performance, revenue, and a plethora of usage statistics. A thorough description of how to design reports and present them to these three eager groups could fill a book of its own, so the best we can do here is to provide a few guidelines. First, evaluate how your affiliates are performing, both as an aggregate unit as well as on an individual basis. These are the nitty-gritty details, which should include the following if you're an e-merchant:

- Number of hits/visitors/unique visitors per day or week
- Click-through rates
- Number of items ordered
- Name of item(s) ordered
- Revenue generated per item
- Referral fee amount for each item
- Total amount earned by the affiliate

From these data, you'll be able to derive a list of your money-makers (in other words, the best-performing affiliates and products). You'll need this list before you can make such managerial decisions as offering additional incentives, removing nonperformers, optimizing your affiliate approval process, and so on. Furthermore, you'll want to make much of this information available to your affiliates so that they will be able to better manage their links that point users to your site. Many homegrown affiliate programs send affiliates a regular report via e-mail, like the one from Amazon.com shown in Figure 11.2 (Amazon now provides Web-based reports as well).

### Marketing

Once you have established your affiliate program, how will you promote it? If your site already draws heavy traffic, then placing a big button on your home page (linking to a page explaining why and how to join your program) is probably your single best solution.

Beyond promotion on your own site, there are other options. First take a look at advertising on venues related to affiliation in general, such as directories like Refer-It.com, Associate-It, and ClickQuick. And of course consider traditional online marketing activities, such as banner advertising (or participating in banner exchanges), provided you can find sites whose audience is likely to be interested in becoming your affiliates. (Refer to Chapter 10, "Increasing Hits and Selling More on Your Web Site," for more on Web promotion in general.)

## Order Processing and Follow-Up

Most merchants have already solved the problem of order processing by the time they set up an affiliate program, but if you're new to selling online, you'll need to make sure you can handle the additional traffic your affiliates send to your site. Your affiliates are depending on you to provide their referrals with

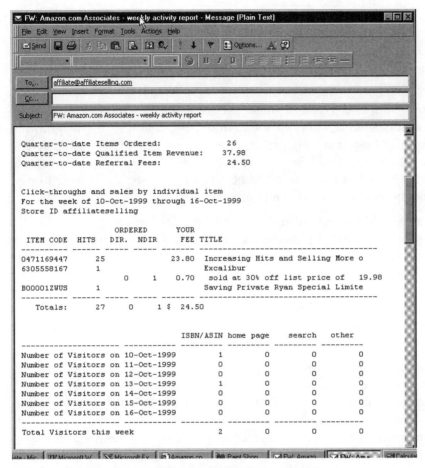

**Figure 11.2** A quarterly activity report from Amazon.com.

timely, accurate, secure order processing. Here's a checklist for those new to the fulfillment game:

**Credit card processing.** Your affiliates are driving traffic to your new e-commerce site, but how are you planning to fill all of the new orders? While it requires more effort to accept credit cards than it does to receive checks, in this day and age, not accepting credit cards online is a nonstarter. Not only have consumers come to expect the convenience and instant gratification afforded by Web-based credit card transactions, failure to accept cards marks any site as unprofessional, unwilling to make a serious investment in its business. This perception may be okay for hobbyist sites, small nonprofit organizations, and the like, but even they will suffer eventually by the absence of this near-ubiquitous convenience. But we're assuming that if you're reading this, at a minimum you almost certainly need to accept credit cards on your site. Beyond that, keep your ears to the ground for signs that digital wallet, micropayment, or other payment mechanisms are making headway in the market. As any new money-transfer standard becomes widely adopted, you'll want to support it also.

**Customer support.** If your affiliate program is at all successful, you can expect to see an upsurge in traffic and sales, followed by a significant increase in customer support/service calls or e-mails. Ensure that you have a dedicated phone line (preferably a toll-free number) and an e-mail address (something like service@merchant.com) used exclusively to support customers both during and after the sale.

**Fulfillment, shipping, and delivery.** Making the ordering process quick and simple is one thing; delivering in a timely manner is another. Be sure that you offer reasonable shipping fees and services (include second-day and over-night delivery, for an extra fee). Sometimes a successful impulse purchase is completely dependent on how fast the customer can get his or her hands on the item. Let the customer decide how desperate he or she is to receive the new toy. Finally, choose a delivery company that you can depend on to ship your products on time and in good condition.

**Returns.** Establish a return policy and post it clearly to your customers. Perhaps insert it on (or one click away from) your order-processing page(s). Also make sure that your affiliate agreement states in no uncertain terms how you intend to handle returns with respect to accounting for affiliate commissions. Let's say, for instance, you pay an affiliate his or her commission but then the customer returns the product for which that commission was earned. Do you have a plan in place for handling this? Will you send a bill to the affiliate? Though not ideal, this is how some programs handle this problem. Will you deduct that amount from a future commission check? The simplest and best solution is to withhold making commission payments until the item's return period has expired (typically 30 days). And note: Affiliate reports that list up-to-the-minute commissions should include a clearly visible disclaimer that details your practice of reducing commissions for any products returned by customers.

**Affiliate revenue tracking.** As previously mentioned, you must track the sales generated by each affiliate, in order to log their commissions accurately. Some merchants choose to provide real-time online reporting tools to affiliates so that the affiliates can check the status of their account as frequently as they like. The more self-service tools you provide, the lower will be your costs associated with supplying manual affiliate customer service and support. For instance, providing a report that shows when an affiliate's check was mailed will prevent the majority of phone calls asking that question. Make sure to make such reports and features easy to find on your affiliate's administration pages. Log your customer support calls to see which additional features can be automated on the Web; and use your phone system's audio directory ("Press 1 for more options") to point callers to self-service features on the Web, to prevent their using your costly phone support personnel for things they prefer to do online anyway. True, it will cost you to develop a full suite of online reporting tools, but these features are important differentiators in the race against your competitors, who are also trying to sign every potential affiliate out there. If you lack the resources to build such features internally, consider using a third-party service to provide it on your behalf.

**Commission accounting and check cutting.** It costs about $5 to cut a commission check. This $5 covers the accounting software, the accountant running the software, and the postage. This unavoidable cost of doing business is the reason so many merchants require their affiliates to meet a payout threshold of anywhere from $25 to $100 before sending them their commissions check. Let's face it, it is pretty inefficient to spend $5 to send a check for $1. (Note: At this time, very few merchants offer direct deposit into affiliate checking accounts.)

**Follow-up.** Many costs associated with paying affiliates and cutting checks can be amortized and justified if you think in terms of customer acquisition (review the first part of this chapter). Whether you pay an affiliate or pay the customer to buy from you, you are paying for that initial mindshare, and, with luck, a regular customer. To that end, merchants are well advised to follow up with their new-found customers—if for no other reason than to ask if they received their product on time and in satisfactory condition. The Vitamin Shoppe, for example, currently sends periodic follow-up e-mails to its customers, containing a $10-off coupon. When the e-mail is received, customers are already familiar with the site and may have other items in mind to purchase in the near future. The $10 coupon goes a long way toward encouraging customers to make that next purchase immediately. (See Chapter 10 for more tips on building repeat customers.)

## Choosing the Right Affiliates

When it comes to affiliates, more doesn't necessarily mean better. It's important that you use the right people to drive the right kind of traffic to your site. Do you care if one of your affiliates is the Webmaster for a popular adult site if you're selling games for kids? A no-brainer. What if an affiliate's site promotes offensive or even illegal behavior? Or draws only 100 pageviews during a busy month? The point is, you have to make many decisions when choosing the affiliates to partner with.

Whether you sign up with an affiliate solutions provider or build your own program from scratch, you'll need to decide if you're going to screen each applicant and how you'll do that. Will you automatically accept all applications? Or screen using questions like: "What does your site offer?" "How many pageviews do you receive per month?" Or will you personally visit each and every Web site to determine whether it will make a satisfactory partner? If you choose the first option, you'll likely end up with some questionable sites and/or poor performers. If you choose the second option, be prepared to hire a slew of interns or other cheap labor and hope they don't get distracted easily. Given the high labor costs associated with manually screening sites (and the ease of foiling such means—an affiliate could change the site's content the day after you check it out), many sites reserve the right to cancel affiliation status (and any unpaid commissions) in the event of discovering a violation of the affiliate agreement. And, unfortunately, the most likely way you'll make such a discovery is via a complaint e-mail from a customer.

## Your Brand

It's important that you view your affiliates as business partners. After all, they'll be placing on their sites the most important indicator of your brand— your logo—along with a link to your site. Their visitors (and your future customers) will correctly assume a partnership. Given that, answer the question: "With which sites do I want my customers to identify me?" An adult site? A site where violence is promoted? How about a site where extreme political opinions are shared? Anything that can be considered highly controversial in any way?

Don't get us wrong, we're not condoning widespread censorship; we're recommending responsible stewardship of your brand. If you're selling children's toys on your e-commerce site, you'll want to filter out applications completed by the Webmaster of a site that promotes hate crimes. Granted, most such sites probably won't be signing up with toy-related affiliate programs. We're using this extreme example to demonstrate how seriously your association with affiliates can impact your brand.

## Poor Performers

As previously mentioned, many merchants require their affiliate to meet a specified payout threshold before cutting a check. However, it's important to keep in mind that even if one of your affiliates fails to meet the $25 (or whatever) threshold by the end of the pay period, you must still settle the balance, whatever it is, at the end of the fiscal year. This means that if one of your affiliates has a balance of $1 commission, you must cut a check for that $1 and mail it at the end of the fiscal year to ensure that your books are in order. This also means that, in effect, you will have to pay $6 for that one new customer. Add affiliate customer service costs (such as phone support) to the equation, and you can see that non- or poor-performing affiliates can become a substantive drain on profitability.

According to Jupiter Communications, about 15 percent of affiliates produce 85 percent of the revenue generated by the typical affiliate program. Given that, many merchants strive to predetermine which sites comprise those top 15 to 20 percent of performers and to weed out the other 85 percent that end up costing them money. Most weeding out (filtering) is performed during the affiliate's application process. Merchants filter performers by requesting: the URL for the Web site where the affiliate link will be placed, the number of unique visitors per month, or some number of pageviews during a given time period. For example, DVD Express currently requires that applicants receive 500 unique visitors each day. (Whether in practice merchants can enforce such criteria is questionable.) Naturally, if an affiliate cannot deliver a significant number of pageviews, then it's unlikely that it will deliver a significant number of customers to your Web site.

One argument against screening out nonperformers is that, collectively, they help build your brand awareness even if they do not drive significant revenues. Most sites would be happy to have their logos appear on the bumperstickers of 100,000 random cars, even if all of those bumper stickers didn't lead directly to a sale. Getting one's name out there as widely as possible is of paramount importance to many sites that do not have the luxury of hand-picking each site on which they'd like to be promoted. Unlike Disney, Bloomingdale's, or Neiman-Marcus, most sites will take whatever exposure they can get.

## Silly Mistakes

We've touched on some basics for defining and building an affiliate program, but we've saved what could possibly be the most valuable section of this chapter to the end: silly mistakes. Here we list some common mistakes merchants make with their affiliate programs.

**NOTE** The foundation for this list was provided by Allan Gardyne, owner and Webmaster of AssociatePrograms.com, and supplemented by Lois Robinson of Creative Computing (www.creativecomputing1.com). Allan's list of mistakes can be found in his Associate Programs Newsletter, #65 and #66. Merchants and affiliates alike will benefit by signing up to receive this free weekly newsletter at www.associateprograms.com/search/newsletter.shtml.

**Not having an affiliate agreement.** Believe it or not, companies launch affiliate programs without first drawing up an agreement for potential associates to read. An agreement is a necessary legal instrument. Without it, no enforceable relationship can or does exist.

**Failing to mention major facts missing in the agreement.** Too many contracts fail to mention the commission affiliates will be paid and/or when they'll be paid. Don't just cut and paste a standard contract from theaffiliateprogram.com. Add details pertinent to your program.

**Inconsistently stating agreement details.** If you decide to increase your payout just prior to your program launch, remember to update your affiliate agreement, too. We've seen a 10 percent commission offered on the affiliate sign-up page, and 8 percent offered in the agreement.

**Not correcting spelling and typing mistakes.** Get help from someone (or hire someone) who knows how to proofread, and instruct that person to go over your site with a fine-toothed comb. We remember one credit card merchant that launched its program on a beautifully designed site, which was ruined by glaring typing mistakes in the first few sentences on the main page.

**Hiding links.** If you don't want the link to your affiliate program to be obvious to your main customers, that's fair enough; but if you want Webmasters to be able to find the link, make sure it exists. Yes, some people actually forget to make the sign-up page accessible from anywhere.

**Not adding a FAQ page.** In addition to your main FAQ, it's an excellent idea to have another list of frequently asked questions specifically for affiliates. If you don't have any questions to put on it yet, show your site to a few friends and write down their questions. Don't have friends? Anticipate questions that your affiliates might have.

**Not providing your name and address.** If you forget—or aren't willing—to publish your name and physical address on your site, don't expect people to trust you. They will wonder what you have to hide.

**Not including a privacy statement.** What are you planning to do with the names and e-mail addresses you collect? Your affiliates have a right to know. You can create a privacy policy by using the TRUSTe wizard at www.etrust.org/wizard/ or write your own. Better yet, fully commit to online privacy by joining the TRUSTe program; it costs from $299 to $4,999 per year, based on revenue.

**Not correcting all the usual errors.** All the usual advice on usability and navigation apply if you want to avoid annoying people. Will it really matter if you delay another day or two while you improve your site? Yes, it will matter. In a good way.

**Using nonoptimized graphics.** Lois Robinson says, "One big gripe I have with merchants is that they fail to optimize their graphics." "When you optimize your graphics, it allows them to load quickly. Keeping graphics small (byte size) is very important! I'd rather just post a text link than take up the space and time [it takes] to load huge graphics."

Here is Lois's list of online resources for optimizing your graphics:

- GIF Cruncher—free GIF Optimizer
  www.gifcruncher.com/

- JPEGCruncher
  www.jpegcruncher.com/cgi-bin/jc/jcrunch.cgi?mode=select

- Web Site Garage's GIF LUBE
  www.websitegarage.com/ref.cgi?banner=ref30d32e55

- NetMechanic Image Optimization
  www.netmechanic.com/GIFBot.htm

- The Online JPEG Wizard by Pegasus Imaging
  www.jpegwizard.com/

- Web Reference's JPEG Wizard
  www.webreference.com/services/graphics/jw/

**Failing to use proper image tags.** Lois also reminds merchants to use proper image tags when supplying graphic code (height, width, and ALT tags):

- "State the size of your graphics," Lois says. "With sizing tags, a browser can download the text of the page, note the image sizes, and know the page layout right away. Your page text will be visible to your visitors while the graphics continue to load. Many banner exchanges fail to use sizing tags, and therefore pages are blank while waiting for access to their servers."

- "ALT tags should contain a short description of the link, not the graphic name," she says. This helps your visitors to identify your link. Place your ALT tag in brackets so the nongraphical browsers can identify your links. For example:

```
<img src="images/valid32.gif" width=119 height=28
alt="[ HTML 3.2 Validated ] " border=0 align=middle>
```

**Not displaying banner file size.** When supplying graphic links for others to use, be sure to state the size of the graphic in bytes. This helps affiliates make a decision as to which graphic to use. If Webmasters are following page-size limitation guidelines, knowing the number of bytes the image contains is important.

**Failing to also offer small buttons.** Don't neglect to offer small buttons or icons that can easily be placed in various locations. This is an excellent way to enable the scattering of your links on many pages.

**Not supplying marketing verbiage.** Always include a brief description of your product or service. Don't leave the catchy marketing phrases totally up to the affiliates. Supply examples that define your site.

**Including unvalidated code.** Only use coding that is viewable in all browsers. This is important for all Webmasters. Using HTML 3.2 coding is the surest way to have your sites viewable by the largest Internet audience. "I highly recommend using DJ Delorie for being able to see how your coding will read in nongraphical browsers," Lois says. "He has several excellent tests you can run on your site. An excellent way to test your coding for use by all visitors" (www.delorie.com/web/).

**Making affiliates guess.** "Explain exactly how your tracking system works," Lois advises. Many people do not accept cookies. Some Internet travelers do not enable Java or JavaScript in their browser. It's important for potential affiliates to know exactly how you are going to be tracking sales. "I've had offers to join programs, and then when I questioned how their sales were tracked they could not provide answers," Lois says.

**Forgetting to inform affiliates.** It seems blindingly obvious, but companies get it wrong: Don VanZant adds that some affiliate program managers have changed hosts or Web addresses without notifying affiliates. Maybe they don't want you to find them.

## Summary

Affiliate programs are an excellent, low-cost way for e-merchants and other commercial sites to attract new visitors, compete in a wider variety of markets, and increase sales. As affiliation becomes more commonplace on the Web, firms will need to offer programs just to keep up with their competitors offering that capability.

Before deciding how to implement your affiliate program, you need to consider your objectives, your target audience, how much you are willing to pay affiliates, how much you can spend to develop the program, how fast you need it, how you'll promote it, whether you have the requisite resources, what technical problems you may have to overcome, and how such a program will conflict with your other business relationships.

If you enlist the services of an affiliate solutions provider, be sure to investigate BeFree, Commission Junction, and LinkShare. If you opt to use a third-party tool, check out AffiliateZone.com, The Affiliate Program, and Groundbreak.com. If you decide to build your own program from scratch, be mindful of who you'll need on your team, what the costs will be, and how you'll handle the ordinary order-processing and follow-up activities associated with all direct e-commerce.

Finally, regardless of how you build your affiliate program, be mindful of the affiliates you choose to do business with, and be sure to avoid the most common mistakes associated with launching an affiliate program.

# Fifty Affiliate Picks

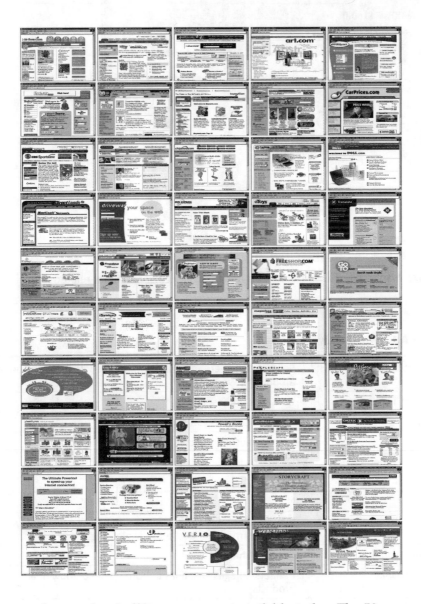

There are thousands of affiliate programs available today. The 50 we review here were chosen based on their commission structure, popularity, and product offerings.

# 1-800-Flowers.com

**Figure A.1**   1-800-Flowers.com sells fresh flowers, gifts, and floral-related items.

**Table A.1**   Program Overview

| | |
|---|---|
| Product/Services | Sells fresh flowers, gifts, and floral-related items to customers around the world. |
| Program Type | Commission-based. |
| Terms | 6%–8% commission on net sales. |
| Bonus? | Higher sales, higher commissions. |
| Payment Schedule | Quarterly. |
| Minimum Threshold | $25. |
| Two-Tier? | No. |
| Program Restrictions | "No pornographic or offensive content; easy navigation within site." Sites must be "aesthetically pleasing." |
| Online Reporting Tools | Yes (LinkShare). |
| Types of Links | Banners/images/text links to home page or individual products. |
| Prefabricated Storefront | No. |
| Powered by | LinkShare. |
| Where to Join | www.1800flowers.com; www.linkshare.com. |

# Amazon.com

**Figure A.2** Amazon.com offers links to books, CDs, videos, DVDs, toys, and more.

**Table A.2** Program Overview

| | |
|---|---|
| Product/Services | Sells books, CDs, videos, DVDs, toys, consumer electronics, computer games, sheet music, and many other products. |
| Program Type | Commission (pay-per-sale). |
| Terms | 15% for books in print and not highly discounted; 5% for CDs, videos, DVDs, and consumer electronics. |
| Bonus? | No. |
| Payment Schedule | Quarterly. |
| Minimum Threshold | $100. |
| Two-Tier? | No. |
| Program Restrictions | No adult sites; no hate sites. Doesn't pay referral fees on any products added to a customer's shopping cart or purchased via the One-Click feature after the customer has reentered its site (other than through an affiliate link), even if the customer previously followed a link from your site to the Amazon site. Gift certificate and items listed as out-of-print or "hard to find" are not eligible for referral fees. |
| Online Reporting Tools | Yes (also, weekly report via e-mail). |
| Types of Links | Banners/images or text links to home page or products; search boxes. |
| Prefabricated Storefront | No. |
| Powered by | Amazon.com. |
| Where to Join | www.amazon.com. |

# Ancestry.com

**Figure A.3** Ancestry.com puts people in touch with their past and earns you a flat fee for membership referrals.

**Table A.3** Program Overview

| | |
|---|---|
| Product/Services | Ancestry.com, MyFamily.com, and FamilyHistory.com offer resources for tracing family history, and private Web sites where families can hold family discussions, create online family photo albums, and maintain a calendar of family events. |
| Program Type | Flat fee (bounty). |
| Terms | $3–$6 per new subscriber to Ancestry.com. |
| Bonus? | More subscribers, higher bounty. |
| Payment Schedule | Quarterly. |
| Minimum Threshold | $10. |
| Two-Tier? | No. |
| Program Restrictions | Qualified subscribers must 1) join Ancestry.com as paying members, as a result of performing a search or linking to Ancestry.com from an affiliate site, and 2) not cancel their accounts during the 30-day trial period for annual subscriptions. |
| Online Reporting Tools | Yes (BeFree's Reporting.net). |
| Types of Links | Banners/text links to home page; search boxes. |
| Prefabricated Storefront | No. |
| Powered by | BeFree. |
| Where to Join | www.ancestry.com; www.befree.com. |

# Art.com

**Figure A.4** Art.com offers links to discounted framed and unframed art.

**Table A.4** Program Overview

| | |
|---|---|
| Product/Services | Sells discounted framed and unframed art. Customers select from available prints, which they can view displayed in different mats and frames. |
| Program Type | Commission-based (pay-per-sale). |
| Terms | 10% of net sales. |
| Bonus? | N/A. |
| Payment Schedule | Monthly (60 days following the end of each month). |
| Minimum Threshold | $50. |
| Two-Tier? | Yes; 2% commission for 90 days on sales made by new affiliates referred by your site. |
| Program Restrictions | No adult sites; no hate sites. affiliates may not post on newsgroups, message boards, or bulletin boards. |
| Online Reporting Tools | Yes (LinkShare). |
| Types of Links | Text, banners, buttons for links to front page or specific products; search box. |
| Prefabricated Storefront | Yes. |
| Powered by | LinkShare. |
| Where to Join | www.art.com; www.linkshare.com. |

# Astrology.net

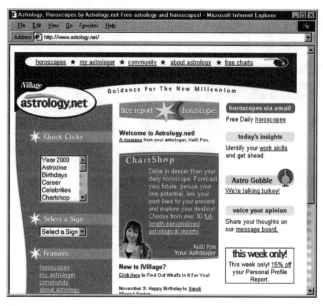

**Figure A.5**   Astrology.net offers personalized astrology reports, as well as commissions.

**Table A.5**   Program Overview

| | |
|---|---|
| Product/Services | Offers customers personalized astrology reports; offers three different affiliate programs: commission, content, and combo. The content and combo programs enable affiliates to display free daily horoscopes on their Web sites. The combo program requires affiliates to provide a byline for Astrology.net, as well as a text or banner ad. |
| Program Type | Three: Commission (pay-per-sale), content (free exchange), and combination of commission and content. |
| Terms | 12%, none, 12%–20%, respectively according to program type. |
| Bonus? | Yes; commissions scale to 20% for high-volume sites in combo program. |
| Payment Schedule | Monthly (60 days following the end of each month), for commission program only. |
| Minimum Threshold | $25, for commission program only. |
| Two-Tier? | No. |
| Program Restrictions | No adult sites; no hate sites. For content/combo programs, affiliates must have 300,000 pageviews per month. |
| Online Reporting Tools | Yes (LinkShare). |
| Types of Links | Banner, text, or icon to horoscopes/astrological readings. |
| Prefabricated Storefront | No. |
| Powered by | LinkShare. |
| Where to Join | www.astrology.net; www.linkshare.com. |

# BabyCenter.com

**Figure A.6**   BabyCenter.com, the leading site for new and expectant parents, provides links to specific products and topics of interest.

**Table A.6**   Program Overview

| Product/Services | The leading Web site for new and expectant parents that offers advice, a baby store (including products for the mom-to-be), product reviews, a gift registry, and more. |
|---|---|
| Program Type | Commission (pay-per-sale). |
| Terms | 15% of affiliate sales. |
| Bonus? | Unlike many programs, you can legitimately earn commissions by buying through your own affiliate links. |
| Payment Schedule | Quarterly. |
| Minimum Threshold | $25. |
| Two-Tier? | No. |
| Program Restrictions | No "objectionable materials" permitted on affiliate sites. |
| Online Reporting Tools | Yes (BeFree's Reporting.net). |
| Types of Links | Banners/images/text links to the home page, specific products, or topics (e.g., "Bottle Feeding"). |
| Prefabricated Storefront | Yes. |
| Powered by | BeFree. |
| Where to Join | www.babycenter.com; www.befree.com. |

# BarnesandNoble.com

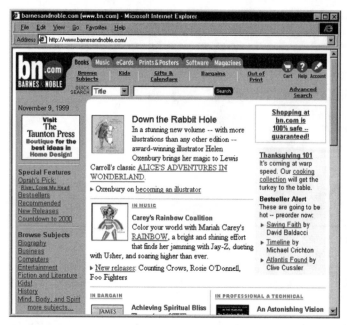

**Figure A.7**   BarnesandNoble.com offers both "traditional" affiliate links as well as e-mail-based affiliate links to books, CDs, videos, DVDs, and more.

**Table A.7**   Program Overview

| Product/Services | A leading offline and online book reseller that offers books, CDs, videos, and DVDs. |
|---|---|
| Program Type | Commission (pay-per-sale). |
| Terms | 15% of affiliate sales. |
| Bonus? | No. |
| Payment Schedule | Quarterly. |
| Minimum Threshold | $25. |
| Two-Tier? | No. |
| Program Restrictions | B&N must be the exclusive bookseller on your site. No "objectionable materials" allowed on affiliate sites. |
| Online Reporting Tools | Yes (BeFree's Reporting.net). |
| Types of Links | Banners/images/text/e-mail links to the home page or specific products; search boxes. |
| Prefabricated Storefront | No. |
| Powered by | BeFree. |
| Where to Join | www.bn.com; www.befree.com. |

# Beyond.com

**Figure A.8** Beyond.com offers links to more than 53,000 physical software titles, 1.6 million downloadable software titles, and more.

**Table A.8** Program Overview

| | |
|---|---|
| Product/Services | Offers more than 53,000 physical software titles, 1.6 million downloadable software titles, hardware, books, gifts, hand-helds, etc. |
| Program Type | Commission (pay-per-sale). |
| Terms | 5–10% commission on gross sale for every software title; 2% for every hardware product (Compaq products not included). |
| Bonus? | Yes; discounts at Crucial Technology, SmartClicks, and PC Flowers. |
| Payment Schedule | Quarterly. |
| Minimum Threshold | $75. |
| Two-Tier? | No. |
| Program Restrictions | Affiliate sites may not promote violence, discrimination, unlawful activities, use of spam, or pyramid schemes; they may not contain obscene or fraudulent content, nudity or pornographic materials. |
| Online Reporting Tools | No (quarterly sales reports are sent via e-mail). |
| Types of Links | Banners/images/text links to home page, specific products, a product center (e.g., games); search boxes. |
| Prefabricated Storefront | No. |
| Powered by | Beyond.com. |
| Where to Join | www.beyond.com. |

# Bigstar.com

**Figure A.9** Bigstar offers links to more than 100,000 video, DVD and laserdisc titles.

**Table A.9** Program Overview

| | |
|---|---|
| Product/Services | Bigstar is an online video, DVD, and laserdisc superstore with 100,000 titles in more than 400 categories. |
| Program Type | Commission-based (pay-per-sale). |
| Terms | 8%–12% commission on sales. |
| Bonus? | $5 coupon upon signup; higher sales, higher commissions. |
| Payment Schedule | Quarterly. |
| Minimum Threshold | $90. |
| Two-Tier? | No. |
| Program Restrictions | Affiliate sites may not contain "unlawful, harmful, threatening, defamatory, obscene, harassing, or racially, ethnically, or otherwise objectionable" content. Commission fees are based on the "value of the sale" (does not include taxes, service charges, shipping and handling charges, discounts, gift certificates, credits, credit card processing fees, and chargebacks). |
| Online Reporting Tools | No. |
| Types of Links | Banner/images/text links to home page and products. |
| Prefabricated Storefront | Yes (Movie Store Wiz). |
| Powered by | Bigstar. |
| Where to Join | www.bigstar.com. |

# CarPrices.com

**Figure A.10** CarPrices.com pays a flat fee for quotes for cars, car financing, and car insurance that your referrals request.

**Table A.10** Program Overview

| | |
|---|---|
| Product/Services: | Offers consumers free price quotes on cars, car financing, and car insurance; also provides ratings, load calculators, etc. |
| Program Type | Flat fee (bounty). |
| Terms | $1.20 for each qualified insurance quote; $2.50 for each qualified finance quote; $3 for each qualified new car price quote. |
| Bonus? | No. |
| Payment Schedule | Monthly. |
| Minimum Threshold | $10. |
| Two-Tier? | Yes (You can earn an additional 10% commission on leads from affiliates you refer to them). |
| Program Restrictions | To qualify, you must complete valid forms; no duplicates, etc. (1 form out of 10 is qualified). This is a month-to-month relationship. |
| Online Reporting Tools | Yes (BeFree's Reporting.net). |
| Types of Links | Banners/buttons/text that link to home page. |
| Prefabricated Storefront | No. |
| Powered by | BeFree. |
| Where to Join | www.carprices.com; www.befree.com. |

# CBS SportsLine.com

**Figure A.11**   CBS SportsLine online store offers free sporting news content and links to more than 10,000 premier sports-related products.

**Table A.11**   Program Overview

| | |
|---|---|
| Product/Services | A sports-related online store that sells more than 10,000 products relating to every team in every league in all major sports. |
| Program Type | Affiliate can choose from two programs: News Program offers you sporting news highlights, scores, etc. The Merchandise Program offers 5% commission on sales made in the SportsLine store. |
| Terms | Free content/5% commission on sales. |
| Bonus? | No. |
| Payment Schedule | Monthly. |
| Minimum Threshold | $25. |
| Two-Tier? | No. |
| Program Restrictions | Affiliates may not promote links to other online sports-related stores. CBS SportsLine will "refuse any site that contains objectionable material." |
| Online Reporting Tools | Yes (LinkShare). |
| Types of Links | Banners/images/text links to home page and individual products; search boxes. |
| Prefabricated Storefront | Yes (LinkShare). |
| Powered by | LinkShare. |
| Where to Join | www.cbssportsline.com; www.linkshare.com. |

# CDNOW

**Figure A.12**   Go to CDNOW for music, music news, videos, and DVDs. Affiliates can take their earnings in Cosmic Credit or commissions.

**Table A.12**   Program Overview

| | |
|---|---|
| Product/Services | CDNOW offers more than 300,000 music-related items, videos, and DVDs. |
| Program Type | Cosmic Credit (store credit) for fan sites; commission-based for C2 program (CDNOW's affiliate program for the corporate community). |
| Terms | Cosmic Credit is calculated by taking 7%–15% of the cost of all purchases made through your link. (percentage is based on sales performance); C2 partners earn 7%–15% commission on sales. |
| Bonus? | $10 for first sale; monthly bonuses are given out to high-producing members. |
| Payment Schedule | Cosmic Credit accounts are credited weekly, but if you earn more than $100 of Cosmic Credit, you'll receive a check for your earnings at the end of the calendar quarter. For C2 program, payout is quarterly. |
| Minimum Threshold | N/A for Cosmic Credit; $100 for C2. |
| Two-Tier? | No. |
| Program Restrictions | You may not promote your CDNOW links through unsolicited e-mailing (i.e., spamming), newsgroup postings, nor any other method of mass communication. Your site may not contain offensive content. You can't earn Cosmic Credit on the purchase of gift certificates. |
| Online Reporting Tools | Yes; available at www.cdnow.com/members for Cosmic Credit and at cdnow.com/c2 for C2 affiliates. |
| Types of Links | Text/image/banners/logo links to any area of the store; artist/band pages, album pages, movie pages, contests, or promotions; search boxes. |
| Prefabricated Storefront | No. |
| Powered by | CDNOW. |
| Where to Join | www.cdnow.com. |

# Chipshot.com

**Figure A.13**   Chipshop.com offers custom-built golf equipment to consumers and an escalating commission structure to affiliates.

**Table A.13**   Program Overview

| | |
|---|---|
| Product/Services | Sells custom-built golf equipment and accessories; also serves as a direct retailer of brand-name products. |
| Program Type | Commission-based (pay-per-sale). |
| Terms | 20% commission for sales over $1,500 per quarter; 15% commission for sales between $300–$1,500 per quarter; 10% commission for sales up to $300 per quarter; 1% commission on all brand-name products. |
| Bonus? | No. |
| Payment Schedule | Quarterly. |
| Minimum Threshold | $100. |
| Two-Tier? | No. |
| Program Restrictions | You must place one of Chipshot's three corporate banners on your home page. Your site may not promote violence, discrimination, or illegal activities, nor display sexually explicit material. Your site may not contain any libelous, defamatory, or disparaging materials. Your site must contain a significant amount of content (which means they want more than their banner displayed on a page with others). |
| Online Reporting Tools | No (quarterly reports are sent via e-mail). |
| Types of Links | Banners to any page on Chipshot.com. |
| Prefabricated Storefront | No. |
| Powered by | Chipshot.com. |
| Where to Join | www.chipshot.com. |

# Cooking.com

**Figure A.14**   Cook up some cash with Cooking.com's affiliate program.

**Table A.14**   Program Overview

| | |
|---|---|
| Product/Services | A one-stop cooking site that provides visitors with convenient shopping, great recipes, and cooking tips from today's top chefs. |
| Program Type | Commission (pay-per-sale). |
| Terms | 20% commission on sales. |
| Bonus? | No. |
| Payment Schedule | Quarterly. |
| Minimum Threshold | $100. |
| Two-Tier? | No. |
| Program Restrictions | Your site may not contain "sexually explicit" material; promote discrimination, illegal activities, or pyramid schemes; and may not contain defamatory/fraudulent content. If your referrals place items in their shopping carts and buy them later, you will not earn a commission. You may not display on your site cooking.com discount or other coupons that you receive from any other source. |
| Online Reporting Tools | Yes (www.cookingaffiliates.com). |
| Types of Links | Banners/images/text links to home page and individual products; search boxes. |
| Prefabricated Storefront | No. |
| Powered by | LinkShare. |
| Where to Join | www.cooking.com; www.linkshare.com. |

# Dell.com

**Figure A.15**  Dell, the world's leading direct-sales computer systems company, offers 1 percent commission to affiliates.

**Table A.15**  Program Overview

| | |
| --- | --- |
| Product/Services | The world's leading direct-sales computer systems company. |
| Program Type | Commission-based (pay-per-sale). |
| Terms | 1% on sales made on dell.com or gigabuys.com. |
| Bonus? | No. |
| Payment Schedule | Quarterly. |
| Minimum Threshold | $50. |
| Two-Tier? | No. |
| Program Restrictions | Referral sales must be completed online at dell.com for affiliates to qualify for the referral fee. Affiliate sites may not contain offensive material, and must have traffic of more than 500 unique visitors per day. |
| Online Reporting Tools | Yes (LinkShare). |
| Types of Links | Banners/images/textual/e-mail link to home page or products. |
| Prefabricated Storefront | Yes. |
| Powered by | LinkShare. |
| Where to Join | www.dell.com; www.linkshare.com. |

# DirectLeads

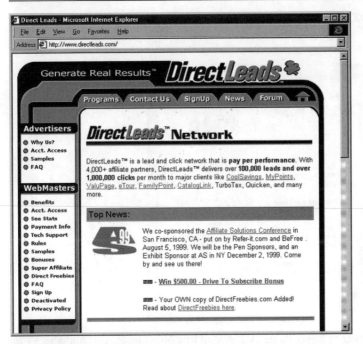

**Figure A.16** DirectLeads.com, an advertising network that pays affiliates for qualified leads for its advertisers.

**Table A.16** Program Overview

| | |
|---|---|
| Product/Services | An advertising network whose sole form of advertising and affiliating is via lead generation. |
| Commission Type/Amount | Pay-per-lead; $.05–$4+ per qualified lead. |
| Bonus? | Yes; 2% if more than $1,000/month; 3% if more than $5,000/month; 4% if more than $7,000/month. |
| Payment Schedule | 60 days after request from affiliate. |
| Minimum Threshold | $20. |
| Two-Tier? | Yes; 10% of the commission of referring sites. |
| Program Restrictions | Affiliate sites must be reporting a minimum of 3,000 unique pageviews per month. Only sites written in English are accepted. No adult or hate sites. Affiliates may not post on newsgroups, message boards, or bulletin board. |
| Online Reporting Tools | Yes (www.directleads.com). |
| Types of Links | Text, banners, buttons, and banner rotations to home page. |
| Prefabricated Storefront | No. |
| Where to Join | www.directleads.com. |

# Driveway.com

**Figure A.17**    Driveway.com offers its users 25MB of free file storage, and affiliates $1 for each new Driveway customer.

**Table A.17**    Program Overview

| | |
|---|---|
| Product/Services | A Web-based service that offers 25MB of free file storage and access. |
| Program Type | Flat fee (bounty). |
| Terms | $1 flat fee per registration. |
| Bonus? | No. |
| Payment Schedule | Quarterly. |
| Minimum Threshold | $200. |
| Two-Tier? | No. |
| Program Restrictions | Affiliate sites must be "aesthetically pleasing"; they may not contain pornographic or offensive content, or promote violence, illegal activities, or discrimination. |
| Online Reporting Tools | Yes (LinkShare). |
| Types of Links | Banners/images/text links to home page. |
| Prefabricated Storefront | No. |
| Powered by | LinkShare. |
| Where to Join | www.driveway.com; www.linkshare.com. |

# DVD Express

**Figure A.18** DVD Express, the first to market DVDs online, offers links to DVDs, videos, music, and movie-related products.

**Table A.18** Program Overview

| | |
|---|---|
| Product/Services | DVD Express was the first online store to sell DVDs. It also offers videos, music, games, and other movie-related products. |
| Program Type | Commission-based (pay-per-sale). |
| Terms | 8% commission. |
| Bonus? | No. |
| Payment Schedule | Quarterly. |
| Minimum Threshold | $100. |
| Two-Tier? | No. |
| Program Restrictions | No pornographic or offensive materials. Content traffic must exceed 500 unique visitors per day; sites must provide easy navigation and be "aesthetically pleasing." |
| Online Reporting Tools | Yes (LinkShare). |
| Types of Links | Banners/images/text links to home page and individual products; search boxes. |
| Prefabricated Storefront | No. |
| Powered by | LinkShare. |
| Where to Join | www.dvdexpress.com; www.linkshare.com. |

# eToys.com

**Figure A.19**   eToys, the leading online toy haven, offers links to toys, games, books, music, clothes, and more.

**Table A.19**   Program Overview

| | |
|---|---|
| Product/Services | The leading online toy store, which offers a plethora of toys, games, books, music, clothes, and more. |
| Program Type | Flat rate (bounty) and commission (pay-per-sale). |
| Terms | $5 for each new customer; 5%–12.5% commission on all sales referred by your site. |
| Bonus? | Yes; commission percentage increases depending on purchase amount per quarter, enabling you to earn up to 12.5%. |
| Payment Schedule | Quarterly. |
| Minimum Threshold | $20. |
| Two-Tier? | No. |
| Program Restrictions | No adult or hate sites; must have "child-safe" content. Must have a Web site before joining and must have a U.S. address to participate. |
| Online Reporting Tools | Yes (BeFree's Reporting.net). |
| Types of Links | Banners/images/icon/text to front door or individual products; search box. |
| Prefabricated Storefront | Yes. |
| Powered by | BeFree. |
| Where to Join | www.etoys.com; www.linkshare.com. |

# eTranslate

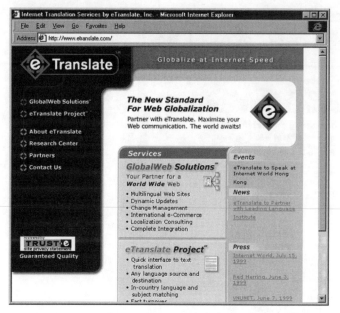

**Figure A.20** eTranslate, a leading online translation company offers affiliates up to 10 percent on commissions.

**Table A.20** Program Overview

| Product/Services | eTranslate offers both traditional (on-site) and Web site translation services. |
| --- | --- |
| Program Type | Commission-based (pay-per-sale). |
| Terms | 5%–10% commission. |
| Bonus? | No. |
| Payment Schedule | Monthly. |
| Minimum Threshold | $100. |
| Two-Tier? | No. |
| Program Restrictions | Affiliate sites cannot contain pornographic or offensive content traffic. They must exceed 500 unique visitors per day, must be easy to navigate, and aesthetically pleasing. |
| Online Reporting Tools | Yes (BeFree's Reporting.net). |
| Types of Links | Banners/images/text to home page or individual products; storefront. |
| Prefabricated Storefront | Yes. |
| Powered by | LinkShare. |
| Where to Join | www.eTranslate.com; www.linkshare.com. |

# Flooz.com

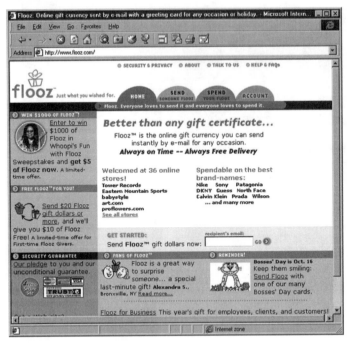

**Figure A.21**  Earn commissions or Flooz gift dollars with affiliate links.

**Table A.21**  Program Overview

| | |
|---|---|
| Product/Services | Offers a "gift currency" that can be used by recipients to shop at more than 36 online stores. |
| Program Type | Commission (pay-per-sale). |
| Terms | 5% cash or 10% in Flooz gift dollars (which can be redeemed at a variety of online stores). |
| Bonus? | No. |
| Payment Schedule | Once every other month. |
| Minimum Threshold | Not specified. |
| Two-Tier? | No. |
| Program Restrictions | No adult or hate sites. |
| Online Reporting Tools | Yes (LinkShare). |
| Types of Links | Banners/images/icon/text to front door or individual products; search box. |
| Prefabricated Storefront | No. |
| Powered by | LinkShare. |
| Where to Join | www.flooz.com; www.linkshare.com. |

# Fogdog Sports

**Figure A.22** Fogdog Sports store offers links to sporting goods and other outdoor products.

**Table A.22** Program Overview

| | |
|---|---|
| Product/Services | One of the largest sporting goods stores on the Internet; a single source for virtually any sports or outdoor product anytime, anywhere. |
| Program Type | Commission (pay-per-sale). |
| Terms | 10% of the sale. |
| Bonus? | 15% if quarterly sales exceed $5,000; 20% if quarterly sales exceed $25,000. |
| Payment Schedule | Quarterly. |
| Minimum Threshold | $100. |
| Two-Tier? | No. |
| Program Restrictions | Your site cannot contain any offensive materials, and must contain a significant amount of content. For each product you display, you must include an image of the product, a description, a review, or other reference. You may not alter the product description or pricing, and you may not list prices for certain manufacturers (see the FAQ for a list). |
| Online Reporting Tools | Yes (BeFree's Reporting.net). |
| Types of Links | Images/banners/text links to general content areas (e.g., Soccer Store). |
| Prefabricated Storefront | No. |
| Powered by | BeFree. |
| Where to Join | www.fogdog.com; www.befree.com. |

# Food.com

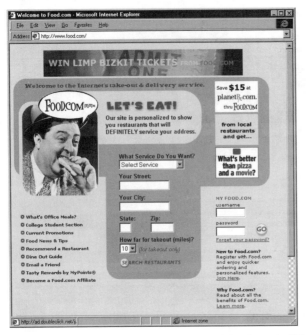

**Figure A.23** Food.com offers you a combination of affiliate programs when you refer customers to its take-out and delivery service.

**Table A.23** Program Overview

| | |
|---|---|
| Product/Services | A Web-based food take-out and delivery service. Also offers food-related tips, makes restaurant recommendations, and more. |
| Program Type | Combination of flat-fee and click-through program. |
| Terms | $.10 per click-through, $1.00 per registration, $5.00 per order for referrals. |
| Bonus? | No. |
| Payment Schedule | Monthly. |
| Minimum Threshold | $50. |
| Two-Tier? | No. |
| Program Restrictions | Your site must be "aesthetically pleasing," and may not "display content that may be deemed pornographic or offensive." |
| Online Reporting Tools | Yes (LinkShare). |
| Types of Links | Banners/images/text links to home page; banners can be rotated. |
| Prefabricated Storefront | No. |
| Powered by | LinkShare. |
| Where to Join | www.food.com; www.linkshare. |

# FreeShop.com

**Figure A.24** FreeShop.com offers customers access to thousands of free offers, and affiliates a combination of affiliate programs.

**Table A.24** Program Overview

| Product/Services | A direct marketing service that offers more than 1.5 million visitors access to thousands of free and trial offers. |
| --- | --- |
| Program Type | Combination of pay-per-click and commission-based. |
| Terms | $.05 for each click-through, then an additional 30%–50% of the fees generated from your referred orders. |
| Bonus? | Yes; three program levels: Bronze earns 30% commission (for sales from $1–$500), Silver earns 40% commission (for sales from $501–$1,000), and Gold earns 50% commission (for sales from $1,001+). |
| Payment Schedule | Quarterly. |
| Minimum Threshold | $10. |
| Two-Tier? | No. |
| Program Restrictions | Your site may not display sexually explicit material or contain defamatory information; it may not promote violence, discrimination, illegal activities; it may not violate intellectual property rights. Your site may not be a warez, ROM, or emulator site (in other words, your site can't contain pirated copies or simulated versions of software/gaming programs). |
| Online Reporting Tools | Yes (LinkShare). |
| Types of Links | Banners/images/text links to home page and individual products; storefront. |
| Prefabricated Storefront | Yes. |
| Powered by | LinkShare. |
| Where to Join | www.freeshop.com; www.linkshare.com. |

# GoTo.com

**Figure A.25** GoTo.com will pay you to integrate its premier search engine into your site.

**Table A.25** Program Overview

| | |
|---|---|
| Product/Services | GoTo.com is a leading search engine/portal. As an affiliate, you can create a search box that displays the results on a site at GoTo.com. |
| Program Type | Click-through. |
| Terms | $.03 per search performed on your site. |
| Bonus? | No. |
| Payment Schedule | Quarterly. |
| Minimum Threshold | $25. |
| Two-Tier? | No. |
| Program Restrictions | N/A. |
| Online Reporting Tools | Yes (BeFree's Reporting.net). |
| Types of Links | Images/text to search box or GoTo.com's home page. |
| Prefabricated Storefront | No. |
| Powered by | BeFree. |
| Where to Join | www.goto.com; www.befree.com. |

# Greeting-cards.com

**Figure A.26**   Greeting-cards.com sells animated musical greeting cards, and offers affiliates residual commissions.

**Table A.26**   Program Overview

| | |
|---|---|
| Product/Services | "The Internet's finest animated musical greeting cards and gifts." |
| Program Type | Commission-based (pay-per-sale) A custom animated musical greeting store is available to sites that host more than 15,000 visitors to their sites each day. |
| Terms | 20%. |
| Bonus? | If your site visitors make their first purchase from your site, then make subsequent visits from Greeting-cards.com, you will make a commission—up to a year later! You also purchase through your own affiliate links. |
| Payment Schedule | Quarterly. |
| Minimum Threshold | $50. |
| Two-Tier? | Yes; if *your* affiliates become affiliates, you get 2% of their sales. |
| Program Restrictions | N/A. |
| Online Reporting Tools | Yes. |
| Types of Links | A link to your Greeting-cards.com co-branded store. |
| Prefabricated Storefront | Yes (stored on the Greeting-card server). |
| Powered by | Greeting-cards.com. |
| Where to Join | www.greeting-cards.com. |

# iSyndicate

**Figure A.27** iSyndicate offers you free dynamic news content for adding affiliate links to your site.

**Table A.27** Program Overview

| | |
|---|---|
| Product/Services | A Web content syndication service. Hundreds of leading news and information Web services use iSyndicate to transmit dynamic content to their site visitors. |
| Program Type | Syndication (free content). |
| Terms | Free content. |
| Bonus? | N/A. |
| Payment Schedule | N/A. |
| Minimum Threshold | N/A. |
| Two-Tier? | No. |
| Program Restrictions | Will not display content to sites containing nudity, pornographic content, or "grossly offensive" material, or that exploit children under the age of 18 or promote illegal activities. |
| Online Reporting Tools | No. |
| Types of Links | Photos/graphics/textual links to news articles; search boxes; headlines. |
| Prefabricated Storefront | No. |
| Powered by | iSyndicate. |
| Where to Join | www.isyndicate.com (Shop for Content). |

# The Lycos Network

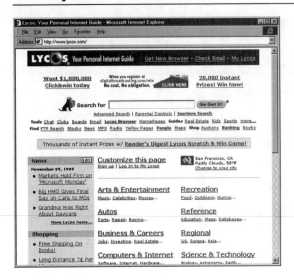

**Figure A.28** The Lycos Network offers affiliates content boxes (search and information look-up) and up to $.03 each time the boxes are used by affiliate site visitors.

**Table A.28** Program Overview

| | |
|---|---|
| Product/Services | The Lycos Network includes 12 Web entities, including: Tripod.com and Angelfire.com, which offer free home page-building tools; Quote.com, which provides financial market data through delayed and real-time quotes; WhoWhere.com, which provides online e-mail, phone, and address directories; MailCity.com, which provides free Web-based e-mail; Hotwired.com, which is a leading provider of technology news; Wired.com, which provides daily news and analysis of high-tech companies and the people who work in them; Hotbot.com, a popular search engine; Sonique, the makers of a Windows audio player; WebMonkey, a leading source of info for Web developers, and Suck.som, one of the Web's longest-running daily columns that provides sardonic commentary on media and culture.<br>    The Lycos Traffic Affiliate Program enables you to place content boxes (i.e., search boxes and other information look-up boxes). |
| Program Type | Click-through. |
| Terms | $.02 per click-through to Hotbot; $.03 per click-through for all other content boxes. |
| Bonus? | No. |
| Payment Schedule | Quarterly. |
| Minimum Threshold | $50. |
| Two-Tier? | No. |
| Program Restrictions | To participate, you must register for the Lycos Traffic Affiliate Program with a unique username and password, even if you're currently signed up as a BeFree affiliate; and you must reside in one of the eligible countries (see the program agreement for a complete list). Your site may not contain "illegal, racist, or hate content." Lycos may require you to provide records and data to determine click-through legitimacy. |
| Online Reporting Tools | Yes (BeFree's Reporting.net). |
| Types of Links | Content boxes. |
| Prefabricated Storefront | No. |
| Powered by | BeFree.com. |
| Where to Join | www.lycos.com; www.befree.com. |

# Magazines.com

**Figure A.29** Magazines.com offers customers more than 1,200 magazines, and offers affiliates commissions for referred subscriptions.

**Table A.29** Program Overview

| Product/Services | Offers discounted subscriptions to more than 1,200 magazine titles. |
|---|---|
| Program Type | Commission-based (pay-per-sale). |
| Terms | 25% on every magazine subscription purchased from an affiliate link. |
| Bonus? | No. |
| Payment Schedule | Quarterly (receive check 30 days following the end of each quarter). |
| Minimum Threshold | $50. |
| Two-Tier? | No. |
| Program Restrictions | Magazines.com must be the exclusive magazine seller on your site. "Unsuitable" sites are ineligible from program participation; unsuitable sites include "those that promote sexually explicit materials; promote violence; promote discrimination based on race, sex, religion, nationality, disability, sexual orientation, or age; promote illegal activities; or violate intellectual property rights." |
| Online Reporting Tools | No. |
| Types of Links | Image/text/e-mail links to home page, category page, Magazines with Free Gifts page, Gift Center page, specific magazines, and more. |
| Prefabricated Storefront | No. |
| Powered by | Magazines.com. |
| Where to Join | www.magazines.com. |

# MotherNature.com

**Figure A.30** MotherNature.com offers discounted health food products, advice, and 12 percent of net sales to affiliates.

**Table A.30** Program Overview

| | |
|---|---|
| Product/Services | Offers thousands of discounted health food products, health/medical advice, and more. |
| Program Type | Commission-based. |
| Terms | 12% of net sales. |
| Bonus? | No. |
| Payment Schedule | Quarterly. |
| Minimum Threshold | $50. |
| Two-Tier? | No. |
| Program Restrictions | You may not include price information in your descriptions; your site must be "suitable," as defined by MotherNature.com. |
| Online Reporting Tools | Yes (BeFree's Reporting.net). |
| Types of Links | Images/text link to home page, products, search box, or departments (e.g., Weight Loss Products). |
| Prefabricated Storefront | No. |
| Powered by | BeFree. |
| Where to Join | www.mothernature.com; www.befree.com. |

# NextCard

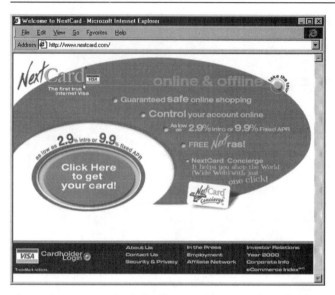

**Figure A.31** NextCard, the first true Internet Visa, gives customers online buying power, and affiliates $20 for introducing them.

**Table A.31** Program Overview

| | |
|---|---|
| Product/Services | Offers "the first true Internet Visa" to customers who want to shop online. |
| Program Type | Flat fee/bounty. |
| Terms | $20 per new NextCard Visa account. |
| Bonus? | Gold Affiliates (affiliates who generate a lot of traffic) earn $25 per new account. |
| Payment Schedule | Quarterly. |
| Minimum Threshold | $20. |
| Two-Tier? | No. |
| Program Restrictions | NextCard will "reject any site that does not feature customer-friendly site navigation, contains offensive content (including pornographic or hateful content)." Also, "all information relating to the calculation of the quarterly amounts paid to you [the affiliate], including but not limited to the number of accounts booked by NextCard, shall be considered proprietary information of NextCard." |
| Online Reporting Tools | No (e-mail-based). |
| Types of Links | Banners and text links. |
| Prefabricated Storefront | No. |
| Powered by | NextCard. |
| Where to Join | www.nextcard.com; associate-it.com. |

# One & Only

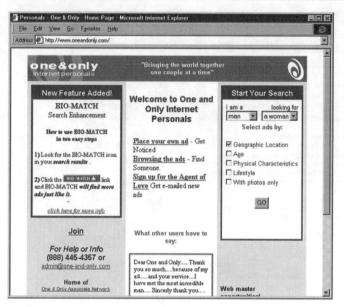

**Figure A.32** One & Only helps users find their soulmates and gives affiliates the chance to earn commissions for membership subscriptions.

**Table A.32** Program Overview

| | |
|---|---|
| Product/Services | A leading online subscriptions-based matchmaking (personal ad placement) service. |
| Program Type | Commission-based. |
| Terms | 15% of gross revenue from new and renewed All You Can E-mail club membership subscriptions. |
| Bonus? | Earn 33.3% of your Webmaster referral commissions and Premier Pass subscriptions. |
| Payment Schedule | Monthly. |
| Minimum Threshold | None. |
| Two-Tier? | Yes; earn 33.3% of your Webmaster referral commissions. |
| Program Restrictions | Your site may not promote sexually explicit material, violence, discrimination, or illegal activities. No spamming. |
| Online Reporting Tools | Yes (Daily Activity Report sent via e-mail). |
| Types of Links | Banners/text links to your own page on One & Only's server. |
| Prefabricated Storefront | No. |
| Powered by | One & Only. |
| Where to Join | www.oneandonly.com. |

# Outpost.com

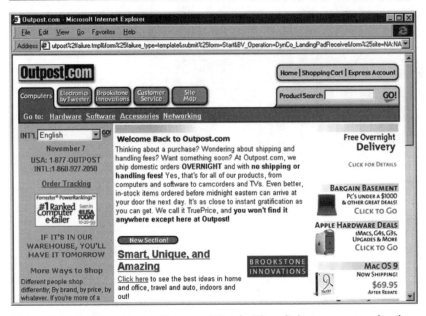

**Figure A.33** Outpost.com, offers specialized affiliate links to computer hardware, software, peripherals, and accessories.

**Table A.33** Program Overview

| | |
|---|---|
| Product/Services | A leading Web-based retailer that offers competitively priced computer hardware, software, peripherals, and accessories. |
| Program Type | Commission-based (pay-per-sale) or store credit. |
| Terms | 3% cash or 5% store credit commission. |
| Bonus? | $1.50 for every new affiliate you send to Outpost via the sign-up page. |
| Payment Schedule | Monthly (60 days following the end of each month). |
| Minimum Threshold | $100. |
| Two-Tier? | No. |
| Program Restrictions | Your site may not contain pornographic or offensive content or promote violence, illegal activities, or discrimination. |
| Online Reporting Tools | Yes (LinkShare). |
| Types of Links | Banners/images/text/e-mail links to home page or specific products; search boxes, storefront, drop-down menus, and more. |
| Prefabricated Storefront | Yes. |
| Powered by | LinkShare. |
| Where to Join | www.outpost.com; www.linkshare.com. |

# PeopleScape

**Figure A.34**   PeopleScape.com helps hi-tech firms find qualified employees, and pays affiliates $2 per qualified lead.

**Table A.34**   Program Overview

| | |
|---|---|
| Product/Services | A next-generation employment company offering a new model for hiring sales, marketing, and technical professionals. |
| Program Type | Pay-per-lead. |
| Terms | $2. |
| Bonus? | No. |
| Payment Schedule | Monthly. |
| Minimum Threshold | None. |
| Two-Tier? | No. |
| Program Restrictions | Your referral must be a sales, marketing or technical professional currently working in the Internet, NewMedia, eCommerce or hi-tech industry. |
| Online Reporting Tools | Yes (Commission Junction). |
| Types of Links | Banners and links to home page. |
| Prefabricated Storefront | No. |
| Powered by | Commission Junction. |
| Where to Join | www.peoplescape.com; www.cj.com. |

# Petstore.com

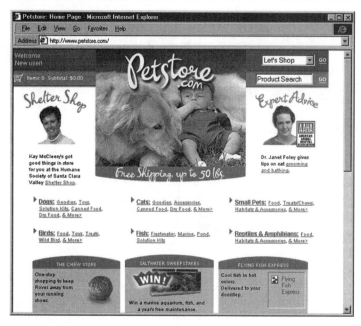

**Figure A.35** Petstore.com offers advice, gifts, training guides, and more for your pet and 10 percent of sales for affiliated pet lovers.

**Table A.35** Program Overview

| | |
|---|---|
| Product/Services | A leading pet supply site that offers advice on animal care, a gift store, a training store, pet therapy tips, and food and accessories for dogs, cats, fish, birds, "small pets," reptiles, and others. |
| Program Type | Commission (pay-per-sale). |
| Terms | 10% of sales. |
| Bonus? | $5 for new customers. |
| Payment Schedule | Monthly. |
| Minimum Threshold | $20. |
| Two-Tier? | No. |
| Program Restrictions | Your site may not contain or link to "inappropriate" material. |
| Online Reporting Tools | Yes (BeFree's Reporting.net). |
| Types of Links | Banners/images/text links to home page. |
| Prefabricated Storefront | No. |
| Powered by | BeFree. |
| Where to Join | www.petstore.com; www.befree.com. |

# PlanetRx

**Figure A.36**   PlanetRx, a leading online pharmacy, pays affiliates commissions for nonprescription medicine sales.

**Table A.36**   Program Overview

| | |
|---|---|
| Product/Services | A leading online pharmacy and drugstore that fills prescriptions, and sells over-the-counter medicines, vitamins, herbs, beauty products, personal care items, and more. |
| Program Type | Commission-based (pay-per-sale). |
| Terms | 15% on nonprescription sales. |
| Bonus? | The Affiliate of the Month receives a $50 shopping spree at PlanetRx; all affiliates get $5 for every new customer they refer who makes a nonprescription medicine purchase. |
| Payment Schedule | Quarterly. |
| Minimum Threshold | $50. |
| Two-Tier? | No. |
| Program Restrictions | Healthcare providers do not qualify for the program. Prescription sales are precluded from the program. Your site may not contain "objectionable material, including pornography, explicit language or content, violence, or discrimination. |
| Online Reporting Tools | Yes (BeFree's Reporting.net). |
| Types of Links | Banners/images/text links to home page, specific products, special promotions, and eCenters—specialized pages with products and information about specific medical conditions (e.g., diabetes, allergies, cancer) or for specific audiences (women, children, seniors). |
| Prefabricated Storefront | No. |
| Powered by | BeFree. |
| Where to Join | www.planetrx.com; www.befree.com. |

# Playboy.com

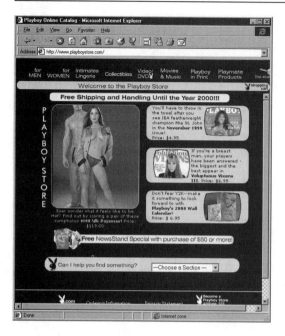

**Figure A.37**  Playboy.com doesn't offer affiliate links to its main attraction (the great articles, of course), but it does offer 10 percent commission for items purchased from the site store.

**Table A.37**  Program Overview

| | |
|---|---|
| Product / Services | The Playboy Store contains products that previously were sold exclusively through its offline catalog. Products include women's and men's loungewear and lingerie, jewelry, videos, CD-ROMs, exotic body oils, and more. |
| Program Type | Percentage commission (pay-per-sale). |
| Terms | 10% of sale (does not include magazine subscriptions). |
| Bonus? | No. |
| Payment Schedule | Quarterly. |
| Minimum Threshold | $50. |
| Two-Tier? | No. |
| Program Restrictions | Affiliates "must have an existing Web site," which must enable "easy navigation" and be "professionally written and aesthetically pleasing." Affiliate sites may not contain offensive material. (Playboy.com presumably has a unique definition of "offensive," which probably differs somewhat from that of the other programs included in this appendix. Follow the Playboy style and you should be safe.)<br>    The program doesn't pay referral fees on any products added to a customer's shopping cart and purchased after the customer has reentered the site (other than through an affiliate link), even if the customer previously followed a link from your site to the Playboy site. In addition, gift certificates are not eligible for referral fees, and affiliates may not buy from their own links. |
| Online Reporting Tools | Yes (LinkShare). |
| Types of Links | Banners/images/text to home page or online store. |
| Prefabricated Storefront | No. |
| Powered by | LinkShare. |
| Where to Join | www.playboy.com; www.linkshare.com. |

# Powell's Books

**Figure A.38** Powell's Books sells new, used, and hard-to-find titles and offers affiliates two program options.

**Table A.38** Program Overview

| | |
|---|---|
| Product/Services | An online bookstore selling new, used, and out-of-print books. |
| Program Type | Commission-based (pay-per-sale) on books; flat rate (bounty) for newsletter subscribers. |
| Terms | 10% commission on sales; $0.25 for each new newsletter subscriber. |
| Bonus? | No. |
| Payment Schedule | Quarterly. |
| Minimum Threshold | $100. |
| Two-Tier? | No. |
| Program Restrictions | Your site may not contain illegal, defamatory, sexually explicit, harassing, violent, discriminatory, or otherwise objectionable materials. |
| Online Reporting Tools | No. |
| Types of Links | Images/text links to the home page, specific author, specific book(s), or online catalog book section or subsections; search box; newsletter banner. |
| Prefabricated Storefront | No. |
| Powered by | Powells.com. |
| Where to Join | www.powells.com. |

# Priceline.com

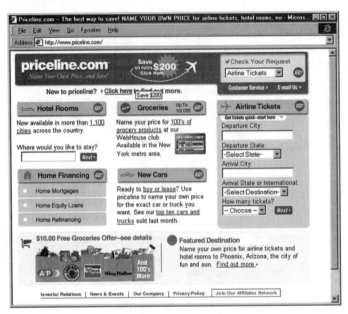

**Figure A.39** Priceline.com lets users bid for their travel reservations and enables affiliates to earn $1 for each qualified bid.

**Table A.39** Program Overview

| | |
|---|---|
| Product/Services | Enables visitors to name their own price (i.e., bid) for rental cars, air travel, hotel reservations—even groceries in some states. |
| Program Type | Flat fee/bounty. |
| Terms | $1 each time a visitor from your site posts a qualified offer. |
| Bonus? | $10 for your first qualified offer; $2 per qualified offer for each over 50 per calendar month. |
| Payment Schedule | Quarterly. |
| Minimum Threshold | $50. |
| Two-Tier? | No. |
| Program Restrictions | Visitors must post qualified offers (see www.priceline.com for details). |
| Online Reporting Tools | Yes (BeFree's Reporting.net). |
| Types of Links | Image/text links to home page, ticket page, hotel page; special reports. |
| Prefabricated Storefront | Yes (Special Report). |
| Powered by | BeFree. |
| Where to Join | www.priceline.com; www.befree.com. |

# Quicken.com

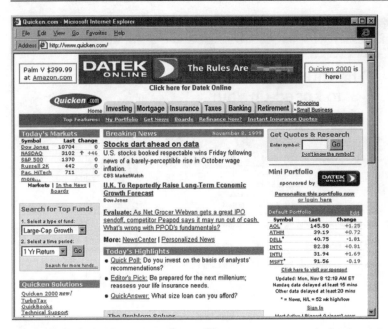

**Figure A.40** Quicken.com offers affiliates access to tools for investing, insurance, and retirement planning, and a penny each time a visitor uses one of its tools.

**Table A.40** Program Overview

| | |
|---|---|
| Product/Services | A leading provider of tools for and information about investing, insurance, mortgage, taxes, banking, retirement planning, and other personal finance issues. |
| Program Type | Click-through. |
| Terms | $.01 each time a Quicken tool is used on your site. |
| Bonus? | No. |
| Payment Schedule | Quarterly. |
| Minimum Threshold | $25. |
| Two-Tier? | No. |
| Program Restrictions | Your site must be deemed "suitable" by Quicken. |
| Online Reporting Tools | Yes (BeFree's Reporting.net). |
| Types of Links | Links to retirement info, insurance quote look-up boxes, mutual fund finder utility and more. |
| Prefabricated Storefront | No. |
| Powered by | BeFree. |
| Where to Join | www.quicken.com; www.befree.com. |

# Speedlane

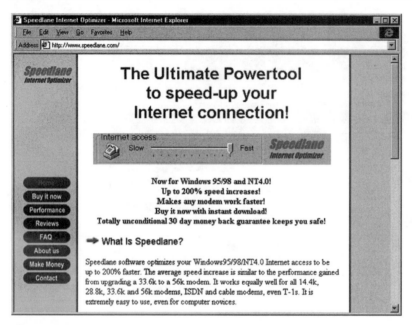

**Figure A.41** Speedlane lets users dial up faster and enables affiliates to earn 33 percent commissions.

**Table A.41** Program Overview

| | |
|---|---|
| Product/Services | Speedlane offers its consumers software to optimize their Windows95/98/NT4.0 Internet access up to 200% faster. |
| Program Type | Commission-based (pay-per-sale). |
| Terms | 33% commissions. |
| Bonus? | No. |
| Payment Schedule | Monthly. |
| Minimum Threshold | None. |
| Two-Tier? | No. |
| Program Restrictions | Affiliates must get permission to resize the Speedlane banner or add descriptive text near it. Affiliates may not use spam to promote Speedlane or post ads to Speedlane on newsgroups or discussion groups unless permitted by the groups. |
| Online Reporting Tools | No. |
| Types of Links | Banner to the home page. |
| Prefabricated Storefront | No. |
| Powered by | Speedlane. |
| Where to Join | www.speedlane.com. |

# Stamps.com

**Figure A.42** Stamps.com gives consumers easy access to postage and enables affiliates to earn $5 to $10 for referring new members.

**Table A.42** Program Overview

| | |
|---|---|
| Product/Services | A service that enables small businesses and consumers to purchase and print postage from the Internet. |
| Program Type | Flat rate (bounty). |
| Terms | $5 for each referral who signs up for the Stamps.com personal plan; $10 for each new referral who signs up for the business plan. |
| Bonus? | Entry into $3,500 sweepstakes. |
| Payment Schedule | Quarterly. |
| Minimum Threshold | $50. |
| Two-Tier? | No. |
| Program Restrictions | An affiliate may not transmit "interstitial advertising" (pop-up ads) to users as they link from the affiliate's site to the Stamps.com site, nor frame or otherwise create a border environment or browser around the Stamps.com site. Affiliate sites may not "promote sexually explicit materials; promote violence; promote discrimination based on race, sex, religion, nationality, disability, sexual orientation or age; promote illegal activities; or violate intellectual property rights." |
| Online Reporting Tools | Yes (BeFree's Reporting.net). |
| Types of Links | Banners/images/text links to the home page. |
| Prefabricated Storefront | No. |
| Powered by | BeFree. |
| Where to Join | www.stamps.com; www.befree.com. |

# Staples.com

**Figure A.43** Staples.com sells 6,000-plus office supplies and allows affiliates to make up to 7 percent commission in Staples "dollars."

**Table A.43** Program Overview

| | |
|---|---|
| Product/Services | Staples sells more than 6,000 office products, from computers and business machines to paper and business card services. |
| Program Type | Flat rate (bounty) and commission-based (pay-per-sale). |
| Terms | $10 for each new customer referral; up to 7% commission in Staples dollars. |
| Bonus? | Charter members earn $15 per new customer. |
| Payment Schedule | Quarterly. |
| Minimum Threshold | $100.00. |
| Two-Tier? | No. |
| Program Restrictions | Your site may not contain content that is unlawful, harmful, threatening, defamatory, obscene, harassing, or racially, ethnically, or otherwise objectionable. |
| Online Reporting Tools | Yes (BeFree's Reporting.net). |
| Types of Links | Banners/images/text links to the home page. |
| Prefabricated Storefront | No. |
| Powered by | BeFree. |
| Where to Join | www.staples.com; www.befree.com. |

# StoryCraft

**Figure A.44**  StoryCraft software helps customers create stories and affiliates generate commissions.

**Table A.44**  Program Overview

| | |
|---|---|
| Product/Services | StoryCraft offers story-development software and courses for novelists and screenwriters. |
| Program Type | Commission-based (pay-per-sale). |
| Terms | 20%. |
| Bonus? | N/A. |
| Payment Schedule | Quarterly. |
| Minimum Threshold | $50. |
| Two-Tier? | No. |
| Program Restrictions | These site types are prohibited from participating in the StoryCraft affiliate program: adult sites; sites that display adult banners; bikini sites, warez, ROM, or emulator sites; sites with no discernible content. Furthermore, affiliates may not place links in newsgroups, unsolicited e-mail, chat rooms, or guestbooks. |
| Online Reporting Tools | Yes (ClickTrade). |
| Types of Links | Banners/text links to the StoryCraft software on writerspage.com. |
| Prefabricated Storefront | No. |
| Powered by | ClickTrade. |
| Where to Join | www.writerspage.com; www.clicktrade.com. |

# TheSmokeShop.com

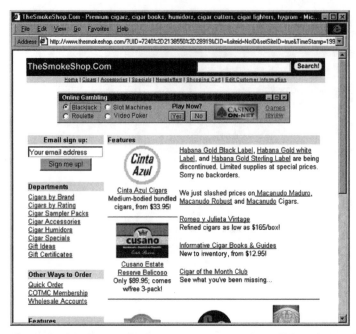

**Figure A.45** TheSmokeShop.com caters to cigar aficionados and offers affiliates a combination program.

**Table A.45** Program Overview

| | |
|---|---|
| Product/Services | TheSmokeShop.com sells cigars, books about cigars, and cigar accessories. |
| Program Type | Commission-based (pay-per-sale) and click-through. |
| Terms | 7% commission/$.07 per click-through. |
| Bonus? | N/A. |
| Payment Schedule | Monthly. |
| Minimum Threshold | $10. |
| Two-Tier? | No. |
| Program Restrictions | Your site cannot be targeted toward minors. Additionally, your site cannot contain content intended to defame TheSmokeShop.com or content that discourages one from visiting TheSmokeShop.com. Furthermore, your site cannot contain text, graphics, or any combination thereof that might mislead a person as to the nature of TheSmokeShop.com site. |
| Online Reporting Tools | Yes (LinkShare). |
| Types of Links | Banners/images/text links to home page and individual products; search boxes; storefront. |
| Prefabricated Storefront | Yes (LinkShare). |
| Powered by | LinkShare. |
| Where to Join | www.thesmokeshop.com; www.linkshare.com. |

# Travelocity.com

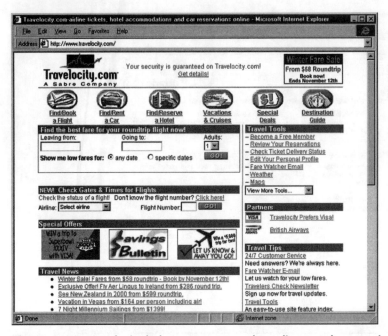

**Figure A.46**  Travelocity helps customers make online travel reservations and pays affiliates $2 per referred booking.

**Table A.46**  Program Overview

| | |
|---|---|
| Product/Services | A leading online travel reservation service where customers can make airline and train, hotel, and rental car reservations. |
| Program Type | Flat fee (bounty). |
| Terms | $2 per airline or VIA Rail Canada ticket booking. |
| Bonus? | No. |
| Payment Schedule | Quarterly. |
| Minimum Threshold | $50. |
| Two-Tier? | No. |
| Program Restrictions | Travelocity reserves the right to "deny any application for any reason, including applications for sites that contain content that could be classified as defamatory, harassing, harmful, obscene, racially objectionable, or unlawful." |
| Online Reporting Tools | Yes (BeFree's Reporting.net). |
| Types of Links | Banners/images/text links to home page, Visa Partners Network, online reservation center, special promotions, reservation tools (e.g., Fare Watcher Email), travel guides, and travel-related news; search boxes, storefront. |
| Prefabricated Storefront | Yes (BeFree). |
| Powered by | BeFree. |
| Where to Join | www.travelocity.com; www.befree.com. |

# Utrade.com

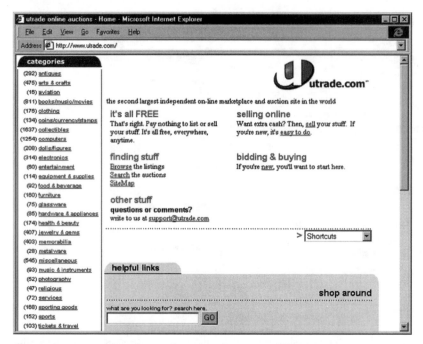

**Figure A.47**   Utrade, where referred traders earn affiliates up to 15 percent in commission.

**Table A.47**   Program Overview

| | |
|---|---|
| Product/Services | An auction site launched by One & Only (also included in this appendix) that offers visitors free and paid auction listings, and enables affiliates to create their own customized auction house. |
| Program Type | Commission-based (pay-per-sale). |
| Terms | 15% commission on auction sales. |
| Bonus? | No. |
| Payment Schedule | Monthly. |
| Minimum Threshold | None. |
| Two-Tier? | Yes; earn 33.3% of your Webmaster referral commissions. |
| Program Restrictions | Affiliate sites may not promote sexually explicit material, violence, discrimination, or illegal activities. No spamming. |
| Online Reporting Tools | Yes (Daily Activity Report sent via e-mail). |
| Types of Links | Banners/text links to customized auction page. |
| Prefabricated Storefront | No. |
| Powered by | One & Only. |
| Where to Join | www.oneandonly.com. |

# Verio

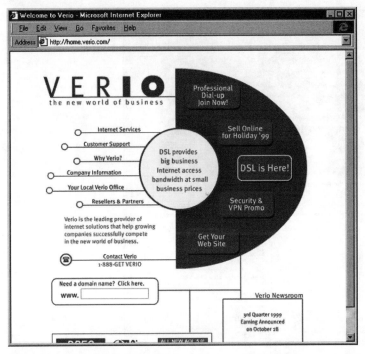

**Figure A.48**  Verio, a Web hosting service, offers affiliates up to $30 per new customer.

**Table A.48**  Program Overview

| Product/Services | A Web hosting service. |
|---|---|
| Program Type | Flat fee (bounty). |
| Terms | $25 for domain name registrations; $30 for all Web hosting services. |
| Bonus? | No. |
| Payment Schedule | Monthly. |
| Minimum Threshold | $100. |
| Two-Tier? | No. |
| Program Restrictions | Your site may not contain offensive material. |
| Online Reporting Tools | Yes (LinkShare). |
| Types of Links | Banners/images/text links to home page. |
| Prefabricated Storefront | No. |
| Powered by | LinkShare. |
| Where to Join | www.verio.com; www.linkshare.com. |

# WebTrends

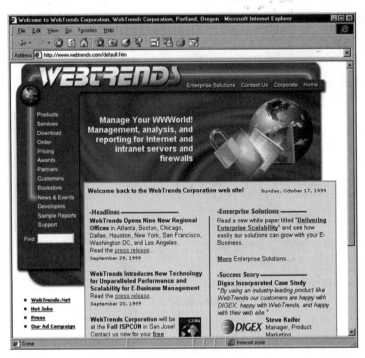

**Figure A.49** WebTrends helps Webmasters monitor their Web logs and earn a bounty for referring new customers.

**Table A.49** Program Overview

| | |
|---|---|
| Product/Services | A leading developer of Internet, intranet, and extranet software management products, offering complete solutions for IT/IS professionals and Webmasters. |
| Program Type | Flat fee/bounty. |
| Terms | $3 per software download/registration for Log Analyzer; $4 for Enterprise Suite, Professional Suite, Suite for Lotus Domino, and WebTrends for Firewalls and VPNs. |
| Bonus? | No. |
| Payment Schedule | Monthly. |
| Minimum Threshold | $20. |
| Two-Tier? | No. |
| Program Restrictions | Your site may not contain content that is "in any way unlawful, harmful, threatening, defamatory, obscene, harassing, or racially, ethnically, or otherwise objectionable." |
| Online Reporting Tools | Yes (BeFree's Reporting.net). |
| Types of Links | Images for links to specific products. |
| Prefabricated Storefront | No. |
| Powered by | BeFree. |
| Where to Join | www.webtrends.com; www.befree.com. |

# Wine.com

**Figure A.50** Wine.com lets affiliates link to its home page, to product categories, or to their favorite Merlot.

**Table A.50** Program Overview

| | |
|---|---|
| Product/Services | Provides in-depth information about wines and the people who produce them; offers wine recommendation, wine club participation, and wine/gift shop. (Note: The site was previously known as VirtualVineyard.) |
| Program Type | Commission-based (pay-per-sale). |
| Terms | 8% of net sales. |
| Bonus? | N/A. |
| Payment Schedule | Monthly (60 days following the end of each month). |
| Minimum Threshold | $50. |
| Two-Tier? | No. |
| Program Restrictions | No adult or hate sites may participate, and all sites must be "aesthetically pleasing." |
| Online Reporting Tools | Yes (LinkShare). |
| Types of Links | Text, banners, buttons for links to front page or specific products; search box. |
| Prefabricated Storefront | No. |
| Powered by | LinkShare. |
| Where to Join | www.wine.com; www.linkshare.com. |

# What's on the Web Site

"They" say that one year in the real world equals seven "Internet years," the reason being that things change on the Web really quickly. We wanted this book's companion site to be more than just a place to promote the book. We're assuming that most of the traffic will comprise people who have read the book and are eager to stay up to speed on affiliate programs and e-commerce. Our goal is to provide you with the tools you need to make your affiliate relationships successful.

Our Web site at www.affiliateselling.com contains the following information (or links to information).

## The Latest Scoop

The latest scoop includes:

- Affiliate survey statistics—who's making money and how?
- Definitions for the latest e-commerce terminology.
- "Content for Hire"—the latest scoop on content syndicators.

# Program Reviews

These reviews cover:

- Categorized list of affiliate programs available for nonprofit Web sites.
- Links to the 50 affiliate programs highlighted in the appendix of this book.
- Links to the best affiliate program review sites, including Associate-It, AssociatePrograms.com, and CashPile.
- Links and reviews for the top affiliate solutions providers, including BeFree, LinkShare, and Commission Junction.

# Resources to Help You Get Started

Here you'll find:

- Links to startup consultants who can help you build your business model around affiliate revenue opportunities.
- A list of affiliate-related newsletters, mailing lists, and newsgroups (and links to references about proper Usenet netiquette).
- Links to Web services offering free Web sites, and virtual storefront providers.
- Excerpts from Greg Helmstetter's book *Increasing Hits and Selling More on Your Web Site.*
- Resources for submitting your homepage URL to the best search engines.
- Links to site-building tools, traffic analysis software, and affiliate program-building tools.
- Much more!

# Glossary

**Ad** On the Web, an ad is almost always in banner form, a graphic image of a designated size that, for a fee, is displayed on one site to drive traffic to another site.

**Ad rotation** The regular alteration of banner ads that appear on a Web page at any given moment. This is usually done automatically by a software program on the hosting Web site or through a third-party syndicator.

**Ad space** Area on a Web page (usually in a margin) that is reserved for ads.

**Ad view** Synonymous with *ad impression*; the appearance of an ad (usually full view without scrolling) on a Web page.

**Affiliate** A Web site that partners with an online merchant by including links to promote the merchant's products or services. In exchange, the affiliate receives a commission, flat fee, or other incentive for all valid transactions it refers to its partner that generate a sale, a sales lead, or some other user action.

**Affiliate solutions providers** Online companies that provide solutions to merchants seeking to provide affiliate programs. Affiliate solutions providers also enable affiliates to review and join prescreened affiliate programs and manage their participation in such programs.

**B-to-B** Abbreviation for business-to-business commerce or other industrial relationships; also B2B. Compare with B-to-C.

**B-to-C** Abbreviation for business-to-consumer commerce, or simply "retail"; also B2C. On the Web, retailing is sometimes called e-tailing, which is practiced by e-tailers.

**Banner**   A hyperlink image (usually in GIF format) that is placed in the margin or other advertising space on a Web page. Some banners are animated; others are static. Banners come in a variety of shapes and sizes (the most common being 468 × 60 pixels).

**Bounty program**   A program that pays affiliates a predetermined flat fee for every new visitor the affiliate delivers; also known as a *flat-fee program*.

**Brand and branding**   A brand is the unique identity of a product, service, concept, or other commercial entity. The brand, which comprises all associations that the public has with the entity (logo, colors, style, perceptions, taglines, and so on) is intended to distinguish the entity from others, particularly competitors. Branding is the process of creating, communicating, and disseminating the brand into public awareness; thus, *brand awareness* is the degree to which consumers recognize or remember a brand.

**Brick-and-mortar**   Refers to traditional, physical, as opposed to digital, structures and vehicles—factories, warehouses, trucks, and retail outlets. A brick-and-mortar company is one with little or no significant Web presence. *See also* click-and-mortar, pure-play.

**C-to-C**   Abbreviation for consumer-to-consumer commerce; that is, commerce with no middle businesspeople. The most notable examples are Web-based auction and classified ad sites. Most large venues for such models (for example, eBay and Classifieds2000) are quickly permeated by consumers who participate so actively and regularly that they become small businesses for them. The presence of these quasi-consumers and the obvious businesses that sell through these sites blurs the distinction between B-to-C and pure C-to-C.

**C/I ratio**   Abbreviation for clicks per impression or, more commonly, click-through rate.

**Click/Click-through**   (n.) The act of clicking with a computer pointing device (typically, a mouse) on a banner ad or link. Currently, ad industry guidelines recommend defining a click as "when a visitor interacts with an advertisement," but this precludes the relevance to affiliate product links. It does, however, capture the idea that users may see hundreds of links/ads but only "interact" with one of them by clicking on it. As such, click-through rates are a good measure of an ad's or link's effectiveness.

**Click-and-mortar**   Business models that are a hybrid between Web-based and traditional (brick-and-mortar) business models. The term is attributed to David Pottruck, co-CEO of Charles Schwab, a firm whose Web services are tightly integrated with its traditional, physical, customer service-oriented offices.

**Click-through rate**   The number of clicks on a link/ad as a percentage of the number of times that the ad was seen (its *impressions*). For example, if 1 out of 20 people to whom a link was displayed actually clicked on it, the click-through rate for that page would be 5 percent. *See also* C/I ratio.

**Click-through program/Pay-per-click program**   A program in which affiliates are paid a small amount of money for each individual visitor they drive to a merchant's site, whether the visitor makes a purchase or not.

**Clip** A bundle of links created and managed in Clip2.com, any of which can be a link to affiliated products or services.

**Code** On the Web, typically refers to HTML code (though programming purists point out that HTML does not compile and is therefore merely a markup language, not true code). Affiliate solutions providers have online tools that provide affiliates with the lines of code they need to add affiliate links to their Web pages and/or *clips*. Affiliates can simply copy the appropriate code and paste it into their own HTML pages (or add it as a link in Clip2.com).

**Co-brand** On the Web, usually refers to two (or more) companies displaying their logos (hence, their brands) together so that the viewer considers the site or feature to be a joint enterprise. Occasionally, affiliates are able to include their own logo and other branding elements on the pages to which they send visitors; for example, services like CrossCommerce.com. Typically, the affiliate logo is placed in a frame at the top of the Web page.

**Commission** The compensation paid to affiliates for participation in a merchant's affiliate program. Commission rates vary from merchant to merchant. Technically, flat fees are a form of commission, but most affiliate programs (and this book) use the word commission to refer to compensations based on a *percentage* of the sales price. *See* revenue share.

**Commission-based program** A program that pays a predetermined percentage commission on the revenue generated by the sale of a product or service to a visitor who came from the referring affiliate's site.

**Conversion rate** The percentage of visitors to a merchant's site who actually make a purchase during that visit. High conversion rates suggest high-quality or prequalified shoppers, those more likely to buy, as opposed to random visitors. Providing helpful information alongside affiliate links (such as reviews of the products) tends to weed out the uninterested, while motivating the interested to click through to the merchant to buy. *See also* O/C ratio.

**Cookie** A block of data stored by a Web server on a client system, and used to identify users to enable the customization of Web content. When a user returns to the same Web site, the browser sends of copy of the cookie back to the server. Cookies are necessary for repeat-visit and multipage processes, such as using a shopping cart. Some ad rotation software uses cookies to determine which ad the user has just seen to ensure that a different ad will be rotated into the next pageview. Many affiliate programs use cookies to track referrals.

**CPM** Acronym for cost per thousand ad impressions, the standard industry measure for pricing and selling ads on Web sites. For example, if a site charges a CPM of $10, it will cost an advertiser 1 cent each time a person views the advertiser's banner ad ($10 ÷ 1,000 = $.01).

**Cross-sell** To recommend or display related or additional products to a customer who has already exhibited interest in a particular product type. Examples include: a grocery store displaying salsa next to chips; and the Travelocity site offering the option to rent a car to somebody who just purchased an airline ticket online.

**Disintermediation** The removal (or obsolescence) of one or more intermediary roles on the value chain between manufacturers and consumers. An example is Hewlett-Packard's creation of a Web site that sells direct to end users, thereby circumventing its traditional resellers.

**E-mail link** For the purpose of this book, an e-mail link is an affiliate link included in e-mail, such as e-mailed newsletters or personal correspondence. Affiliates can place links in e-mail to a merchant site that will direct users to specific products. E-mail links have proven to be an effective way to generate sales, but they must be used in accordance with netiquette, to prevent spamming recipients; that is, sending mail they do not want to receive (*see* Chapter 10).

**E-merchants** Companies that sell products or services directly through their Web site. E-merchants that target end consumers (as opposed to other businesses) are sometimes called *e-tailers*, short for e-retailers.

**eShelf** A CrossCommerce.com feature. A rectangular-shaped allotment of on-screen real estate on an affiliate Web page, into which CrossCommerce delivers real-time product information. Affiliates can hand-pick products and have prices updated automatically, or they can have CrossCommerce update which products appear based on rules defined by the affiliate (such as top-selling golf clubs).

**E-tailers** *See* e-merchants.

**Eyeballs** Web industry jargon (borrowed from Shakespeare) that refers to visitors, impressions, or site traffic in general.

**Flat-fee program** A program that pays affiliates a predetermined amount (as opposed to a percentage) for every visitor (or first-time visitor) they send to the program-provider merchant's site (also known as *bounty program*).

**Host** To store a Web site or other data on a machine (a Web server) and deliver (serve) its content via the Internet whenever a user requests it (by visiting the site).

**Hyperenablement** A possible future scenario in which every function on the value chain from manufacturer to consumer can be outsourced to a third party who participates in a revenue share. A hyperenabled e-commerce industry would allow any company (or person) to appear to operate an e-commerce site of grand scale.

**Impression** An instance of display of a link or banner to a user. *See* Ad view.

**Incentive** In the context of this book, a reward, typically non-cash (e.g., store credit) that an affiliate receives for sending visitors to the program-provider merchant's site.

**Infomediary** A third-party content syndicator or aggregator who coordinates the flow of content created at many sources and distributed to many outlets.

**Intermediation** The interjection of another party (an intermediary) between two other parties. In a business context, this typically refers to the introduction of an intermediary between manufacturers and consumers. Examples of intermediaries include distributors, value-added resellers, and retailers.

**Loss leader** An item priced below the retailer's cost, meaning the merchant loses money on each unit sold. In both traditional as well as Web commerce, loss leaders are offered to draw customers into the store, where in theory they will also buy enough profitable items (during that visit or future visits). In this way, the merchant makes more money on the whole than if the customer had never stopped by.

**Merchant**  For the purposes of this book, a person or company that sells products or services directly on the Web.

**O/C ratio**  In this book, the abbreviation for orders per click. Same as *conversion rate.*

**OEM**  Acronym for original equipment manufacturer; in this book, used as both a noun and a verb. The term originated in the hardware industry. As a noun, it is used to refer to a company that produces equipment from components bought from other manufacturers. As a verb, "to OEM" is the process of producing a physical product from the parts made and sold by their original manufacturer(s). For example, your WizBang brand laser printer might actually be composed of parts made by Canon, even if Canon's logo appears nowhere on the printer. In the Web world, the Wiz-Bang Portal that lets you search the entire Web is probably using another company's search capability without your knowing it. So on the Web, OEM usually applies to applications, that is, forms or displays that interact with the user and do something. However, there is a gray area between functionality and content (real-time stock-quote lookup is both, for instance); and you might hear OEM used to refer not only to functionality/technology licensing, but to pure content licensing as well. Incidentally, if the original manufacturer logo appears on the final product, then the arrangement is usually called *co-branded* rather than OEM. A gray area exists between these terms as well, particularly with respect to the relative visibility given to each party's brand.

**Offer**  (n.) In this book, the terms of the deal offered to an affiliate by a merchant. These can include commissions based on a percentage of the sale, a flat fee paid for each impression, or click-through, something more exotic (like noncash incentives), or a combination of these. The details of a merchant's offer are typically provided either by the merchant or by the affiliate solutions provider representing the merchant after an affiliate has been approved to join a merchant's program.

**Pageview**  The delivery of a Web page to a user's browser. This is a measure of page delivery only; it does not indicate whether the user actually viewed the page. Some users might click through to the next page before the first page finishes downloading, and the first page would still register as one pageview.

**Payment terms**  The terms agreed to between affiliates and merchants for affiliate compensation, such as flat fee, per-click rate, percentage of sale, and others.

**Payout**  The amount of money paid to an affiliate in exchange for driving visitors to a merchant's site.

**Pay-per-click model**  A compensation model by which affiliates are paid a fixed rate per click-through to the merchant's site. *See* click-through program.

**Pay-per-lead model**  A compensation model by which affiliates are paid a fixed rate or commission for each lead generated by a merchant's site, usually recognized when the referred visitor submits a form at the merchant site, such as a request for more information.

**Pay-per-sale model**  A compensation model by which affiliates are paid a fixed rate or commission for a sale made to a visitor they send to the merchant's site. *See* commission-based program.

**Portal**  A Web site (usually large) that attempts to provide multiple kinds of content and services to a group of Web users, the objective being to become the starting or key entry point for that group of users. For instance, Women.com is a portal site for women, meaning that women can quickly and easily find any Web resources oriented specifically toward women at the site.

**Private offer**  An offer from a merchant that is made only to a particular affiliate or group of affiliates.

**Program level**  A tier in an affiliate program that offers different compensation types or amounts to different affiliates. For instance, CDNOW offers store credit to small affiliates (usually individuals) but cash to large affiliates (usually companies).

**Pure-play company**  A Web company that operates exclusively on the Web. For example, (at this time) eToys, is a pure-play Web company in that it has no brick-and-mortar retail stores—though it does have traditional warehouses from which it ships products ordered online by users.

**Push** (n.)  A content distribution model pioneered by PointCast in which the user personalizes a browser and then automatically receives (is "pushed") customized content at some regular interval. Contrast this with content the user has to go looking for (called *pull*). Due largely to the squandered bandwidth and storage required for content updates—most of which went unseen—the push model has fallen out of favor. The concept of customized automated access to information was resurrected with "my page" features at various portals, using a more economical adaptation called *smart pull*, whereby prescreened headlines are pushed but the majority of targeted content is not transmitted unless the user clicks on a link.

**Reintermediation**  The act of changing which party delivers (and gets paid for) various components in the value chain from manufacturer to consumer. An example is affiliates that get paid for sales referred to merchants, as opposed to, say, Wal-Mart taking that percentage for selling to consumers through its brick-and-mortar stores. The key distinction here is not that intermediaries have been eliminated (*see* disintermediation), but that the party now doing the work is different.

**Report**  In this book, a document containing affiliate traffic and sales information presented in a format that allows affiliates to understand how their affiliate links are performing. Most merchants and virtually all affiliate solutions providers provide tools that allow affiliates to generate a wide variety of reports. Affiliates can use these reports to track their earnings, identify trends and patterns, and learn how to improve their performance.

**Revenue share**  In commission-based agreements, refers to the amount of money each party gets, as negotiated between strategic partners. It is possible for more than two parties to share revenue.

**Rotation**  In this book, refers to the automated shuffling of banners on a site so that returning visitors don't see the same thing for too long. Under the terms of some merchant affiliate programs, you can choose to rotate all of the banners they provide or you can select only specific banners you want to appear.

**Search box** A link that allows visitors at an affiliate site to perform a search of part of or all the entire inventory of a merchant's site. The visitor types a keyword into the text box provided on your site and then clicks Search (or Go, or something similar). The user is taken to the merchant's site where a Search Results page displays, containing links to the appropriate places on the merchant's site. This is a good way to provide your visitors direct access to the products they are interested in, thus increasing the likelihood that they will make a purchase.

**Smart pull** A content distribution model by which criteria are applied to automatically deliver customized content. CrossCommerce.com's method of delivering dynamic, criteria-based products (such as "today's top-selling golf club") to an affiliate's site in real time is an example of smart pull.

**Special offer** Deals offered to affiliates that are typically linked to a specific promotion (such as a product, a holiday, etc.). These deals can be public or private offers that are available for a limited time, at increased commission, for a particular product or products, or a combination of these.

**Storefront** E-commerce-enabled Web pages that are hosted elsewhere (that is, they are not part of your site's URL) and display products for sale, to facilitate transactions. Many affiliate solutions providers enable affiliates to use storefronts that are dynamically updated; however the ability to modify the design of these pages (to match your own site look-and-feel) is quite limited (as of this writing).

**Storelet** Prepackaged selections of hand-picked products in a rectangular format that can be dropped onto any affiliate page alongside the affiliate's content; a Cross-Commerce.com feature. Like storefronts, storelets automatically receive updated content. Unlike storefronts, storelets reside on your page and can be modified to match your site design.

**Subaffiliate** Variously, refers to an affiliate's affiliate in a multi-tier program or to multiple accounts at multiple Web sites owned by one affiliate.

**Terms of agreement/service** An agreement created by a merchant (or its affiliate solutions provider) that describes the contractual obligations of both the merchant and the affiliate for the affiliate program.

**Text link** In this book, a hyperlink pointing to a merchant's site that is not accompanied by a graphical image. Affiliates can use text links rather than graphical links (banners) on their sites. Text links are easy to use, require little space on the page, save download time, enhance usability, and are the most clicked-on types of links available. Text links also enable affiliates to link to a merchant's site from a word or phrase; for example, from within a paragraph of body text.

**Unique visitor** A user who enters a Web site for the first time on a given day or some other arbitrary time period (this varies from company to company). Unique visitors are identified by their address (the number assigned to the computer they used to access the Internet); this precludes their being counted twice if they return more than once on the same day or other specified time period. As a traffic metric, the number of unique visitors is important to site owners, who need to know, for instance, if the latest 100 pageviews comprised 100 people viewing one page each, or one person viewing 100 pages.

**Value chain**   The sequence of involvement of parties in the production and distribution of goods from raw resources to the end consumer (for example: iron ore mining → steel manufacturing → subassembly manufacturer → automobile production → car dealership → consumer). In theory, each party along the chain takes a percentage of the final sales price, proportionate to the amount of value it adds (or power it wields). The Web has introduced fundamental change to the relative importance of different players on the value chain, allowing, for example, manufacturers to sell direct to end consumers, thereby circumventing traditional channels of distribution. *See also*, disintermediation and reintermediation.

**Visit**   In this book, a visitor session at a Web site, regardless of how many pages he or she views during that session. A visit can be a somewhat arbitrary measurement with respect to repeat viewers, in that a period of inactivity must be assigned (by the site owners) to define what constitutes a new and distinct visit. For instance, if 30 minutes of inactivity has been assigned as the end of a user session, and a user visits a site, hunts around, takes an hour-long lunch break, and picks up right where he or she left off, then the site's traffic reports will show this user's activity as two separate visits.

**Web ring**   A popular form of relationship whereby a group of Web sites elects to make all of their sites accessible from other sites within the group. By agreeing to place links to some, all, or randomly selected members of the group, sites form a "ring" that is easily navigated by users. Web rings can be big or small, inclusive or exclusive (not every site can join), and are usually made up of sites related by some common theme or topic.

# Index